KT-406-838

LANDSCAPES FOR THE WORLD

WITHDRAWN FROM
THE LIBRARY
UNIVERSITY OF
WINCHESTER

KA 0290027 0

LANDSCAPES FOR THE WORLD

Conserving a Global Heritage

Peter Fowler

WIND*gather*
PRESS

Landscapes for the World: Conserving a Global Heritage

© Peter Fowler, 2004

All rights reserved.
No part of this publication may be reproduced, stored in a retrieval system, or transmitted in any form or by any means (whether electronic, mechanical, photocopying or recording) or otherwise without the written permission of both the publisher and the copyright holder.

Published by: Windgather Press Ltd, 29 Bishop Road, Bollington, Macclesfield, Cheshire SK10 5NX, UK

Distributed by: Central Books Ltd, 99 Wallis Road, London E9 5LN

British Library Cataloguing-in-Publication Data
A catalogue record for this book is available from the British Library

ISBN 0-9545575-9-X

Designed, typeset and originated by Carnegie Publishing Ltd, Chatsworth Road, Lancaster
Printed and bound by Cambridge University Press

UNIVERSITY COLLEGE
WINCHESTER

02900270   363·69
              FOW

to

Henry

with whom I have been over so much old ground

Contents

List of Illustrations

List of Illustrations

Figures

Tables

Acknowledgements

No-one is responsible for this book except the author, but numerous colleagues have, usually unconsciously, helped significantly in its emergence. I thank them all, throughout the conservation world and around the geographical world. I owe a huge debt to many who have, safely so far, made and implemented my travel arrangements, and welcomed me to their landscapes, often laying on 4WD vehicles, monoplanes and helicopters to improve the access and the view, e.g. Plates 3, 5.

My greatest personal debt is to Dr Henry Cleere, World Heritage Co-ordinator 1992–2002, ICOMOS (Figure 1), who suggested I be invited to the first World Heritage cultural landscapes meeting in 1992, and who introduced me in 1993 to the nuances of an ICOMOS evaluation mission, happily to the Boyne Valley in Ireland as far as I remember. Our friendly, though always vibrant, collaboration on various matters goes back much further than that, however, and, recently retired from the latest of at least four successful careers, he will accept the dedication, I hope, in the spirit of admiration in which it is offered. I know, with satisfaction, that he will disagree with much of this text, and will tell me so.

Two other particular individuals have greatly helped me explore some of the world's great landscapes, actually and metaphorically. Dr. Mechtild Rössler, in charge of cultural landscapes at the World Heritage Centre, UNESCO, Paris, has always encouraged my interest, often in the most practical way. Professor Adrian Phillips, wearing his IUCN hat and also personally, has attempted to keep me up to the mark theoretically and naturally in matters to do with World Heritage landscapes. Numerous other friends in both the World Heritage Centre and the ICOMOS headquarters, Paris, have significantly supported my efforts and been engaging colleagues. The book could not have been created without ready access to files, library and photographic archive in the ICOMOS Documentation Centre, Paris, and extensive use here of materials therefrom. I appreciate the tri-lingual co-operation of José Garcia. I also happily acknowledge various WHC publications, particularly its *Brief Descriptions*, as a fruitful source of paraphrases and quotations.

Most of the photographs are by the author but I am particularly indebted to Henry Cleere for Plates 2 and 9 and Figures 3b, 9, 18, 19, 21, 28, 36, 37, 50, 63; Dr Christopher Young (English Heritage; Figure 24); María Mercedes

Podestá (Instituto Nacional de Antropología y Pensamiento Latinamericano, Buenos Aires, Figures 64, 65): Alessandro Balsama (World Heritage Centre, Plate 12, Figure 66); Pierre-Marie Tricaud (Institut d'Amènagement et d'Urbanism de la Région d'Île-de-France, Paris; Figure 27); Danny Waygood (Figure 49); and colleagues in the Publications Unit, UNESCO, who made it possible to use the images (Copyright UNESCO) Figures 20, 22, 25, 35, 39 and 59. Plate 1 is copyright Virtual New Zealand.

It would be both unrealistic and ungracious not to acknowledge also the significant role of Richard Purslow as publisher, editor, encourager – and supplier of Figure 29 – in making this book actually happen.

Merci beaucoup à tous.

Abbreviations

Brief Descriptions	*Brief Descriptions of Sites Inscribed on the World Heritage List*, WHC.01/15, January 2001 (the edition used here); rev. edn to include July 2003 inscriptions, 2003)
CL:	cultural landscape
Guidelines: (Operational Guidelines):	WHC 1999: Intergovernmental Committee for the Protection of the World Cultural and Natural Heritage, *Operational Guidelines for the Implementation of the World Heritage Convention*, UNESCO, World Heritage Centre, Paris (WHC–99/2, revised March 1999)
ICCROM:	International Centre for the Study of the Preservation and Restoration of Cultural Property
ICOMOS:	International Council on Monuments and Sites
IUCN:	International Union for the Conservation of Nature, now the World Conservation Union
UN:	the United Nations
UNESCO:	the United Nations Educational, Scientific and Cultural Organisation
WHC:	World Heritage Centre
WHCommittee:	World Heritage Committee

FIGURE 1.
An ICOMOS mission early in the development of the World Heritage cultural landscape idea: Henry Cleere in typical pose inspecting rock art with his guide at Uluru, Australia, April, 1994.

Preface

....

I ended another book recently, based on the excruciating minutiae of a particular local landscape in England, by commenting on '... ideas, ideas about archaeology and research, about the place and history, and about abstractions such as resource, stewardship and World Heritage'. My rather grandiose conclusion was that 'It might give pause for thought ... that the study of a parish pump ends with such a global, and noble, concept.'

This book is about that 'global, noble concept' as expressed in terms of landscape. Given that the metaphor of the English parish pump conveys the meaning of something of local importance but of little interest elsewhere, the concept of World Heritage might well appear at first sight to be at the opposite end of the range of different heritages; but this is not so. A large conference at Venice in November, 2002, celebrated the thirtieth anniversary of the World Heritage Convention, 1972, by identifying that the local was a key component of the global. One of the many topics featuring there, and the subject of its own three-day 'workshop' at Ferrara beforehand, was 'cultural landscapes'. New to many people, the concept was only adopted as a suitable one for consideration as World Heritage by the World Heritage Committee in 1992. 'World Heritage cultural landscape', a daunting phrase, embraces the concept of a global idea, while rejoicing that every landscape is local to, and valued by, someone. It embraces too another fundamental idea which we discuss at length in this book.

The World Heritage concept is founded, I believe, on the idea of a world-wide heritage of, for and belonging to everyone. It seems to me the sort of idea for which there is great need in the early twenty-first century. Collectively, we try to express this particular concept in official terms through the idea of World Heritage, one of the most successful of UNESCO's programmes over the last thirty years. Since 1972, when the World Heritage Convention was approved, 754 places have been inscribed on the World Heritage List (July 2003; Table 1). I am particularly interested in the role of landscape in the theory and implementation of this idea, a topic which has exercised many scholars, officials and local communities for decades but which has only seriously been tackled since 1992.

I was lucky: during the 1990s and into the twenty-first century, I happened to be in the right place at the right time as landscape was first formally recognised and then defined as increasingly appropriate to a dynamic vision of 'World Heritage'. Individual landscapes began to be identified in their countries by signatories to the World Heritage Convention and proposed as 'cultural landscapes' to the UNESCO World Heritage Centre in Paris. This meant they had to be visited, assessed and, finally in some cases, officially approved as worthy of inscription on the World Heritage List (Table 2). This process, still in its infancy, has nevertheless meant that the first 36 such landscapes have inevitably raised interesting questions about the nature of both landscape and World Heritage, while at the same time helping refine in practice the original definition adopted by the World Heritage Committee.

Fortunately for me, in one way or another, I was involved with most of the 'cultural landscapes' to have arisen in this World Heritage context during the first decade of implementation. All of the chapters contain material from that experience; some are based on, or are edited versions of, lectures I was invited to give at various World Heritage and other conferences and seminars during that decade. The lectures in particular were usually lectures abroad, and even when in Britain, were usually for mixed, not specifically academic, audiences. My subtext was usually to try to persuade, administrators and politicians for example, as well as to explain. None of the chapters here are of texts exactly as given (I seldom spoke from a written script) or as published in conference proceedings and specialist journals, for obviously I have removed the considerable amount of repetition within and overlap between them. This applies particularly with regard to UNESCO organisation, methods and definitions in the field of World Heritage and cultural landscapes where the explanations in Chapter 1 cover the whole book.

The chapters here reflect two, interwoven lines of development, both personal or at least as seen in a personal perspective. On the one hand is the idea and implementation of 'cultural landscape' as an integral element of the concept of World Heritage. On the other are some thoughts and experiences which have come to me in this field during 1992–2003.

A version of this book was complete by the end of 2001, but then followed a year of intensive work on cultural landscapes for ICOMOS and the World Heritage Centre (Fowler 2003b), climaxing at Ferrara (WHC 2003c). In December, 2001, I was commissioned by the World Heritage Centre at UNESCO, Paris, to review that first decade and indicate future lines of development in World Heritage cultural landscapes. My report was handed over in October, 2002, in time for the Ferrara 'workshop' referred to above (Fowler 2003a), and then revised in the light of Ferrara and other events, finally being completed after peer review in March, 2003. Inevitably, some of this book has crept into that *Review* (Fowler 2003b), and vice versa, especially when I have judged the needs of what I imagine will be two rather different audiences; but in general I have consciously tried to avoid substantial repetition – goodness knows there is enough to say. The two publications are conceived as essentially complementary. In the *Review*, for example, I have been conscious of its 'official' status, addressed by a consultant to, *inter alia*, the World Heritage Committee, whereas in this book my approach and style are more relaxed for what I hope will be some students and people just interested in landscape. I have deliberately dealt only briefly with the management of these landscapes (Chapter 10), because another book is simultaneously covering the topic (ICCROM forthcoming).

Where I have visited a Site, the text here reflects my experience, but all the descriptions of World Heritage cultural landscapes owe at least something to others' perceptions and writings. In particular, all these accounts draw heavily on documents generated by the World Heritage Centre and ICOMOS (some drafted by this author but most by others). All are now in the public domain, either published conventionally or on the web or available in and from the ICOMOS library, Paris; but it would make for tedious reading indeed to reference every quotation, paraphrase, summary and abstract, so only the main references are given here in the text. Much of the bibliographic infrastructure, with comment, is in the Notes at the end of the book. In terms of much of the material I have used, the Site name and/or its number on the World Heritage List are in fact references which will take an enquirer to the appropriate file(s), by country (French spelling) alphabetically, and then by site name, in the ICOMOS Library (the catalogue of which is on the web). There is also an embryonic archive room in the World Heritage Centre.

Much of the content here is not attempting to push back the frontiers of landscape knowledge through reporting on new research. Rather is it using known archaeological/historical/topographic information to further, through dialogue, the purposes of landscape awareness, appreciation and conservation. The material is arranged chronologically in terms of World Heritage cultural landscapes for the first part of the book (Introduction and Inscription, Chapters 1–5). Thereafter I use a thematic approach, discussing Britain (Chapters 6–8) and management and conservation (Chapters 9–10) before concluding with an assessment of World Heritage and cultural landscape so far. Clearly, this book contains an element of subjective exploration over a decade of a particular sort of landscape from a personal point of view. This exploration is built on my long-standing interest in landscape and agrarian history (Fowler 1983, 2000, 2002), recently in parallel with work for ICOMOS and the WHC. Obviously, I have drawn very much on the experience and some of the data made available and generated by those circumstances.

This book, then, entirely unofficial, is at least a sort of personal stock-taking as I begin my second decade living with cultural landscapes – so far enjoyable, part-time but always challenging. This text is the product of significant revision in 2003 in the light of all the above. For statistical and tabulation purposes, the World Heritage data used are as at 3 July, 2003, the date at which the results of the World Heritage Committee's meeting in Paris were released.

However grand the idea or the actual landscape in view, in my pursuit of the 'global, noble concept' which is, I believe, at the core of World Heritage, I am everywhere impressed by the ubiquity of the parish pump and people's need of it: in reality, of course, and also metaphorically.

Clerkenwell, Paris and le Bédos July, 2003

CHAPTER I

Landscape and World Heritage

FIGURE 2.
The picture does not
express the cacophony
of natural sound as
dawn breaks, but
watchers are being
closely watched – in
the foreground by a
mostly submerged part
of the biodiversity in
the wetland of Spring-
time Kakadu, Australia.

Landscape belongs to everyone. This book is about a way of trying to bring about a realisation of that truism, for at least some of the world's outstanding landscapes. I do not, however, seek to own, nationalise or internationalise land itself, the stuff physically existing over the part of the surface of the globe which is not covered by sea; we recognize the legal property rights of landowners and respect a particular philosophical stance in these matters. My premise, however, is that no one individual or corporation can possibly own landscape, a curious phenomenon embracing that physical stuff which we can sense by sight, smell and touch while overlayering it with a myriad personal and communal connotations. One of the significances of any landscape is as a locality. It 'means' something to everyone and every individual who values it for what he or she perceives to be its particular character, its singularity of place. The concept of 'cultural landscapes' as World Heritage Sites embraces ideas of belonging, outstanding, significance, locality, meaning, value as well as singularity of place. In a complementary way, it is also provoking thought about the concept of World Heritage itself, for cultural landscapes can now be a kind of World Heritage site and their recognition, inscription and management ask questions about ideas and practicalities.

The particular approach pursued here to one of the world's greatest resources – landscape as a social and personal value – has implicit within it one very important fact: the 'global, noble concept' of World Heritage, now with some landscapes of global distinction included, is not the opposite of a place thought to be of only local interest; for every landscape finds a validity as a local place, however much it may be overlain with more prestigious designations like 'National Park' or 'World Heritage Site'. Yet, whatever the local value, a potential World Heritage Site must satisfy the criterion of being of 'universal value'. That alone, however the phrase be interpreted, should make it different, and in the case of a World Heritage 'cultural landscape' give it a demonstrable quality over and above the merits of a local 'treasure' alone. In 1992, the World Heritage Convention became the first international legal instrument to recognize and protect cultural landscapes – provided they could be shown to be 'of universal value'.

'World Heritage' comes rather late into a landscape already crowded, some would say overcrowded, with conservation designations. World Heritage Sites are not technically 'designated' like an Area of Outstanding Natural Beauty in the UK but are 'inscribed' on a list maintained in Paris by the United Nations Educational, Scientific and Cultural Organisation (UNESCO). It has been doing this since 1972 when UNESCO somewhat presciently agreed the World Heritage Convention in the wake of a growing awareness that all over the world major sites, natural and cultural, were threatened and being destroyed. The twenty-first century has sadly begun by emphasizing the urgency of this mission.

UNESCO itself had in 1972 recently driven through a major rescue programme in Egypt, saving monuments in advance of the construction of the Aswan dam. It was not entirely a co-incidence that 'Rescue, the Trust for British Archaeology' came into being at the same time, motivated by the urgency of archaeological destruction in the British landscape. Within five years, it had changed government financing of and attitudes to that insular problem. Similarly, from the mid-seventies onwards, governments ('States Parties' in UNESCO-speak) around the world slowly, and then with increasing enthusiasm, began to sign the Convention. By July 2003, the Convention had been ratified by 175 States Parties, and 754 properties in 129 countries had been inscribed on the World Heritage List.

Table 1. Number and categories of properties inscribed on the World Heritage List (at 3 July 2003).

Type of property	Total number
Cultural properties	582
Natural properties	149
Mixed cultural and natural properties	23
TOTAL	754

Over the decade 1993–2003, that total of 754 has been approached at annual additions of 33 (1993), 29, 29, 37, 46 (1997), 30, 48, 61, 31, 9 and 24 (2003) – by a curious quirk of numbers, exactly half (377) of the total. In other words, the rate of inscription in the decade 1993–2003 has been twice that of the previous twenty years. Either the world is much richer in heritage than previously thought, or the concept of 'world heritage' is changing, or factors other than simple world-class merit e.g. politics, have come into play. One major development involving all three of those perspectives concerns the emergence of 'cultural landscapes'.

In 1992 there were no World Heritage cultural landscapes; by July, 2003, 36 World Heritage Sites from 25 countries had been formally identified as cultural landscapes (Table 2). This book is primarily about them, the ideas behind them, and some reflections they have prompted.

Table 2. The official list of World Heritage cultural landscapes
(with abbreviated names), arranged by their year of inscription and
World Heritage number

Year	WH no.	State party	Short title
1993	421	New Zealand	Tongariro
1994	447	Australia	Uluru
1995	722	Philippines	Cordilleras
	723	Portugal	Sintra
1996	763	Czech Republic	Lednice
1997	773	France/Spain	Mont Perdu
	806	Austria	Hallstatt
	826	Italy	Cinque Terre
	830	Italy	Amalfitana
1998	842	Italy	Cilento
	850	Lebanon	Quadisha
1999	474	Hungary	Hortobagy
	840	Cuba	Viñales
	905	Poland	Kalwaria
	932	France	St Emilion
	938	Nigeria	Sukur
2000	534	Germany	Dessau-
	933	France	Loire valley (part)
	968	Sweden	Öland
	970	Austria	Wachau
	984	UK	Blaenavon
	994	Lithuania/Rus	Curonian Spit
	1008	Cuba	Plantations
2001	481	Laos	Vat Phou
	772	Austria/Hungary	Fertö-Neu. Lake
	950	Madagascar	Ambohimango
	1044	Spain	Aranjuez
	1046	Portugal	Alto Douro
2002	1063	Hungary	Tokaj
	1066	Germany	Rhine valley (part)
2003	208	Afghanistan	Bamiyan valley
	925	India	Bhimbetka
	1068	Italy	Sacri Monti
	1099	South Africa	Mapungubwe
	1084	United Kingdom	Kew
	306	Zimbabwe	Matobo Hills

Despite this quantitative and spatial success, the Convention has had to justify itself over its thirty years of existence, both because World Heritage status bestows no legal protection as such and because it was a late-comer into the field of conservation. For a century and more, all over the world responsible governments have been passing laws and taking other steps to protect their heritage, natural and cultural. As a result, in the UK alone, for example, hundreds of thousands of 'listed' buildings, hundreds of thousands of acres of land conserved in some way (about ten per cent of the national land area) and some 20,000 Scheduled Ancient Monuments (working towards a 'viable sample' of *c.* 50,000) jostle in a conservation landscape overlaid on the physical one. There are in fact a multitude of criteria for widely different types of dozens of different designations across the natural and cultural fields. This means that World Heritage, the grandest concept of them all, might well be seen as the last straw, crushing even lower the already overloaded desks of the conservation bureaucracy, official and voluntary.

In fact, governments and people generally seem to like the idea and, increasingly during the last two decades of the twentieth century, they were queuing up to offer their best sites for the world's delectation and judgement. The idea of 'cultural landscapes' added to that perception in 1992. This is healthy and encouraging, for the countries which have voluntarily signed the World Heritage Convention are indeed expected to take it seriously and must face the consequences of their signature seriously. But what is it exactly that they have signed up to?

The World Heritage List

The idea of World Heritage was expressed clearly in the 1972 UNESCO *Convention concerning the Protection of the World Cultural and Natural Heritage.* The purpose of the *Convention* is to ensure the identification, protection, conservation, presentation and transmission to future generations of cultural and natural heritage of "outstanding universal value". A whole library now exists on what that phrase means (see the Bibliography).

Reflecting thinking that had been the norm but which was already becoming archaic in the 1960s, the Convention divided potential World Heritage Sites into two sorts: natural and cultural. These sorts were considered opposites, almost antagonists, for at the time nature conservationists thought that the less human interference there had been with an area, the 'better' it was. Similarly, 'cultural' most readily embraced individual monuments and structures, towns and ruins as isolated phenomena largely in the minds of architects, architectural historians and those of an aesthetic tendency, with little thought of context and the landscape itself.

Potential cultural World Heritage Sites have to meet one or more criteria. Exactly the same basic criteria apply to cultural landscapes as to any other potential cultural World Heritage Sites. They are spelt out in paras. 23–24 of the World Heritage Centre's *Operational Guidelines* (WHC 1999; these *Guidelines* are currently under revision). The six crucial criteria, here abbreviated, ask that the site be one or more of the following:

(i) a masterpiece of human creative genius

(ii) an important interchange of human value, over a span of time or within a cultural area of the world, on developments in architecture or technology, monumental arts, town-planning or landscape design

(iii) a unique or at least exceptional testimony to a cultural tradition or civilization, living or disappeared

(iv) an outstanding example of a type of building or architectural or technological ensemble or landscape which – a key, and much misunderstood phrase, this – illustrates (a) significant stage(s) in human history

(v) an outstanding example of a traditional human settlement or land-use, representative of a culture (or cultures), especially when under threat

(vi) be directly or tangibly associated with events or living traditions, with ideas, or with beliefs, with artistic and literary works of outstanding universal significance

In addition, all cultural sites have to meet criteria of authenticity 'and in the case of cultural landscapes [of] their distinctive character and components'; and to enjoy adequate legal, contractual or traditional protection (and nowadays, in effect, a management plan). These criteria play an important role in the discussion of specific landscapes that follows in this book.

What is authenticity? What is 'integrity', another quality asked for in nomination documents and much favoured in World Heritage circles? These are the most difficult of questions to answer, and several World Heritage conferences have tried to find answers. The *Operational Guidelines* state that meeting the test of authenticity involves matters of design, material, workmanship or setting. Reconstruction is only acceptable if it is carried out on the basis of complete and detailed documentation on the original and to no extent on conjecture. Yet, by and large, despite the philosophical agonisings and the clear consensus that there is no one answer, it is relatively easy to recognize authenticity and integrity when you meet them (Plate 1, Figure 3).

'Integrity' is usually taken to mean physical and/or contextual and/or environmental integrity, matters often blurred into issues of authenticity. Examples would include an architectural complex which was either more or less complete, or was a ruin which had not been subsequently affected by later development. Development around a site, or within a landscape, injurious to the site's essential quality, would be considered, in World Heritage terms, to have diminished the integrity. A main road dividing an architectural masterpiece from its park and gardens, for example, would have caused a property to have lost much of its integrity. On the other hand, appropriate development, say for example a sequence of buildings erected over time and all performing the traditional functions of a site, could be considered to have maintained the integrity (and added significantly to its historical interest).

'Authenticity' is much more difficult, not least because different cultures have different ideas of what is and is not 'authentic'. The introduction of

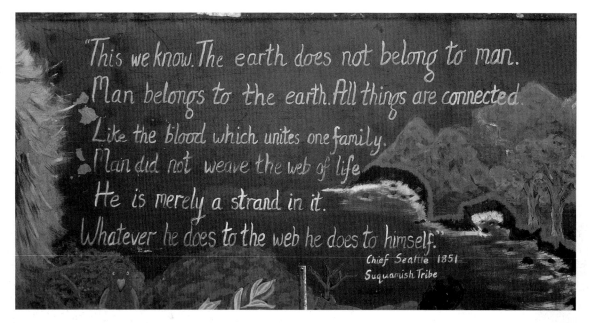

FIGURE 3.

a. (*above*) Philosophic mural, quoting the words of Chief Seattle of the Suquamish Tribe in 1851, overlooking the recently-restored sea-front at Roseau, Dominica, 2000.

b. (*below*) Head-Smashed-In Buffalo Jump, Alberta, Canada, inscribed in 1981, is a good example of a pre-1992 World Heritage site which could now be re-considered as a cultural landscape because of its involvement in a specialized hunting technique dependent on a close, long-term relationship between people, topography and a knowledge of animal behaviour.

c. (*opposite*) Classic restoration of the Temple of Piety and its watery context at Studley Royal, UK, with Fountains Abbey part of a World Heritage site inscribed before 1992 and, with the benefit of hindsight, a good example of a category 1 cultural landscape.

modern materials, like concrete and steel into a timber-framed building, for example, would seriously impair a monument's authenticity. So would re-construction, as distinct from 'consolidate as found.' Authenticity really involves both the positive and the negative: on the one hand the presence of much of the original in terms of design, materials and perhaps management, and on the other the absence of inappropriate intrusions, whether they be in the form of poor later workmanship or of additions to the setting which make the experience of appreciating or using the property significantly different from that which it was meant to promote. For example, modern buildings around and close to a seventeenth century set of military defences may now not only dominate the environment in which the defences were originally dominant but, rather more subtly, may also block the fields of fire which particular gun batteries were designed to cover, thereby largely negating the 'authenticity' of the structure. Sometimes used seriously, but here mentioned flippantly, concepts such as 'particularly authentic' are not entirely unknown.

World Heritage mixed cultural and natural heritage properties

Table 1 on page 2 contains a third category of Site, 'mixed cultural and natural properties'.

The twenty-three properties currently included in the World Heritage List on the basis of both their natural and cultural values are known as "mixed properties". Paragraph 18 of the *Guidelines* states that "States Parties should as far as possible endeavour to include in their submissions properties which derive their outstanding universal value from a particularly significant combination of cultural and natural features". From early on some overlap between the two supposedly distinct categories was encountered in practice, and from this reality emerged the intellectually messy idea of the 'mixed site'. Being a pragmatic, not theoretical, idea, bureaucracy can cope with it, and the 'mixed site' persists as a third category of World Heritage Site (Table 3).

Three of those mixed sites – Uluru-Kata Tjuta National Park, Pyrénées-Mont Perdu and Tongariro National Park – have subsequently been recognized as cultural landscapes, though their 'mixed site' status apparently continues too. Perhaps most of the others should also be re-examined as potential 'cultural landscapes'.

In coming to its decisions the World Heritage Committee bears many factors in mind, not all of them perhaps with a 'noble, global concept' to the fore. Professionally, it is supported by the staff of the World Heritage Centre at UNESCO in Paris, and by the Advisory Bodies. They are the International Council on Monuments and Sites (ICOMOS: head office Paris), the International Union for the Conservation of Nature (IUCN: Berne), and the International Council for the Conservation and Restoration of Monuments (ICCROM: Rome). All three have an official role in advising the World Heritage Committee. ICOMOS is the lead body in the case of cultural landscapes, working closely with IUCN. In various ways, including site inspections, it assesses each cultural nomination and offers its advice to the Committee (which does not always accept it).

Fortunately in practice much of the world positively wants World Heritage Sites, whatever the finer points of their definition and the labour involved in making a nomination. People crave their World Heritage inscription; enormous efforts, great ambitions and, frankly, wildly optimistic economic dreams cluster around the World Heritage concept among governments in some cases, and at numerous places and their inhabitants elsewhere in the face of government indifference or incompetence.

Expectations and consequences of World Heritage inscription

Expectations and consequences of 'inscription' vary, even when we are theoretically dealing in an even-handed way with a supposedly uniform 'gold standard' of heritage. One of the lessons that the World Heritage Committee

Table 3. The 23 mixed cultural and natural properties inscribed on the World Heritage List (at 3 July 2003)

Name of mixed property	State party	Cultural criteria	Natural criteria
Tassili n'Ajjer	Algeria	i, iii	ii, iii
Kakadu National Park	Australia	i, vi	ii, iii, iv
Willandra Lakes Region	Australia	iii	i
Tasmanian Wilderness	Australia	iii, iv, vi	i, ii, iii, iv
Uluru-Kata Tjuta National Park	Australia	v, vi	ii,iii
Mount Taishan	China	i, ii, iii, iv, v, vi	iii
Mount Huangshan	China	ii	iii, iv
Mt Emei Scenic Area, including Leshan Giant Buddha Scenic Area	China	iv, vi	iv
Mount Wuyi	China	iii, vi	iii, iv
Ohrid Region with its Cultural and Historical Aspect and its Natural Environment	Former Yugoslav Republic of Macedonia	i, iii, iv	iii
Pyrénées – Mont Perdu	France–Spain	iii, iv, v	i, iii
Meteora	Greece	i, ii, iv, v	iii
Mount Athos	Greece	i, ii, iv, v, vi	iii
Tikal National Park	Guatemala	i, iii, iv	ii,iv
Cliff of Bandiagara (Land of the Dogons)	Mali	v	iii
Tongariro National Park	New Zealand	vi	ii,iii
Historic Sanctuary of Machu Picchu	Peru	i, iii	ii, iii
Rio Abiseo National Park	Peru	iii	ii, iii, iv
Ukhahlamba/Drakensberg	South Africa	i, iii	iii, iv
Ibiza, biodiversity and culture	Spain	ii, iii, iv	ii, iv
The Laponian Area	Sweden	iii, v	i, ii, iii
Göreme National Park and the Rock Sites of Cappadocia	Turkey	i, iii, v	iii
Hierapolis-Pamukkale	Turkey	iii, iv	iii

has learnt the hard way, and now values, is that underneath the blanket of World Heritage application and designation is the most important quality of all – diversity. The uniformity comes in the expectation of excellence, however that quality manifests itself; and in the expected standards of management in its widest sense. The following brief analysis applies to World Heritage Sites as a whole and, though some points may be more appropriate to single structures, are in general relevant to cultural landscapes. It reads, I fear, as something of a list of bullet points; but the reader will, I hope, find it a useful reference area in considering what follows:

Expectations of inscription arise in several quarters, and can be categorised as those:

    (1) of THE WORLD HERITAGE COMMITTEE:

* that, as required by the Convention, the nominated WHS is of 'outstanding universal value'

* that the nomination itself is in the form of a professionally competent document, with or without video, visual and audio accompaniments

* that the nomination arrives on its agenda with a clear assessment, preferably concluding with a firm recommendation by one or more of the Advisory Bodies, as a result of a stringent review process over the preceding year or longer

* that the nominating State has the means to manage the Site e.g. a State heritage service, an appropriate legal system

* that it will use those means effectively, which now means having a Management Plan preferably developed with local partnership

* that public access will be encouraged and catered for

* that, following inscription, good periodic reports about the management, condition and use of the WHS will be received.

With respect to cultural landscapes specifically, the World Heritage Committee's expectations are stated as requirements in paragraphs 36–42 of the *Operational Guidelines* (1999), here summarized and deconstructed to bring out the many elements involved. Cultural landscapes must:

* represent the "combined works of nature and of man" (para 36)

* be illustrative of the evolution of human society and settlement over time, under the influence of:
  † the physical constraints and/or opportunities presented by their natural environment
  † successive social, economic and cultural forces,
  † both external and internal

* be selected for:
  † their outstanding universal value
  † their representativity in terms of a clearly defined geo-cultural region

† and their capacity to illustrate the essential and distinct cultural elements of such regions

* demonstrate a diversity of manifestations of the interaction between humankind and its natural environment (37)

* reflect specific techniques of sustainable land-use, considering the characteristics and limits of the natural environment they are established in (38)

* reflect a specific spiritual relation to nature

The *Guidelines* also note that:

* the protection of cultural landscapes can contribute to modern techniques of sustainable land-use, and can maintain or enhance natural values in the landscape

* the continued existence of traditional forms of land-use supports biological diversity in many regions of the world

* the protection of traditional cultural landscapes is therefore helpful in maintaining biological diversity

* the extent [of a cultural landscape] is relative to its functionality and intelligibility (40)

* the sample [of landscape] selected [by the nominating State Party] must be substantial enough to represent adequately the totality of the cultural landscape that it illustrates

* the possibility of designating long linear areas which represent culturally significant transport and communication networks should not be excluded

* the general criteria for conservation and management laid down in paragraph 24(b)(ii) (*see* Chapter 10) are equally applicable to cultural landscapes (41)

* due attention must be paid to the full range of values represented in the landscape, both cultural and natural

* nominations should be prepared in collaboration with and the full approval of local communities

* the existence of a category of "cultural landscape", included on the World Heritage List on the basis of the criteria set out in paragraph 24, does not exclude the possibility of sites of exceptional importance in relation to both cultural and natural criteria continuing to be included (42). In such cases, their outstanding universal significance must be justified under both sets of criteria.

Clearly, the Committee's expectations are both high and demanding, at least in theory. In practice, many a nomination has been accepted despite falling short of at least some of these expectations; but, thankfully, experience with cultural landscapes has so far been rigorous, both in the preparatory phase by the Advisory Bodies and the Centre and in Committee, a practice illustrated right up to the time of writing when the July 2003 meeting of the Committee 'referred' back to the nominating States Parties i.e. did not accept without further work, several potential cultural landscapes. The euphemism 'defer' is used for in effect an outright refusal.

(2) of the STATE PARTY:
* that inscription will serve political ends e.g. enable the State to keep up with peers and neighbours in cultural affairs, enhance the image of the State externally, enhance the image of the government, enhance the reputation of a minister, give the government clout in various negotiations, be prestigious for visiting dignitaries
* that inscription will provide access to various international funding sources e.g. UNESCO, World Bank, International Monetary Fund
* that inscription will be useful in one or more of several ways, notably in helping the tourist industry but also, for example, in providing an image to put on stamps (an important point in countries with an economic interest in philately)
* that inscription will foster/re-inforce a sense of national pride and/or identity and increase citizens' respect for the national patrimony
* that in some vague way inscription might help keep the populace content and perhaps encourage some form of local participation

(3) of LOCAL PEOPLE:
* that inscription will rapidly lead to local and personal financial improvement, initially in the form of grants from the UN and generally as a mechanism for accessing Western capitalism
* that inscription will boost tourism, leading to improvements in the local economy by the creation of jobs in tourism and its infrastructure e.g. in construction, and by the injection of tourists' cash
* that overall a WH Site will act as a catalyst for rapid and drastic changes towards something better
* in contrast, that inscription will attract too many visitors who

will have the effect of 'spoiling' local amenities and generally lead to a degradation of local life

* in contrast too is the expectation that inscription will act as a ring-fence against radical change and will re-inforce the maintenance of traditional ways of life e.g. by insisting that age-old methods of cultivation and herding continue, and by providing opportunities to welcome visitors and show off local traditions

(4) of VISITORS and TOURISTS:

* that they are going to the best in the world as well the very best of a particular country

* that the Site will be of global natural and/or human significance

* that a WH Site is worth going a long way to see, not least because by definition it should possess characteristics such as uniqueness, historical significance, impressiveness, even beauty, and/or a deep aesthetic value

* that an inscribed Site will:

  † be well-conserved and maintained

  † exhibit the highest standards of presentation and interpretation

  † provide them with high-class versions of the normal visitor facilities (visitor centre, rest-rooms etc.) now expected at a tourist destination (an expectation potentially clearly at odds with the whole point of inscribing some Sites)

  † for at least some visitors, demonstrate robust 'green' and 'sustainability' credentials

(5) of CONSERVATIONISTS, SCHOLARS and 'EXPERTS'

* that the WH status of the Site can be justified on scientific grounds e.g. that it demonstrably contains one of the best geological sequences in the world, or is a particularly good example of a significant habitat now becoming rare

* that the management regime, particularly in respect of conservation, is appropriate to the particular values for which the Site has acquired WH status e.g. that the tourism strategy does not endanger wildlife qualities, and that the structural restoration programme is based on research, fact and understanding, not fantasy, populist opportunism or ignorance

* that maintenance of the research potential of the Site is a

management priority which, while encouraging new work within a well-informed research design, includes rigorous control of projects involving resource depletion e.g. floral and geological collection, archaeological excavation

* that, whatever the formal constitution of the Site's organisational framework, it demonstrates a facility and willingness to receive and act on informed scientific and conservation advice.

That must suffice as a brief introduction to World Heritage and its List of sites. Now we turn specifically to cultural landscapes.

CHAPTER 2

The Idea of Cultural Landscape

Historical background

'Cultural landscape' has never been a popular term and even in academia, where it seems to have been invented, its use has been limited both in time and space. The term, and a particular idea it embraced, were promoted by Professor Carl Sauer and the 'Berkeley' school of geographers in the USA in the 1920s and '30s, but its conceptual origins lie at least a half-century earlier than that in the writings of German historians and French geographers. Scholars such as Michelet in mid-nineteenth-century France do not appear to have used the actual phrase 'cultural landscape' but they were thinking of land-scape not just as Nature but as the product of a long process involving people and natural circumstances. This was in contrast to other ways of conceiving of and looking at landscape. The 'Biblical view', for example, taught that all landscape was created in one Divine act; the 'Classical' view saw landscape as something arranged, indeed arrangeable, as a static stage-set, a view fashion-able in eighteenth-century Europe; a 'scientific' view of long-term geological and geomorphological sequence developed from observational opportunities initially provided by early deep mining and gravel quarrying; and the 'Romantic' perspective, personified by William Wordsworth as prose-writer as well as poet, saw landscape as natural, meaningful and stimulating of higher thoughts and sensibilities among its human occupants.

Sauer understood 'cultural landscape' in a particular way, but in essence his meaning was similar to ours, at least in World Heritage terms:

> 'The cultural landscape is fashioned from a natural landscape by a culture group. Culture is the agent, the natural area the medium, the cultural landscape the result.'
>
> *Sauer 1926*

The human geography, or cultural anthropology, which Sauer espoused was a leading-edge academic discipline for a generation. The idea of cultural land-scapes was influential in several related fields, not least in some parts of archaeology. The 'landscapes with personality' of Fox (1933) and the 'field archaeology' of Crawford (1953) (who briefly studied geography at Oxford) and in the 1930s–1950s were conceptually not far away even if the inspiration was unconscious; and the phrase continued to be used in some places, for example:

> 'Cultural landscapes will always remain elusive expressions of "a persistent desire to make the earth over in the image of some heaven."'
>
> *(Jackson 1952)*

More prosaic was a definition of a decade later but one which, though now 40 years old, could still stand as an expression of the basic idea underpinning the World Heritage concept:

> 'Cultural Landscape – a concrete and characteristic product of the interplay between a given human community, embodying certain cultural preferences and potentials, and a particular set of natural circumstances. It is a heritage of many eras of natural evolution and of many generations of human effort.'
>
> *(Wagner and Mikesell 1962)*

Such approaches were pushed aside by the hard, cutting edges of the 'New Geography' in the 1960s when landscape, like other matters, was reduced to, and explained by, mathematical models. The general rise of environmental awareness, and some new science, not least that of a palaeo-environmental nature concerning such matters as past climates, soil history and former florae, nevertheless began to emphasise the aridity of such perspectives, however beautiful the methodology and useful some of the results. It seemed to many working in the landscape that a more holistic perspective was needed, to take account of the very long time patently necessary to form the landscape with which we engaged on a daily basis. Time was also needed to allow for the changes, not merely those which had already occurred, but also those which we were ourselves making happen, communally and individually. Furthermore, reverting almost to the Romantic notion, there was and is the strong urge to make the landscape 'mean' something – it is not just there, a compound of physics and chemistry, but ought to have a significance to the human mind and sensibilities. In parts of the world, in much of Africa, for example, it has scarcely been otherwise (Munjeri 2000, 38).

As such thoughts began to re-emerge into the Western mainstream in the 1980s, Sauer's old idea was re-stated for a new generation:

> '… The cultural landscape is a tangible manifestation of human actions and beliefs set against and within the natural landscape.'
>
> *(Melnick 1984, 2).*

Over the next decade cultural landscape began to establish itself as academically respectable again. This did not, however, happen in time – rather, not with sufficient impact at first – to sway the World Heritage Committee when it considered whether, in the wake of the failure of the UK nomination of the Lake District, it needed to embrace man-influenced landscapes as well as natural landscapes and man-made structures. Nevertheless, informed opinion was changing and becoming more influential. One of the most respected of English countryside academics, Oliver Rackham (1988, 77) wrote:

> 'The individuality of the British and Irish cultural landscape is attributed to climatic, historical and edaphic factors ...'

– a meaning embraced fairly precisely in the single French word 'terroir'.

Most influential was a major conference in Sogndal, western Norway, which resulted in the thick book called *The Cultural Landscape – past, present and future* (Birks *et al.* 1988). Most significant political and bureaucratic steps have to be backed by an authoritative study – though neither politicians not administrators will willingly admit it – and in the case of cultural landscape and World Heritage, this book was it. About the same time, a particularly 'philosophical' definition appeared:

> 'Cultural landscape is a transformed part of free nature resulting from man's intervention to shape it according to particular concepts of culture.'
>
> *(Svobodova 1990, 24)*

The phrase after 'resulting from' was and is absolutely to the point. Despite a reluctance by certain interests (which persists in some quarters), the author-itative World Conservation Union (= the International Union for the Conservation of Nature: IUCN) addressed precisely the same point in moving towards its own view of landscape as it defined its own categories. Category V, Protected Landscape/Seascape, is an area 'where the interaction of people and nature over time has produced an area of distinct character with significant aesthetic, ecological and/or cultural value ...'. Its own perspective came in the immediately following words '... and often with high biological diversity.' It goes on, 'safeguarding the integrity of this traditional interaction is vital to the protection, maintenance and evolution of such an area.' (IUCN 1994a). This definition silently acknowledged that, by the early 1990s, a very similar definition of 'cultural landscape', one which saw landscape as neither God-given nor purely natural but as the product of the interaction between nature and culture, was in operation at the international level, at least for World Heritage purposes.

The World Heritage version of cultural landscape

Such thoughts were the common ground shared by a small group of people, of 'natural' as well as 'cultural' backgrounds, from several walks of life and from all round the world, which was invited by the World Heritage Centre to meet in an Alsatian neo-Gothic schloss at La Petite Pierre in October, 1992. The agenda was to consider cultural landscape as a potential type of World Heritage Site, and to advise the World Heritage Committee accordingly.

Fortunately it rained throughout the weekend, so by the Sunday afternoon the delegates had unanimously agreed that cultural landscapes:

> 'are illustrative of the evolution of human society and settlement over time, under the influence of the physical constraints and/or opportunities presented by their natural environment, and of successive social, economic and cultural forces, both external and internal. They should be selected [for World Heritage status] on the basis both of their outstanding universal value and of their representativity in terms of a clearly defined geographical region, and also for their capacity to illustrate the essential and distinct cultural elements of such regions.'

They further agreed to recommend to the World Heritage Committee that 'Cultural landscapes', as defined, fell well within the Convention and that the Committee could add them to its brief as a new category of World Heritage Site, within existing criteria. Furthermore, it recommended that ICOMOS should be the lead Advisory Body in this matter, with an assurance (which has been implemented) that a close working relationship with IUCN would be developed in assessing potential World Heritage cultural landscapes. The recommendations went to the World Heritage Committee that December, 1992, and were accepted. The Convention thus became the first international legal instrument to attempt to identify, protect and conserve cultural land-scapes of outstanding universal value with a view to transmitting them to future generations.

The rest of this book is about some subsequent developments, mainly from a personal perspective; but there were immediate and medium-term bureau-cratic consequences. Between 1992 and 1999, a total of ten expert meetings on cultural landscapes was organized by the World Heritage Centre and others. These expert meetings were milestones in the implementation of the decisions of the Committee by identifying different methods that States Parties might choose to use when nominating cultural landscapes for inclusion on the World Heritage List. Methodologies for identifying cultural landscapes were developed and suggestions made towards the classification and evaluation of cultural landscapes. Specific legal, management, socio-economic and conser-vation issues related to cultural landscapes were also addressed and examples of outstanding cultural landscapes discussed. Most of these meetings made specific recommendations concerning the recognition, identification, protec-tion and management of cultural landscapes in their specific thematic or regional context.

Before we finish with definitions, here are a few which have been put forward since cultural landscapes officially became a type of potential World Heritage Site. One of the urgent tasks of a 1993 meeting at Schorfheide was to expand on the Petite Pierre definition, for all concerned needed to explain what was and was not a 'cultural landscape'. The meeting itself ranged glob-ally and along the interface of nature conservation and cultural dimensions in the landscape. An important paper by David Jacques (1995) soon after reflected some of these issues. The conference proceedings were edited by three of the participants (von Droste, Rössler and Plachter 1995) and have remained the solid rock on which developments in this field were subsequently based.

Two definitions from Schorfheide were:

'Cultural landscapes reflect the interactions between people and their natural environment over space and time. Nature, in this context, is the counterpart to human society; both are dynamic forces, shaping the landscapes ... A cultural landscape is a complex phenomenon with a tangible and intangible identity. The intangible component arises from ideas and interactions which have an impact on the perceptions and shaping of a landscape, such as sacred beliefs closely linked to the landscape and the way it has been perceived over time. Cultural landscapes mirror the cultures which created them.'

(Plachter and Rössler in *von Droste et al. 1995, 15).*

In a paper delivered at the conference, one of the world's leading nature conservationists, Adrian Phillips, and a supporter of cultural landscapes throughout their developmental process, advanced a powerful argument. 'We should see landscape for what it is: a forum where nature and culture meet', he declared. 'Very few – if any – landscapes are truly natural', he continued, a bold and controversial statement coming from a naturalist and one that was still provoking profound disagreement at an Oxford cultural landscapes conference in 2000. Still, every discipline has its backwoodsmen, and sadly biology and ecology are no exception. Phillips made a significant point in remarking that one of the most important long-term benefits of the inclusion of cultural landscapes under the World Heritage Convention is that it should help promote greater awareness in developing regions of landscape issues generally, and of cultural landscapes in particular. His own definition was:

'Cultural landscapes are the everyday landscapes which surround us. They are the result of human intervention in the natural landscape and present a record of human activity and human values.'

There can be little argument with the first sentence there; which emphasizes the point that World Heritage cultural landscapes have to be something more, something special to lift them above the generality. A cultural landscape in this specific sense is therefore more than the result of human intervention but actually the result of an interaction between two dynamic processes – Nature and acculturation – in what is itself a third dynamic.

In the conference volume, the definition has been modified and enlarged:

'Cultural landscapes are to be found in every part of the populated world. They represent a rich and almost infinitely varied part of the human heritage' [and] 'often reflect living models of sustainable use of land and natural resources.'

(Phillips 1995, 381)

Clearly, in only those few words, Phillips' perspective is different in a very welcome way from that of the anthropological approach. In both practice and theory, dealing with cultural landscapes is an intellectual challenge. They embody powerful elements, in the mind as well as on the ground, of various academic disciplines.

My own contribution of a definition at the time, characteristically wordy, was:

> '... anything cultural involves development and process and both those require
> time. A cultural landscape has to have been, by definition therefore,
> dynamic, ... linking not just thought but action about these curious things,
> the relationships between humanity and time and between humanity and
> nature ... essentially the term embodies this relational, processual concept, and
> its meaning is always going to be an exercise in interpretations, in
> significances, in values. Landscape interpretation and cultural landscape go
> together, for both are about ideas and meanings, concepts and interpretations,
> dynamics and dialogues ...'
>
> *(Fowler 1995).*

It has subsequently been interesting to note whether academia has observed the rapid development of one of its own ideas as a tool of international co-operation. As far as I am aware, there has so far been little notice but one exception does comment on World Heritage inscription as well as providing its own nod toward history and its own definition:

> 'The American geographer Carl Sauer first formulated the concept of
> "cultural" landscape as fashioned from the "natural" landscape. Human
> geographers now seek meaning in the landscape as a "repository of human
> striving", and post-modernist perspectives visualize the landscape as a "cultural
> image" whose verbal or written representations provide images, or "texts" of its
> meaning, or "reading".'
>
> *(Ashmore and Knapp 1999, 3).*

Inevitably 'post-modernist' had to come into a modern definition but while the conceptual content there is not new, the definition provides a useful articulation relating the subject to some other issues currently on the socio-logical agenda.

Another recent definition takes us back to the Nature/Man debate which continues to underlie the concept of cultural landscape:

'There are two opposing views with regard to cultural landscapes:

   (1) Landscapes qualify for the term "cultural landscapes" if they
      express the influence of humankind on the environment at the
      landscape level, either visually or with regard to structure. In view
      of the universality of human impact on nature and natural
      resources, basically all landscapes would have to be considered
      "cultural landscapes" ...

(2) Cultural landscapes do not exist as such, or at least, they are not worthy of being protected because the influence of humankind on nature is intrinsically degrading. Thus more than anything, "cultural landscapes" reflect the wanton destruction of nature ...'

(Plachter 1999, 95).

Plachter, a human geographer, airs two ideas in his conventional definition, that evidence of past anthropogenic influence must be visible (with which I agree) and that, because anthropogenic influence is effectively ubiquitous, therefore all landscape is 'cultural' (with which I agree in theory but not in the practice of World Heritage recognition); but he then makes us recognise that, in glorifying the interaction of people and Nature, World Heritage is, in the eyes of some naturalists, glorifying Man's assault on Nature. This is a powerful point, not least at the moment when so many subscribe in at least general terms to a 'green' and more sustainable life-style. Nevertheless, the view to which Plachter draws our attention is itself ultimately unsustainable because it is based on the unstated premise not only that Nature is more important than we are but also that the Nature/Man relationship is only one of conflict. Neither is true, because we are ourselves part of Nature.

The concept of cultural landscape is, then, of a living phenomenon, changing its shape and its colours rather than its essential nature, and very much to do with people. I have tried to incorporate the human dimension in two of the several definitions I have attempted:

'A cultural landscape is a memorial to the unknown labourer'

and

'... a cultural landscape is a very personal thing.' (Figure 4)

The concept of cultural landscape links not just thought but action about these curious places, places to be curious about and places which affect us in curious ways. They are places where we can be aware of relationships between humanity and time, and between humanity and nature; yet a cultural land-scape should speak to us not just of pasts and has-beens but also of futures and possibilities. By definition, a cultural landscape has to have a past; to be of any value, it has to have a future, most importantly for our successors to contemplate tomorrow. So a cultural landscape is not just an idea; it should also be something of practical use. We as a species need communal reference points, to check where we are going to as well as coming from; as individuals, we similarly need our own little bits of heritage to give us personal identity and to act as our lodestone.

'Cultural landscape' is a cumbersome phrase. Since its perception is not intrinsic but very much of the human mind, then maybe a better phrase, borrowing from the Jellicoes (1975, 374), would be 'humanistic landscape'.

FIGURE 4.
'Heritage is a very
personal thing', as
exemplified by personal
possession of Mont-
Perdu, France/Spain.

They warn of 'the blindness that follows sheer lack of appreciation and the consequent destruction of those values in history that together are symbolic of a single great idea.' (*op. cit.*). Perhaps such a humanistic interpretation of landscape, melded with all that we now know about landscape scientifically, offers a way forward: a humbling eco-history, rather than a retreat to the simplistic opposites of romantic natural history or machismo cultural history. The phrase itself matters not a lot. Awkward or otherwise, the words should speak to us of experiences, of places remembered, of ideas such as scientific reservoir, memory-bank and desirable destination; and of one concept to take us forward in our understanding of ourselves, among the fauna on a floral, fragile planet.

The nature of World Heritage cultural landscapes

So much for the idea of cultural landscapes in general; World Heritage cultural landscapes have a particular meaning. Or rather should one say that they have two broad areas of potential different meaning, one the official definitions of what they should be, or at least were expected to be, the other how they have collectively defined themselves as being. With 36 to play with now, it is interesting to compare these two meanings, the intended and the actual.

'World Heritage' has inched its way into the world's consciousness over the last twenty years (Pressouyre 1993, 1996), importantly for cultural landscapes since it has given that concept both status and a practical definition. World Heritage cultural landscapes are now inscribed on the World Heritage List for a purpose specified on the World Heritage Centre's web page as: 'to reveal and sustain the great diversity of the interactions between humans and their environment, to protect living traditional cultures and preserve the traces of those which have disappeared ...'. Cultural landscapes are inscribed on the List on the basis of the cultural heritage criteria of the World Heritage Convention (Chapter 1). Some significant steps can be identified in the World Heritage Committee's journey to this situation (Fowler 2003b, Annexes A and B). Table 4 shows the three categories of World Heritage cultural landscapes defined and adopted by the Committee:

Table 4. Categories of World Heritage cultural landscape

CL category	Definition
1	A **clearly defined landscape** is one designed and created intentionally by man. This embraces garden and parkland landscapes characteristically constructed for aesthetic, social and recreational reasons which are often (but not always) associated with religious or other monumental buildings and ensembles (Pl. 2)
2	An **organically evolved landscape** results from an initial social, economic, administrative, and/or religious imperative and has developed its present form by association with and in response to its natural environment. Such landscapes reflect that process of evolution in their form and component features. They fall into two sub-categories (labelled a and b respectively for the purposes of this review):
	a. a **relict (or fossil) landscape** is one in which an evolutionary process came to an end at some time in the past, either abruptly or over a period. Its significant distinguishing features are, however, still visible in material form (Figure 3b)
	b. a **continuing landscape** is one which retains an active social role in contemporary society closely associated with a traditional way of life. It is continuing to evolve while, at the same time, it exhibits significant material evidence of its historic evolution (Pl. 3)
3	An **associative cultural landscape** is a landscape with definable powerful, religious, artistic or cultural associations with the natural element rather than material cultural evidence, which may be insignificant or even absent (Pl. 1)

We shall explore aspects of these types of landscape as defined in 1992. Regionally and locally, the concept and management of 'cultural landscape', raises issues and prompts debate. We begin by looking at Europe, for many of the issues there illustrate similar ones elsewhere.

Cultural landscape, World Heritage and Europe

It is now generally agreed that, give or take a mountain-top here or there, the whole of the European and British landscape is modified by humanity and is, to a greater or lesser extent, anthropogenic. In this respect European landscape may be more 'used' – indeed be the product of human use – than other parts of the world, but elsewhere too assessors must be careful not to fall into the trap of thinking they are looking at wilderness when in fact their view may well be of landscape at least influenced if not actually modified by people during the last 10,000 years. Most of Europe is in one sense cultural landscape, using that adjective as synonymous with 'man-made.' Throughout the European Landscape Convention, the single word 'landscape' is used in the sense of man-made landscape – which is fine, but confusing if 'cultural land- scape' does not have a distinctive meaning. My view is that the word alone and the word qualified by 'cultural' are not synonymous, and that 'cultural landscape' can and should have its own special significance. Here I try to iden- tify some facets of that potential significance, while flagging that the phrase of course already has its own specific significance in a World Heritage context. It was gratifying nevertheless that in 2000, 'cultural landscapes', which were almost unthought of in English minds even a decade previously, justified a prestigious Oxford conference of their own, and there can be little doubt that it was the influence of World Heritage discourse on the matter which largely brought this about (Kelly *et al* 2001). Delegates eventually produced an 'Oxford Declaration on Landscape' but, to the end, could not agree whether they were talking about 'landscape' or 'cultural landscape'. They almost agreed, however, that the latter was an elite concept. All the more reason, therefore, to stress that such landscapes, the phrase and the concept, are not confined solely to existence in a World Heritage context. 'Cultural landscape' is valid globally, including in Britain (*see* Chapter 6), whether or not partic- ular landscapes acquire the accolade of World Heritage inscription. Further, far from being élite, they are democratic, vernacular and common, in the English sense of belonging to everyone – and hence the title of this book.

A cultural landscape is a very personal thing (Appleton 1986, 1994). My own perception is deeply influenced in particular by what other people consider to be *their* cultural landscapes. My perceptions have been shaped by a journey: from Kakadu through Uluru-Kata Tjuta to Banawe in the Cordilleras; to Hallstatt-Dachstein/Salzkammergut, les Cévennes/Grands Causses in France, and Pyrénées-Mont Perdu on the Spanish/French border; to the Loire Valley, the Vall de Boí in the Spanish Pyrénnées, the northern Andes in Venezuela and Dominica in the Caribbean; to Hawaii, the Everglades, Chaco and Mesa Verde in the USA, the Atlas Mountains and Moroccan coast and, most recently, Avebury in England and the small island of Pico out in the Atlantic among the Azores. In other words, I am privileged to have visited and, in some cases, helped evaluate, places which are now among (and not among!) the world's first World Heritage cultural landscapes.

A Euro-British, particularly English, perspective can refine some of those definitions discussed earlier in this Chapter, so we should niggle away at the concept a little further here. A recent British perspective is also helpfully to hand (Macinnes 1999). 'Cultural landscape' is a concept which can be considered within, not alien to, the long tradition of English rural writings. 'Large sweeping downs, and deep dells here and there, with villages amongst lofty trees' seems a pretty good sketch of a cultural landscape by a writer who considered himself 'incapable of appreciating natural beauty in places where human conditions are poor'. William Cobbett there neatly subsumes the interactive trinity of Nature, land and Man. Nearly two centuries ago he, like us, found inseparable 'the morally acceptable and the aesthetically pleasing.' He also 'saw a significance behind the obvious appearances of the landscape: he too traced causes and effects; and he ... was concerned with the fate of the common people.' Over a century later, but still 70 years ago, H. J. Massingham has a similar view: 'My theme is the relationship between man and nature in our own country, its fruitfulness and the disastrous consequences of disturbing it' and 'I do not really care for landscape which is without sign of any co-operation between Nature and Man'.

The concept of cultural landscape contained in the World Heritage definition is nevertheless new. It could not have been available to earlier generations because they did not possess (in the widest sense of the phrase) our scientific knowledge, our growing understanding of how we ourselves function, or our ability to create and use such concepts as 'process', 'relationships' and 'holistic'. We have in our grasp, not as a result of some phoney idea such as the 'rediscovery' of 'lost knowledge' but on a rational basis, something which offers us not just a new way of looking at scenery and not even a new way of looking at Nature; but a vision which could enable us to perceive ourselves as part of a process creating and constantly changing the environment of which we are an integral part. Cultural landscapes, properly handled as intellectual property and not reduced to mindless items of bureaucratic convenience, could be the nodes of memory for humankind in thinking about that process.

A more specific, deeper sense for the phrase 'cultural landscape' comes wrapped in a global concept. Our hard-won scientific understanding of the British landscape is a product similar to that intellectually-generated in many other parts of the world. Together, bottom-upwards as it were, these many local perceptions merge with the global perception of the strategists who perceive in their perspective the humanising of the whole world's environment. The basic point, fundamental in getting to grips with 'cultural landscape', is that there is now nothing truly natural left on earth. Even equatorial jungles and icy, polar landscapes are Man-effected in some respect. No longer is Nature defined, as so many have believed, by that which is separate from humanity. One of the main reasons why I am so keen on cultural landscape is that it can be, I believe, a significant medium in converting what can so easily be the negativism of such facts into a productive process whereby we find new relationships between human societies and Nature as their matrix.

A stretch of countryside – though almost everything I say can apply to a cityscape and industrial landscape too – can embody and represent such relationships; but we have to be able to perceive that evidence and appreciate its significance. We need to sense the conjunction of physical remains and intangible associations in special places, and be able to recognise that a cultural landscape has been created where previously there was just geography. That line of argument clearly leads to the conclusion that a cultural landscape resides in the human mind, not on the ground. Hallstatt, Austria, for example, has existed for over three thousand years as a significant place but it was only in 1996, when we were ready to receive the idea, that the place transformed itself, not physically but in our minds, into a cultural landscape. The process was even more striking in the case of Orford Ness, Suffolk, England, when in 1994 the National Trust's futuristic perception of significance in a twentieth-century landscape of ugliness and deadly high-tech, lurid beauty and iconographic redundancy, brought a stretch of barren, shingle coast from government dereliction into heritage care. It is not yet a World Heritage cultural landscape but its scientific and historical significances, and expressive, dramatic qualities of natural/human interaction, should bring it into consideration during the twenty-first century.

World Heritage has given cultural landscapes, most of them in Europe, both status and a practical definition; my own believe is that 'cultural landscape' can reciprocally enhance the concept of World Heritage. That concept is indeed a noble thing; in practice its application, as experience has shown, can be fraught with issues which, superficially, appear to be tangential and even irrelevant. But 'heritage' is itself an extremely emotive and powerful subject matter, and that will impinge upon considerations of 'cultural landscape' quite as much as it has to individual archaeological sites and cultural property. Indeed, 'landscape' is a highly-charged subject in any case, involving matters across a range from life-style through property rights to aesthetics and cognitive perception, so it was conceivable that in espousing the sub-set of 'cultural landscape', 'World Heritage' was about to enter a very interesting phase of its development (reviewed in Fowler 2003b).

World Heritage, as we have seen, identifies three main categories of cultural landscape (Table 4) (Plates 1–8). A recent, independent attempt to categorize cultural landscapes also proposes a tripartite division: 'constructed' (category 1. *above*, plus some of 2.), 'conceptualized' (close to 3.) and 'ideational' ('landscapes of the mind': 3. also) (Ashmore and Knapp 1999, 8–13). Category 2.b of the World Heritage *schema* seems not to have been grasped, yet it is likely that that will be the category to prove most popular with the world's people. Britain contains outstanding examples of all three main types of cultural landscape as defined by the World Heritage Committee (Chapter 6). It provokes one immediate *caveat* about *Designed and Associative Landscapes.* Many whole functional landscapes, like the Banawe rice terraces (Figure 5, Cover, Plate 3) which originated at least 2,000 years ago, and the agrarian arrangements on second millennium BC Dartmoor, are quite as much

FIGURE 5.
The stone and earth
rice-terraces near
Banawe, Cordilleras,
Philippines, are under
enormous pressures
from running water
and gravity and require
continuous
maintenance,
traditionally carried out
by the women of the
Ifugao.

'designed and created intentionally by man' as are the great parks and gardens of Stowe, Stourhead and Schönbrunn. And they are rather bigger in scale too. The definition of this first, 'obvious' type of cultural landscape should perhaps have dealt more with recreation and aesthetics rather than emphasising deliberateness alone.

27

That said, most associative cultural landscapes in Britain are probably not of global significance. One that certainly is, however, – and I emphasise that it is as an associative cultural landscape, and not primarily as either a relict or continuing one – is the Lake District. 'Brontë country' around Haworth, North Yorkshire, exemplifies more typically the issue in Britain. It comprises a fine but in many ways typical area of Pennine moorland, not of itself immediately suggestive of world class but certainly a cultural landscape. There is no doubt about the direct physical and creative association between landscape and writers, so any suggestion that the area is a potential World Heritage 'cultural landscape' would depend upon assessment of the literary significance of the Brontë family. Fine writers indeed (though not equally), but are they of sufficient significance globally – in the history of the novel, for example – to carry their home landscape into World Heritage status almost entirely by association? – a nice judgement is required.

One of the points in the idea of 'associative cultural landscapes' – and this applies whether in World Heritage considerations or not – is, in contrast to that last example, to allow for the recognition of what I call 'oral landscapes'. By that I mean, not just landscape with lots of stories inspired by them, as on the moors around Haworth, but landscapes full of stories told about them.

'Relict landscape', category 2a in Table 4, is a familiar concept in Europe. Indeed, so common are excellent examples of 'dead' landscapes in Britain that landscape students and managers there may have become rather blasé about them. Of course, there is no way in which it is possible or desirable to protect them all as of outstanding or universal World Heritage significance; yet, from a world point of view, I would suggest that in the British Isles is a major resource, something of a rarity on a global scale. I would certainly expect to see it contributing significantly to any rational European system of landscape recognition.

This raises several fairly basic questions. One is 'How much land do we have to include to designate "a system"' i.e. enough to understand how the system worked, rather than only enough to contain the visible archaeology or the habitat of one plant or the immediate economic environment of a working community? The question currently arises, for example, in the National Trust's proposal to recreate a wetland in a nature reserve of 14 square miles around the existing 800-acre (324 hectare) Wicken Fen Reserve, Cambridgeshire. There, species depletion continues despite sensitive management because 'it suffers as an island in a sea of hostile farmland and is too small to protect wildlife effectively'. On the Wiltshire Downs east of Avebury, extensive though the archaeological evidence is of highly-organised field systems in long-term farming land-use, the working system of which they were an integral part can only be properly glimpsed if they are viewed in a much broader topographical perspective, certainly much bigger than the current World Heritage Site which partly embraces them.

Upland Britain provides further examples, though exactly the same point could be made by exemplifying agrarian landscapes in Hawaii (defunct) and on Pico in the Azores (Plate 4). A common factor in many prehistoric British examples is that the 'evolutionary process' of the second millennium BC i.e. the agricultural systems which produced the organised landscapes of field, farm, pasture and lane, came to an end around the twelfth and eleventh centuries BC. There are variations: Cheviot, for example, has that Bronze Age phase but much of the landscape was (still or again?) in use in the later centuries BC and the early ones AD. Many early landscapes also show evidence of later, disconnected phases of land-use. Both Dartmoor and Bodmin Moor, for example, have good archaeologies of a quite well-documented phase of marginal farming from 1100 to 1300, and of various metal-ore and stone-quarrying activities thereafter. But such activities, characteristically of limited extent, tend to add interest to the 'old' landscapes already existing rather than damage them too much. The developed landscape of later second millennium BC Dartmoor is truly remarkable, both in what it visibly was and in its state of preservation which, properly studied, enables us to perceive that ancient entity (Fleming 1988). Seeing it, however, is only one dimension of perception, for the human mind also wants to understand how it worked.

What in fact are we looking at? We have to designate enough land to understand how the system worked rather than only enough to contain the visible archaeology. In the case of Dartmoor, impressive and extensive though the archaeological evidence of an essentially stone landscape of built walls is, the working system of which they were an integral part can only be properly glimpsed if they are viewed in a much broader topographical perspective. If Dartmoor were ever to be considered for World Heritage nomination as a cultural landscape – and either or both it and Bodmin Moor would be the obvious examples from England – then very careful consideration would have to be given to extent, preferably on a functional rather than topographical or survival basis. The inscription of the Cordilleras rice-terraces, Philippines, even though that is a 'continuing landscape' example, is a good model, selecting a relatively small, 'working' area from a huge region of montane rice-growing (Villalon 1995).

The other basic question is visibility itself. It is particularly germane to Britain. There, all over the lowlands including river valleys, the equivalents to the systems just described are known to exist but now in an almost totally flattened and buried condition *below* the ground surface. They are, in other words, invisible in normal terms. Yet they are not only visible but recorded with remarkable detail by air photography (e.g. RCHM 1959). And here, once more, we are talking of whole landscapes, not just individual archaeological sites, and multi-period landscapes at that. The scientific value of such landscapes, often additionally significant because of their waterlogged contents, cannot be doubted; but while an invisible cultural landscape is certainly conceivable intellectually and scientifically, could the World Heritage concept absorb an invisible World Heritage cultural landscape? In a sense, it could be argued, whatever the philosophic and bureaucratic difficulties with such an idea, we already have such an 'invisible' cultural landscape, though in a different dimension; for there is very little to be seen at least by Western eyes in the empty but indigenously-crowded landscape of Uluru (Plate 5 and Chapter 3). A landscape's values, its setting, lie in presence, not visual qualities.

Such issues – functionality, extent, survival – are the practical aspects of defining cultural landscape in theory and in words. Some of those concerned are well-aware of the connection between landscape, the associated lifeway and contemporary economics, though the all too characteristic assumption that tourism is the sure-fire way of achieving economic viability is questionable (ICOMOS 1993). Tourism is locally as fragile as a Spring *adonis,* and less reliable; it can soar like an eagle and crash like a meteorite, as was dramatically illustrated by the collapse of rural tourism in Britain in the early months of 2001 in the wake of foot and mouth disease.

The European Landscape Convention toyed in draft with the idea of a list of Landscapes of European significance. Some register of landscapes of European significance could fit neatly in the middle of a three-tier hierarchy between landscapes of national importance and World Heritage cultural landscapes 'of outstanding universal' value. I say this not, however, for bureaucratic convenience but because it will be quite impossible to do justice to Europe's landscapes in terms of World Heritage designation. Some mechanism for recognising landscapes which are part of the European inheritance – and, all other things being equal, similarly on other continents – representing its landscape diversity, for example, would therefore be useful in enabling appreciation of them to be better shared among Europe's peoples.

I have recently been faced with four European cultural landscape claimants on World Heritage status, all rural though all with industrial attachments, all scenically beautiful, and all agrarian. They brought home to me what is blindingly obvious: that Europe is full of stunning landscapes, overwhelmingly of countryside – not surprising, really, given its rural demeanour. Varied and diverse though my four landscapes were, they shared three common factors:

   i. each was an ensemble of natural factors in a combination
      particular to that place;
   ii. the human use of that place, particularly in a labour-intensive,
      non-intensive agrarian economy;
   iii. and the results of the interaction of the first two factors.

What struck me in particular, given the huge areas of Europe still farmed, is how quickly farming technology has changed yet how 'traditional' so much of the landscape still is. The crying need is for some European-wide attempt to identify types of traditional European *agrarian* landscape and then scientifically isolate the outstanding and typical examples – perhaps three? – of each type. If all European landscape is 'cultural', what is so special in European terms, never mind global ones, about 'cultural landscapes'? Where was my European frame of reference for judging these cases continentally as a filter to a World Heritage judgement? How many montane limestone landscapes with abandoned field systems do we need, for example, to illustrate a great European tradition of extensive, low-input but much 'sweat and grief' marginal farming? Where does the Vall de Boí stand in its European rankings? (Plate 6). Was the Mont Perdu assessment of the transhumant validity across two trans-frontier National Parks factually as well as intuitively correct? (Plate 7). In practice an internal European process of assessment of such agrarian landscapes would be so helpful – indeed, it is an urgent priority in my view, if only for European purposes if not for World Heritage ones. Much the same could be argued for other continents.

Conclusion

In general then, we can note that the phrase 'Cultural landscape' incorporates an adjective which, in England, is commonly perceived as having a narrow, elitist meaning. Fortunately, such a nuance is not conveyed in many other places, notably Scandinavia. Unfortunately, however, that particular sense has besmirched the concept of 'cultural landscape' when the phrase, not least in its application in World Heritage terms, means exactly the opposite. Apart from that special World Heritage class of parks and gardens, a cultural landscape must by definition be somewhere created by the long anonymous endeavours of ordinary people. By recognising 'cultural landscapes', we have, almost for the first time, given ourselves the opportunity to recognise places which may well look ordinary but can fill out in our appreciation to become extraordinary. An ability of some places to do that creates monuments to the faceless ones, the people who lived and died unrecorded except unconsciously and collectively by the landscape modified by their labours. A cultural landscape is a memorial to the unknown labourer.

CHAPTER 3

The First World Heritage Cultural Landscapes, 1993–95: Australasia and South East Asia

....

The idea of adding cultural landscape to the type of site which could qualify for World Heritage status represented a coming together of many minds from around the world; just as did the meeting of those few people in Alsace in 1992 who defined what a cultural landscape was for World Heritage purposes. This symbiosis almost certainly reflected the greater attention which, on the whole, had been given to the evolution of rural landscapes in Europe in particular, though there was nothing in fact in the definition which limited cultural landscapes to rural landscapes alone. Nevertheless, for present purposes it was the detailed analyses of rural landscapes by archaeologists, geographers and environmental experts which were influential, though it would be a fundamental misconception to see cultural landscapes as an exclusively Euro-centric phenomenon. The diversity of landscape, as well as the range of ideas around the common theme, were well-represented at Schorfheide-Chorin at the first World Heritage cultural landscape conference after the World Heritage Committee's decision, and that variety is clearly expressed in the resultant book (von Droste *et al.* 1995). It was as expected, therefore, that the first four World Heritage cultural landscapes were nominated from outside Europe. They were from New Zealand, Australia and the Philippines.

Tongariro, New Zealand
The first, Tongariro National Park (Plate 1), was a place and a case which had been a catalyst in stimulating the debate. It had been a natural World Heritage Site (1990) before it was realised that the 'natural' environment was not only the homeland of a human community but also that the natural features were endowed with great significances in human culture. Furthermore, it was the presence of people quietly and subtly 'managing' nature which gave it some of its characteristic qualities. Tongariro had been discussed as a model of an 'associative' landscape at the Petite Pierre meeting which defined the three categories of cultural landscape, so it was no surprise that it was re-submitted in 1993 under cultural criterion vi alone.

That re-nomination quoted the description of a 1907 survey report, still not superseded in its graphic brevity:

The great volcanoes, Ruapehu, Tongariro and Ngauruhoe differed much in character. Ruapehu was a magnificent mountain mass, with glaciers filling the gullies. Its crater, a mile in diameter, was filled with crevassed ice and contained a hot lake ... Ngauruhoe was a perfect cone in shape, and was quite without vegetation from base to summit. The crater contained towards its centre a mud volcano, which not very long ago covered the sides of the mountain for a thousand feet with hot mud ... Tongariro was not one single volcano, but consists of a number of craters, some long since inactive and some still quite ready to eject ashes, whilst steam and sulphurous vapour were continually given off from them ...

Tumu Te Heuheu (1995) gives an inimitable account of this landscape which I can only summarise and quote from, without in any way capturing his indigenous style. 'Culture and language', as he remarks, 'are synonymous.' 'Language', he continues, 'moulds the landscape to fit our culture.' The belief is that Ngatoroirangi, priest and navigator of the Arawa canoe which brought Polynesians to North Island, New Zealand, determined to climb an as yet un-named mountain as he explored his new land. Exhaustion and cold, however, threatened to defeat him at the summit so he called upon his ancestral spirits and his sisters in distant Hawaiki to send fire to warm him: '*Ka riro au ki te tonga, haria mai he ahi maku!*' His call was heard, and fire was sent with the fire-gods Pupu and Te Hoata to rescue him. 'Its fiery course is marked', as the nomination documents states, 'by mud-pools, geysers, steam-pits, and hot streams stretching across Aotearoa (New Zealand) from the original landfall in the Bay of Plenty and culminating in the volcanoes of Tongariro and Ngauruhoe.' In this way the mountain come by its name, Tongariro.

It also came to possess human and superhuman characteristics, bonding 'geography to humanity'. Their power caused passers-by to look the other way to avoid disasters befalling them, a typical aspect 'in the Maori holistic and spiritualistic approach to the natural world.' 'Maori culture has a rich oral history in which the connections between man and the landscape play a central role', observes the ICOMOS assessment, stressing the importance of oral history. 'The formation of the land, of the mountains' violent love for Phhanga (a "female" volcano), and of how fire came to the central North Island are the themes of some of the best known Maori stories. In Maori mythology the first children of Papatuanuku (Earth Mother) and Ranginui (Sky Father) were the spectacular mountains of Aotearoa, and thus linked closely with the last of their offspring, human beings.'

For the Ngati Tuwharetoa *iwi* this is a living landscape with its own *mauri* or life-force. With its active and dormant volcanoes and thermal pools, it is moreover a direct genealogical link with their historical homeland and Hawaiki and with their landing place in the Bay of Plenty. The natural land-scape plays a fundamental role through oral tradition in defining and confirming the cultural identity of the Maori people: the two are indissolubly linked. A basic sense of continuity through *tupuna* (ancestors) is manifested in the form of profound reverence for the peaks. The natural beauty of Tongariro is the spiritual and historical centre of Maori culture. It was as an entity, physical, conceptual and spiritual, that Tongariro came to be recognised by the English colonial government when, to prevent its fragmentation in new land allotments then being arranged, in 1887 it became New Zealand's first National Park, a gift of the Ngati Tuwharetoa as a sacred place under the *mana* of the Queen.

Tongariro's claim to become an associative cultural landscape on the grounds of its intangible, oral significance alone was unambiguous and powerful, and in 1993, only one year after cultural landscapes were formally approved as a concept in World Heritage terms, it became the world's first World Heritage cultural landscape. It was a great significance in clearly signalling at the outset, as those at La Petite Pierre had intended, that Western concepts of landscape were insufficiently catholic to embrace what was meant by cultural landscape. At the centennial celebration in 1997, by which time the Park embraced 79,000 hectares, the Paramount Chief of the Ngati Tuwharetoa said 'these sacred mountains are to be owned by no-one and yet are for everyone', a thought appropriate not only to Tongariro but to the whole concept of cultural landscape. That concept, clearly at the outset a noble, global one, encompassed from the start non-tangible, non-monumental, spiritual and oral values, a point emphasised by the world's second cultural landscape.

Uluru-Kata Tjuta, Australia

Perhaps more familiar to the world as Ayer's Rock, 'Uluru' (Plate 5) as it is otherwise known in shorthand includes for World Heritage purposes not only the familiar, rocky sandstone bulk of Uluru itself but also the Olga mountains. The area of the World Heritage cultural landscape nevertheless is bounded by the limits of the Uluru-Kata Tjuta National Park and is not expansive enough to encompass the 'intelligible spiritual and functional landscape' of the Anangu people (Layton and Titchen 1995, 178). The relationship between the indigenous people and the landscape around the rock outcrops is essentially a compound of two factors: the long-established management of the land by the Anangu, principally by burning (Figure 6) – 'swaling' would be the technical, vernacular word in England; and the 'peopling' of that landscape with ancestral heroes – a cultural tradition 'in which the landscape functions as a mnemonic for historic events'.

That it is a cultural landscape at all, however, is remarkable because the Park was previously inscribed in 1987 as a World Heritage natural site. For some that was sufficient: there was no doubt that the Park justified that status on natural grounds alone. Yet it did not do justice to the cultural significance of the landscape, and a growing Western awareness of that fact. Uluru-Kata Tjuta, like Tongariro, played an important role in shaping the definitions of cultural landscape in 1992 and immediately thereafter. Scientific research was simultaneously reinforcing the claims of Aboriginal people to great antiquity

FIGURE 6.
The limestone scarp
between the plateau
and the wetlands in
Kakadu National Park
and World Heritage
site, Australia, with the
traditional method of
controlling vegetation,
burning, being
practised.

in central Australia (*c* 50,000 BC), while conservation interest in the implications of fire-managed landscape over millennia was being matched by a growing public interest in 'dream-lines' and the 'dream-time'. The approval of cultural landscape for World Heritage purposes therefore provided the opportunity to recognise the relationship between the Anangu and their land and to do so without in any way weakening overt recognition of the Park's natural qualities.

Physically lying in the 'Red Centre' of central Australia, the National Park (132, 566 hectares) is an arid area of sand-dunes and flats extensively covered by 'bush', characteristically mulga woodland. Uluru and the Olgas stick up out of this apparently featureless desert, dramatic punctuations that dominate it visually for long distances in all directions. Both famously change their appearance during the day, and on each day; and this is literally true. Rational explanations would dwell on their geology, shape, striations and erosion, on the way they catch the hard, clear sunlight differentially, accentuating colour (red, orange, black, purple), reflection, shadow; but it is not difficult to begin to attribute qualities of magic, especially at sunrise and sunset or after a deluge of rain. And of course the surroundings are neither featureless nor empty. They contain a myriad of features, significant features, appreciated by the local eye and given value by the local culture. As stated by the Australian Government's (1994, 8) *Renomination of Uluru-Kata Tjuta National Park*, however, 'the significance of the landscape is not measured only by individual locations ... they are interconnected by the *iwara* (tracks) of the heroic beings active during the *Tjukurpa* ('the Law' see below). The *Renomination* summarised (p. 4) the claim of the place on World Heritage as 'The cultural landscape of the A<u>n</u>angu *Tjukurpa* is an outstanding example of the traditional type of settlement and land-use known as hunting and gathering. It is directly and tangibly associated with events, living traditions, ideas and beliefs of outstanding universal significance, and it is a potent example of imbuing the landscape with the values and creative powers of cultural history through the phenomenon of sacred sites.'

In particular, the landscape 'is the representation of "the Law", which describes how the land was given form as a result of the travels of ancestral beings' (*op. cit.*, which the rest of this paragraph follows closely). Indeed, 'the Law' (*Tjukurpa*) defines all aspects of the relationship between people and the land and between people themselves. As a result, for Aboriginal people the landscape is not a 'natural' entity, but a cultural one. Furthermore, the Law establishes an all-encompassing series of laws that bind people, the landscape, the animals and plants into one interconnected world. 'It is a complex concept because it relates not only to the era of the travels of the ancestral figures, but also to the Law as a force in the lives of the living. It does not reflect the Western concept of time.'

Twelve major rock art sites, and hundreds of other painting sites, exist around the base of Uluru in overhangs and rock shelters. Uluru-Ka<u>t</u>a Tju<u>t</u>a is characterised more by rock engravings. The earliest date to some 9,000 years ago and there is no doubt of the antiquity of the artistic tradition; some paintings were still being created in the 1970s, however, and probably most paintings are relatively recent. There has been no detailed archaeological research at the habitation sites in the Park, but the general picture seems to be of transitory occupation before some five thousand years ago. New tool types thereafter, and the appearance of a seed grindstone which enabled grass seeds to be added to the diet, are aspects of an increasing intensification of activity and development in social organisation about four-three thousand years ago. Contact with Europeans was sporadic in the late nineteenth century. An idea to use the area for white settlement and pastoral farming was abandoned, underlining the success of other people, the A<u>n</u>angu, in adapting their culture to, and in modifying, the environment so that a sustainable mode of subsistence, developed millennia previously, had continued into the early twentieth century.

Then, the A<u>n</u>angu resisted attempts to assimilate them into European culture but, from the 1940s, began to rely on tourists as a source of cash. Initially, officialdom did not encourage an A<u>n</u>angu presence at Uluru but in 1973 three crucial recommendations were made: that the early clutch of tourist facilities, including an air strip, close to Uluru itself should be relocated outside the Park (subsequently creating the archaeology by the rock of an early tourism centre, visible from the air, Plate 5); that A<u>n</u>angu sacred sites at Uluru should be protected; and that training should be provided for A<u>n</u>angu rangers. A decade later, the Prime Minister announced that title to the National Park

FIGURE 7.
The local people, who manage the Uluṟu-Kata Tjuta National Park, Australia, ask in a prominent notice at the foot of the mountain that visitors respect the fact that it is sacred in their belief-system.

would be granted to the traditional owners; and in 1986 a Board of Management was established to manage the Park in conjunction with the Director of National Parks and Wildlife. Anangu have a majority on the Board. In 1993 the official name of the park [became] Uluṟu-Kaṯa Tjuṯa National Park at the request of the traditional owners.

An abiding personal memory is of half-opened boxes of stones and bits of rock heaped along the veranda of one of the wooden buildings used by Park staff at the foot of Uluṟu. Their contents, ordinary stones in other contexts, had been returned, mostly by mail, by visitors who, after their visit, sometimes long after their visit, had learnt in numerous ways that Uluṟu was not simply a fun-thing to climb and chip away at on a day out in the outback, but was a holy mountain, sacred to the A_nangu. In remorse, they sent their souvenirs back, often with notes along the lines of 'We simply didn't realise …', 'If only we had known we would never have taken …' and 'We're very sorry, no offence was meant …'. Climbing the rock is of course also an obvious tourist challenge – 'Been there, done that'. 'That' may be acceptable for Ayer's Rock, a British colonial perspective, but it seems inappropriate in the indigenous context of Ulu_ru as a sacred mountain. Yet many visitors, ant-like in their skyline insignificance, were still making the steep ascent in the mid-1990s, despite calls for respect (Figure 7). Nevertheless, a new respect and understanding among visitors, not just for a landscape but for those who inhabit it, might prove in the long term to be one of the merits of cultural landscape as a 'noble, global concept'.

Cordilleras, Philippines

Visually in utter contrast to Ulu_ru-Ka_ta Tju_ta, the rice terraces in the Cordilleras, Philippines (Cover; Plate 3, Figure 5), provide a particularly good example of a continuing, organically-evolved cultural landscape. They were well-known before nomination, having a claim as 'the eighth wonder of the world'. Behind the drama of their appearance, however, lies an economic reality to grow more rice in the mountains, and an intangible heritage resting in the semi-magical, legendary status of the terraces of the rice-fields in the Banawe area, popularly known as the 'Stairway to the Sky' and the 'Stairway of the giants'.

The terraces lie between 700–1900 metres above sea level among the spectacular mountains of Luzon Island, a day's drive north of Manila in the northern Philippines. That is if you can reach Banawe by motorised vehicle. The way is not only mountainous and through what was until not so long ago guerrilla country but the road is mostly unpaved through a landscape subject to volcanic and earthquake action and heavy rainfall. All three, but particularly the last, produce dramatic landslips, and diversions, for example down to a stream bed and up again, are almost inevitably a feature of the journey. Banawe itself, a small town, features in Western writings because it possesses a modern hotel in a landscape mainly of wooden houses, raised and levelled on stilts to counteract the steep slopes. A profound, scientific study of the area and its people, the Ifugao, by an American ethnographer who lived among them (Conklin 1980), is nevertheless the academic source of most of our outsider's understanding of the rice terraces and their workings.

The terraces themselves hang like steps, often on steep slopes, from the edge of rain-forest high on the mountain sides down to the edges of the valley-bottom streams. From just a metre high on valley floor, they can rise to 6 m high on slopes above, sometimes to support only a small terrace perhaps just 2–3 m wide. The terrace systems stretch from valley to valley across a huge area of mountainous landscape, as much as 20,000 km². The earliest archaeological evidence for their creation indicates that construction began some two thousand years ago. Collectively, they represent an enormous, anonymous effort to accumulate a tremendous social asset which enables life to be lived and sustained at this altitude in this environment. The resultant, quite extraordinary landscape, generated by a combination of dramatic topography and a unique man-made alteration of it, suspends vast quantities of water on the mountain sides as the terraced rice-fields are gently irrigated. Control of the water is the key to both the agricultural landscape and the system of working it. Essentially, the terraces are the main components in a simple but effective system of irrigation which is at the same time designed to defy the pull of gravity on the water. An essential factor in the operation of the system is, therefore, that the fronts of the terraces which contain the water, and the channels and bamboo pipes which lace the mountain sides, be maintained and repaired all the time. The main repairs, as when the water-logged front of a terrace slips downhill, is carried out by the women: the work can involve bringing mud and small boulders upslope to rebuild a stone revetment of the sort which characteristically lies inside the grassy scarps bounding the terraces. Indeed, it is estimated that the rice-fields involve some 14,000 miles of walling.

This highly-structured landscape remains, especially around Banawe, a working landscape. On it grows the basis of the local economy deriving from a single annual harvest of *tinawon*, 'a fragrant upland homegrown rice' (Yuson 2000, 32). The local social structure reflects the needs of rice cultivation in this environment, as witnessed by one of the roles of women exemplified *above*. That structure contains, and must continue to contain if the system is to be maintained, skilled, knowledgeable and sympathetic manual labour, with the emphasis on 'manual'; for the fragility and topography of the terrace systems inhibit the use of machines. Here, mechanisation cannot make up a shortfall in field labour, nor can it significantly ease the burden of those who labour by hand. No wonder, therefore, that many of the young people look to a life beyond the mountains: 'The highlands account for seven per cent of the total land area of the Philippines, but are home to less than two per cent of the country's population' (Yuson 2000, 32). Those who remain look to an income from tourism, perhaps to supplement but perhaps even to replace their livelihood from the fields. The danger, however, is obvious, for if the fields are not worked tourists would look at 'dead' remains of a former system, a fossil archaeological landscape rather than a living landscape intimately related to the life and society of those who worked it.

On the other hand, who has the right to condemn any society, any individual, to a life of unremitting labour and penury just for the sake of the tourist gaze or even for the sake of a local, and in this case national, heritage? The local heritage is represented by several traditions, both in the landscape and in social behaviour. Each cluster of terraces, for example, 'is surrounded by a buffer ring of private forests (*muyong*), managed according to tribal practices ... A centrally located ritual rice field is the first parcel to be planted or harvested. Near the dwellings [of one room, raised on four posts and covered by a thatched pyramidical roof (Figure 8)] is the ritual hill, usually

FIGURE 8.
Traditional house on
stilts, Banawe,
Cordilleras, Philippines.

marked by a grove of sacred betel trees where the holy men (*mumbaki*) carry out traditional rites.' (Yuson 2000, 33). In an attempt to stay the erosion of local tradition in the face of Western values and economic reality, a farming ritual called *Patipat* was revived in 2000, fifty six years after its last performance (when the American military and social impact on the area was considerable). It was colourful and symbolic, ushering rats and evils spirits down the treads of the 'stairway to the river' where, as in former days, they were supposedly drowned. But whether such conscious heritagization will actually counteract the powerful forces of materialism and restore an already 'eroded sense of identity' (Yuson 2000, 33) remains to be seen. The event quite properly stressed the basis of the co-existence between the traditional society of the Ifugao and their working landscape: you can't have one without the other. In practice, however, both will have to accept some modification if both are going to survive.

Meanwhile, such is the national pride that the rice terraces are the Philippines' heritage logo. On the world stage, they were also a site which contributed to the debate about cultural landscape leading up to and immediately after the recognition of the category by the World Heritage

FIGURE 9.
Terraced rice-fields in China: representing rice-growing and its many landscapes in South East Asia, yet – with the exception of the Cordilleras – hardly represented on the World Heritage List.

Committee. In a sense, the terraces were the first 'pure' cultural landscape to be inscribed, for their two predecessors were both already on the World Heritage Lists as natural sites. And the terraces of the Ifugao have remained a standard-setter since 1995, for they represent the quality against which all other potential World Heritage cultural landscapes can be judged (Figure 9). None, in my view, has surpassed them. With such an inspiring example leading the way, it is to be hoped that there will be an awakening of interest in cultural landscape issues in the world, perhaps especially in developing countries with special landscapes but little experience of landscape conservation. Indeed one of the most important long-term benefits of the inclusion of cultural landscapes under the World Heritage Convention is that it should help promote everywhere greater awareness of landscape issues generally, and of cultural landscapes in particular. What has happened to the Cordilleras rice terraces in the meantime, however, is very sad.

CHAPTER 4

Inscriptions, 1995–98:
Europe and South West Asia

After the inscription of the first three World Heritage cultural landscapes in 1993–95, all as it happened from one particular (large) portion of the world's surface in Australasia and south east Asia, it could appear now as if the 'old world' determined to set the balance 'right'. The next seven inscriptions, 1995–98, were all from Europe, three of them from Italy.

Regardless of their geographical location and national origins, between them they added significantly to the portfolio of inscribed cultural landscapes, complementing the wide-ranging nature of the first three. Two of them, the fourth and fifth, were formal, park landscapes, though neither was just that; but they nevertheless introduced into the List two examples of what many regard as one of Europe's major contributions to the world's artistic and aesthetic heritage. Then came two mountain landscapes, one on the Franco-Spanish frontier in the Pyrénées, the other in the Austrian Alps: both very different, yet each with much in common. Three Italian nominations then followed, all with their own characteristics of course but all with water as a major element. Sea is common to all three, with either or both irrigation and rivers also integral to their landscapes. We cannot deal with all three even-handedly so will arbitrarily, but with good reason, concentrate on one I have visited, Portovenere. Otherwise, a brief section covers each of the other four, non-Italian landscapes. Europe's first contribution to the list demonstrated the diversity inherent in the concept of cultural landscape, not the homogeneity which often follows from bureaucratic intervention.

FIGURE 10.
Old Quarter of Sintra from the Moorish Castle in the World Heritage cultural landscape of Sintra, Portugal.

Sintra, Portugal

'Sintra was classified as World Heritage Cultural Landscape at 11.05 a.m. on 6th December 1995 at the 19th Session of the UNESCO World Heritage Committee Meeting in Berlin.' (on title page of Ribeiro 1998). Such pride is fortunately typical and, in the case of Sintra (Figure 10), it had been encouraged by inscription and is well justified. But you need to work quite hard, physically and intellectually, to discover the cultural landscape when you visit the place, and to see it as distinct from a motley collection of rather odd buildings scattered around a curiously dislocated town and the flanks of a craggy, afforested minor mountain range. Nevertheless, this was Europe's first World Heritage cultural landscape, and it was and is an appropriate choice.

All has not been easy, however, since inscription. Local dissatisfaction with the treatment of the Site has been expressed. Often a proposal to create a World Heritage Site and approval of inscription provoke local opposition, but in this case the local argument is that the authorities are not taking their World Heritage responsibilities seriously enough. The issues' complexity is illustrated by the content of an ICOMOS re-appraisal of the Site in 2000. It covered the physical geography of Sintra Mountain, the restoration of water systems, re-cycling in the environment, the role of the forest in the cultural landscape, an integrated management plan, interpretation in the management of the World Heritage site and how to improve the management structure: a list which also gives some idea of the nature of the place.

Sintra as a cultural landscape meets all three criteria of *Guidelines*, para 39. It is notably a continuing landscape with an active social role, albeit perhaps in not quite the sense that was envisaged by the drafters of that provision. It is an exclusive dwelling, holiday and retirement place for well-off foreigners as well as Portuguese, and a convenient and accessible 'lung' for a day-out for the nearby urban population of Lisbon. The area can well accommodate such apparently conflicting uses, for they are separated spatially both inside and beyond the inscribed area. As with many other World Heritage sites, the historic town centre – plus a lot of sand – provides a convincing stage set for filming. The needs of a Spanish TV 'soap' during my visit created a somewhat surreal scene early one morning, set off by the fantasy of the Moorish Castle on the skyline above (Plate 8).

Description of the Site

The cultural landscape lies on and around a mountain at the eastern end of a mountain range. Orientated east–west, the massif is only 15km long by 5km wide but, sticking up from the extensive surrounding plateaux, it has always been considered as a real mountain. The geology of the mountain is mainly a magmatic massif that has thrust through tertiary limestone plateaux. Its highest point is Cruz Alta at 528m above sea level. The mountain receives an average of 1000mm of rain per year, the nearby plateaux only 400mm. The mountain is also the meeting-place of a temperate, very humid Atlantic influence (northern slopes) and a hot dry Mediterranean one (southern slopes). The rivers are numerous and contribute greatly to the erosion of the mountain. The top of the mountain is often covered by a kind of mist that gives it the appearance of cloudy tropical forest.

Physically, the cultural landscape consists of an interlinked ensemble of man-made structures, the main cultural monuments being the town of Sintra itself (part of it outside the World Heritage site) with its 'old quarter' and series of outstanding buildings (Figure 10), and, on the surrounding hills, parks and gardens embracing Pena and Monserrat Palaces (Figure 11), Regaleira Quinta, the Moorish Castle, Capuchos Monastery, and hundreds of temples, follies, grottoes, waterfalls, small lakes, ponds and other Romantic and neo-Classical structures. Water, of which there was plenty naturally, was managed, partly to create hydrological conditions for acclimatization of wet sub-tropical or tropical plants, and above all to provide movement and sound-effects in the three-dimensional stage-set which was a Romantic garden: hence the laying and making of kilometres of buried pipes and drains along the sides of paths and walks, and the creation of gushing woodland brooks. A lot of the water system created to achieve these two objectives was by 2000 in a bad state after between 50 and 100 years of poor maintenance; pipes are broken or leaking, drains are eroded and blocked, canals are empty with sand and leaves, streams are polluted, and lakes are in the process of eutrophication.

Numerous private dwellings also occur in the inscribed area, often themselves of architectural interest and characteristically standing in designed, exotic gardens. The place is made for parks and gardens. A unique micro-climate with high rainfall and a temperature range of only *c.* 4–24°C provide an attractive habitat for plants. The climax vegetation contains diverse groups of Mediterranean–Atlantic features. Of the 900 plants considered as part of the natural ecosystem of Sintra Mountain, 51 per cent are Mediterranean or Western-Mediterranean, 11 per cent Mediterranean–Atlantic, and 5 per cent Atlantic. The genuinely indigenous vegetation had, however, been largely destroyed by over-exploitation by the early nineteenth century, and the floral magnificence which has so significantly contributed to Sintra's World Heritage status is almost entirely a creation of the nineteenth and early twentieth centuries when in effect a new landscape was made, structurally as well as in terms of its plants. Those same environmental circumstances encouraged gardeners and the importation of species from around the world. Romanticism introduced, beside local vegetation and built features like waterfalls and grottoes, exotic plants such as *Acer japonicum, Agave mexicana, Araucaria angustifolia* and *Cedrus libani.* Foresters worked mainly with pines, acacias and eucalyptuses. They created architecture as forest and forest as architecture. Forest was an integral part of the various original designs as the originators sought to create their environment in terms of a Romantic ideal. They sought to look out at the practical realization of such Romanticism from the rooms of their castle; they also wanted to discover their castles half hidden by vegetation and mist. The English garden designer Beckford worked here; Byron stayed here. Literary and artistic associations give the place significance, to Portugal as well as Europe, not only in terms of works written locally and of garden design but rather in terms of the standing of the place in the Romantic Movement.

The designed elements of the landscape complement the natural topography; the network of narrow, local roads is a marked feature. Kilometres of these roads within the cultural landscape are characteristically steeply confined and often sunken, either cut down into bare rock or walled. The cuts into and through rock are demanded by the topography; the walls are the outward signs of the estates around the palaces and the *quintas*. With trees arching above, the effect is of moving through a series of sinuous, semi-dark tunnels.

An element of religiosity imbues the landscape as a whole: Sintra Mountain has been and clearly is a 'holy mountain.' Religion is also embedded in numerous sites and monuments throughout the cultural landscape. Two of the major palaces, for example, were originally religious foundations, and one of the private gardens I visited was not only exquisitely beautiful but also designed and ornamented entirely around the theme of religion – Classical, Christian and Muslim. Moorish references elsewhere are also favoured

FIGURE II. Neo-Moorish architecture on an inner balcony of Pena Palace, Sintra, Portugal.

(Figure 11). The Capuchos monastery is significant not only because it carries the feeling of a sacred mountain and represents the transformation of a religious complex into a palace, but also because it retains the reality of a religious place.

The general state of individual monuments, from single monoliths to palace complexes, is often good, owing to the relatively short time since some were abandoned (100–50 years), the absence of frost, and the quite narrow temperature range which reduces the stresses on external surfaces. Decorated tiles on external walls, for example, are often in good condition. On the other hand, the characteristic rain and damp have clearly taken their toll on roofs and fittings in houses and parks. There is a fundamental conflict in this respect: the very moist atmosphere is essential for the development and maintenance of the cultural/natural landscape, but it creates serious problems for architectural monuments.

Extensive (and in places intensive) development has already filled much of the view from the cultural landscape to both north and south. Management of the World Heritage site should, therefore, concentrate on preventing any inappropriate development within the cultural landscape – which appears as a large green oasis in the landscape from outside – and indeed hold the line against intrusions at the outer boundary of the buffer zone.

Between 1995 and 2000, the authorities undertook considerable works, an effort which gives some idea of what is involved in terms of responsibilities and heightened expectations once a cultural landscape, particularly one with major buildings, is inscribed on the World Heritage List. This included two restoration projects, one of the Royal Palace in Sintra and the creation of a car-free zone in front of it, and the other of Pena Palace. It was also planned to open new restaurants and shops in the Parks and to make progress with such practical matters as providing car-parks and better access points to the protected area.

Major problems lie still, however, with structural restoration e.g. at Monserrat Palace, under wraps at the time of my visit, and with the vegetation and the actual structure of the parks and gardens. Here is a huge and long-term challenge, compound of an often poor state of physical repair, a rampant Nature, and great public interest. Vistas, the very structure, however intangible, of a Romantic park, are of urgent concern, for everywhere they are lost or obscured and require careful, sensitive restoration. Vandalism is, perhaps surprisingly, an immediate problem, with arson (at least two important buildings) and widespread graffiti symptoms of frequent misuse of the secrecy and isolation afforded by large parks with extensive woodland.

Sintra, the town, and its major monuments around, constitute a prime tourist attraction, both to the resident population of Lisbon, 40 minutes by train to the east, and the tens of thousands of visitors who come to southern Portugal on holiday. Tourists have, of course, been coming for over two centuries: in one sense this is part of the essence of the place, popularly renowned for its pure air and green spaces as much as for its aesthetic qualities and history. 300,000 visitors go to the Palaces each year; there are huge visitor and traffic problems at the "Palace end" of Sintra itself where, after carefully contrived improvements to facades and street surfaces, the area is nevertheless visually teetering on the edge of becoming just another day-tourist destination, overfull with souvenir shops and the like. Major works already carried out in and around the town – a new railway station, a new bypass – and ambitious plans in hand (including a long underground car park just outside the World Heritage Site), are all driven by the pressures of tourism. Fortunately, properly managed, much of the pressure can be safely and instructively dispersed across the mountains, where management already possesses an asset many another attraction seeks to create. That asset lies in its multiple properties, all potentially separate tourist destinations.

The cultural landscape of Sintra was inscribed on the World Heritage List on the basis of criteria (ii), (iv) and (v). It clearly meets (ii), for overall and in detail it exhibits, both 'over a span of time' and 'within a cultural area of the world', 'an important interchange of human values ... on developments in ... landscape design.' With regard to criterion (iv), it is not difficult to argue that it is an outstanding example of landscape which illustrates a significant stage in human history, although personally I find its claim weak in that respect. Similarly, Sintra's 'fit' with criterion (v) is perhaps also arguable depending on the significance attached to the word 'traditional' i.e. it is not a 'traditional' cultural landscape in the sense that 'traditional' was meant and used in the original document that emerged from La Petite Pierre. On the other hand, Sintra could as easily have been considered under criterion (vi), since it is directly and tangibly 'associated with ideas' and 'beliefs ... of outstanding universal significance.' In addition it is associated with artistic and literary works, and people, which and who are at least arguably significant in the European cultural tradition. As a 'cultural landscape', it meets criteria 39 (i) (a landscape 'designed and created intentionally by man'), (ii) (a continuing landscape with an active social role) and (iii) ('powerful religious, artistic and cultural associations of the natural element').

There is no doubt, then, that Sintra qualifies as a World Heritage cultural landscape but, for a European 'first', it was not perhaps such an overwhelming and 'obvious' example of a cultural landscape as were Tongariro, Uluru and the Cordilleras for their respective regions of the world. It is not as well known outside Portugal as were the others outside their countries, and so does not quite carry their international iconographic qualities. There is too perhaps an element of ambiguity over the main criteria used to justify its inclusion on the List, and perhaps not enough was made originally of its 'associative' elements. It needed a monitoring mission (*see* Chapter 10) to bring those out, something which probably reflected the way thinking about such landscapes had advanced during five years of further cultural landscape experience, 1995–2000 (*cf.* Chapter 5).

We have dealt at length and in detail with Sintra because it was the first European World Heritage cultural landscape. It is also in itself a complex property with major issues of management in terms of restoration, interpretation and access. It therefore raises many of the issues about the nature and conservation of cultural landscapes, even though there is nothing else quite like it among the 36 official World Heritage cultural landscapes. The next two cultural landscape inscriptions, both European, also raised interesting issues.

Lednice, Czech Republic

The Lednice-Valtice Cultural Landscape, Czech Republic, was inscribed in 1996, the first formal park landscape of World Heritage cultural landscape category 1 to be nominated and accepted as such. Though there were a park (full of Gothic and English references) and other ornamental landscapes and gardens within the Sintra cultural landscape, coming after Tongariro, Uluṟu and the Cordilleras rice terraces, Lednice-Valtice represented quite a change. The area lies in southern Moravia, embracing some 200 sq km which make it one of the largest artificial landscapes in Europe. The countryside itself was 'fashioned according to English romantic principles of landscape architecture', says the official citation, and is the setting for the two castles of Lednice and Valtice where Baroque architecture is married with the classical and neo-Gothic styles. The whole was consciously developed by the Dukes of Liechtenstein between the seventeenth and twentieth centuries. It was and is a good first example of the classic European artificial landscape designed primarily for visual effect and pleasure.

Pyrénées-Mont Perdu, Spain/France

In complete contrast was the next (1997–1999) World Heritage cultural landscape, that of Pyrénées-Mont Perdu (Plate 7; Figures 12 and 13). This straddles the French and Spanish frontier in high mountain country some 40 km south of Lourdes. It was actually inscribed in 1999, with an addition approved in 1999, after a double-pronged evaluation. It was first visited by an IUCN mission when it was thought to be primarily a natural site, but the evaluator sensed that there might be more to it than that. He alerted ICOMOS to the possibility of its being a mixed site, even a cultural landscape. As a result, ICOMOS carried out its own evaluation, both on the ground – which I had the privilege of performing – and through its other normal channels, eventually recommending to the World Heritage Committee that the nomination was of a cultural landscape. The site was inscribed, curiously and ambivalently, as both a mixed site under natural criteria (i) and (iii) and cultural criteria (iii), (iv) and (v), and as a cultural landscape, something of a bureaucratic muddle which does nothing to enhance the concept of 'cultural landscape'.

Though not in any sense a park in the Lednice-Valdice sense, the World Heritage area consists of two National Parks, Odesa in Spain, Mont Perdu in France. They share a common boundary along the national frontier. The inscribed area is of 30, 639 ha, encompassing in addition to Mont Perdu itself at 3,352 m in altitude two of Europe's largest, deepest canyons on the Spanish side and three walls of near-vertical rock on the French. The whole is of considerable geological interest, a splendid and visually impressive example of calcareous landforms.

What makes it a cultural landscape of outstanding value, as distinct from one only of geological interest, however great, is the clear interaction of people and environment still continuing as an active process within, and directly as a result of, this geological phenomenon. South of the watershed, the land in general inclines southwards, catches the sun on long slopes, and becomes very dry. North of Perdu, the land faces north, is steeper and more often in shadow, it enjoys a higher rainfall, and it retains more water. As a result, since at least medieval times when it is first documented, transhumance has occurred and still continues: 'Spanish' stock is driven north up into and across the mountains in May-June to spend the summer grazing on 'French' pasture. Those national adjectives are in inverted commas because that is the way we would now think of it; but of course the practice dates back to a time when there

FIGURE 12. Bare summer sheep-pasture abandoned by late October above Gavarnie on the north side of the Pyrénées, Mont-Perdu, France.

FIGURE 13.
Cows still graze in late
October high on the
south side of the
Pyrénées in the Odesa
National Park, Mont-
Perdu, Spain.

was no national frontier and when such terms had not been invented in this context. Indeed, people living on both sides of the mountain range – the World Heritage site itself is almost completely uninhabited – regard the area as their own country, a non-national entity which is neither French nor Spanish. Whatever the nationality of the animals, the effect of their feeding on the valley slopes and mountain pastures in present-day France can everywhere be seen in the flora, most notably in the near-absence of trees, the shape of the bushes – browsed off at animal-eating height – and the composition of the short-grazed herbage (Figure 12).

Among the several issues brought forward with the inscriptions at Lednice and Mont Perdu, management stands out, particularly at Pyrénées-Mont Perdu. Indeed, no management plan for the whole of the World Heritage landscape existed six years after inscription despite requests for one, and an obligation to produce it. Of course, each National Park has its own management plan but experience has shown that there are difficulties in this case in developing an integrated approach in practice, despite an inter-Park Charter of general co-operation. Furthermore, on the French side, a promotional 'Friends' organisation which very much led the way with the National Park in advocating that the Mont Perdu area should become not just a World Heritage Site but an official cultural landscape is now deeply disillusioned with the authorities and their treatment of the World Heritage site. Whatever the rights

51

and wrongs of the situation – which in some respects is not entirely different from that at Sintra – the fact of the absence of integrated, trans-frontier management policies and practices at official level, and of good relations with local people, is a disappointing sign that all is not as it should be in a well-run World Heritage cultural landscape. Among other things, as we discuss in Chapter 10, such a landscape should be a model to other ones in several respects, not least its management as a World Heritage site in addition to a National Park. Meanwhile, however, the annual cycle of transhumance continues in its traditional form and it is very much to the credit, and benefit, of all concerned that the various levels of imposed modern bureaucracy have not impaired that. Curiously, the very next cultural landscape inscription was remarkably similar in some respects to Mont Perdu. It is certainly mountainous.

Hallstatt-Dachstein, Austria

The Hallstatt-Dachstein area lies in the southern Alps, 220 kms (135 miles) west south west of Vienna. It was under snow when I visited it in January, 1997, but brilliant sunshine had the effect of making the whole look scenically excoriating. The World Heritage cultural landscape here is one of visual drama, with huge mountains rising abruptly from narrow valleys. It is a landscape to appeal to Gothic fantasy, hostile yet beautiful. Nature dominates, from the deep lakes to the permanent glaciers high above; yet Man has inhabited the valleys here for over three millennia, eking out a living from the traditional natural resources of valley and montane pasture. On that pasture, and above, the sub-alpine and alpine meadows support a well-recorded range of plants, some currently extending their montane range at their upper limits as the glacial edges retreat even higher. The higher pastures have been used for the summer grazing of sheep and cattle since prehistoric times as part of the process of transhumance, a process which still gives the various valley communities rights of access to specific grazing areas high in the mountains. For at least 3,000 years up to the present, however, the distinctive part of the Hallstatt economy was salt-mining, extracting salt from the Salzbergial, the 'salt-mountain' (Figure 14).

Though the human impact appears to be relatively slight on such an immense landscape, use of the wider landscape by farmer-miners over the centuries has modified it to a degree, while the mining has transformed the inside of the mountain, now honeycombed with man-made galleries, tunnels and caverns. It is the presence of salt, a natural resource essential to human life, which has made this place different; there has been intense human activity in the midst of a largely untamed landscape. A broad swathe of the landscape around Hallstatt Lake forms a buffer zone, in general adequate to protect the Site's setting; but it is what has gone on inside the mountains and beneath the Lake's surface which affords the place outstanding significance. Water and salt below, montane farming (including transhumance) above and an association

FIGURE 14.
The ICOMOS mission with officials and mine staff about to go into the underground salt-mine during the evaluation of Hallstatt, Austria.

with an event of great technological significance, the introduction of iron to central Europe nearly three thousand years ago, combine at Hallstatt-Dachstein to convert beautiful scenery into cultural landscape.

The significance of the glaciated Dachstein mountain, nearly 3000m high, lies in its hydrology, which is of world-class importance both in itself and in terms of the knowledge of it acquired through a long history of exploration, discovery and scientific study. The quality and quantity of the montane water provide a potentially significant resource. The hydrological system is closely connected, literally and scientifically, to the area's speleology, which has attracted and sustained much scientific study aided by a long tradition of self-disciplined volunteer work by cavers and cave-divers. Three caves are open to the public: each is speleologically different but their integrated management allows a range of knowledge and experience to be made available in a coherent programme of conservation, accessibility and interpretation.

Hallstatt is also of great archaeological importance, a heritage of European and indeed global significance. The 'Hallstatt Culture' is the name given to an early iron-using culture that is, in archaeological terms, one of the best defined in the world. Two archaeological sites in particular have produced that definition. Both sites, clearly part of the same complex, are situated in the accessible Salzberg valley, high above the present-day town of Hallstatt. One site is the cemetery that gave the 'Hallstatt Culture' its name, flourishing in the period broadly *c.* 900–600 BC. From the 1,000+ graves excavated so far, mainly in the later nineteenth century, have come jewellery, weapons, bronze and ceramic vessels, ivory, amber and glass, much of the material associated in grave-groups. It is this context which provides its scientific value; the collection also includes highly-decorated items which give the whole an artistic and aesthetic interest. The excavated material is now in the Natural History Museum in Vienna, where many of the grave groups are on display together; other material is attractively displayed in a recently refurbished museum in Hallstatt itself.

The 'Hallstatt Culture' developed in the early centuries of the first millennium BC, based upon the extraction of salt and the Mediterranean/European contacts and wealth that its distribution brought. The late prehistoric archaeology here in a sense heralds the emergence of Europe as a place becoming different in some significant respects from other parts of the world. Thereafter the use of iron became more and more widespread within the continent and the knowledge of how to make it was never lost.

The second site is the salt-mine within the Salzberg, the mountain immediately behind Hallstatt town. Research deep within it in the 1990s demonstrated that systematic salt-mining occurred earlier than the 'Hallstatt culture', in the later second millennium BC (*c.* 1200 BC) and culturally within a mid/late Bronze Age context. I saw, preserved in wet glutinous mud, a recently-discovered gallery, organic material including a rope, and a living area: the miners were certainly mining, digging a gallery from a vertical shaft and apparently living troglodytically with their families while working. Of great interest in the history of salt-extraction and mining, such discoveries are of considerable significance in illuminating the origins of the 'Hallstatt Culture' and in emphasising the importance of the area as a 'scientific reservoir' for further research. Hallstatt can increase our understanding of the development of technology in Europe and its social, economic and artistic ramifications long before the emergence of Rome.

The mine and its surrounds were under royal and state management for four centuries until the end of the twentieth century. The mine itself is still working commercially, but some parts of it are now available to visitors, including areas made safe for display arising from the continuing programme of archaeological investigation. Visitors can enter old galleries and see the clear evidence of movement over the last three thousand years within the mountain which has had the effect of squeezing and squashing previous working spaces; the salt itself preserves organic artefacts. Modern salt production remains as high as ever, though only *c.* 60 men are now employed in a very efficient mining operation which has become highly mechanised and computerised. Salt is extracted as brine which is now piped down-valley to a modern treatment plant at Ebersee.

With the development of the transport network in the nineteenth century the Salzkammergut began to enjoy a flourishing *villégiature* culture in and around Hallstatt. The area has an important place in the history of the

FIGURE 15. Riomaggiore and cliffs from the south on the Ligurian coast, Portovenere, Cinque Terre, and the Islands World Heritage cultural landscape, Italy.

development of tourism, and for a century and more it has been one of the best-known tourist regions in Europe. Hallstatt town itself remains a tourist destination. Picturesquely situated on the edge of its lake, it is best approached across the water by ferry from the valley railway station opposite. Now a (virtually) car-free zone, it contains traditional buildings in stone with barrel vaulting supporting timber-framed upper storeys. The parish church replaced an earlier Romanesque structure, parts of which survive. In the tiny graveyard immediately on its north is a Gothic structure. Its basement, viewable at ground level, contains a neatly-arranged assemblage of human skulls and long bones, the skulls being marked with the name and other details of the deceased. Purely practical considerations dictate this apparently macabre procedure: because the graveyard cannot expand, the skeletal material is regularly removed from the few graves when they need to be used again.

Portovenere, Cinque Terres and the Islands, Italy

This cultural landscape includes the area at the top left hand corner of Italy, the north western coast, just before it begins to curve westwards towards the French Riviera. It lies south of Genoa, forming the coastline south eastwards

from Monterosso towards the great naval base of La Spezia. It is an impressive coast, with steep cliffs broken only by narrow, steep-sided ravines where streams, at times torrential, come tumbling down into the sea. Little, cliff-hanging villages cluster around these tiny estuaries, usually above narrow strands or small, sandy beaches (Figure 15).

The eponymous five villages and their lands are, from north to south, Monterosso, Riomaggiore (Figure 16), Corniglia, Manorola and Vernazza

FIGURE 16.
View up the main street, Riomaggiore, Cinque Terre, Italy.

FIGURE 17.
Vernazza in its
landscape context of
terraced vineyards on
coastal cliffs, as viewed
from the castle, Cinque
Terre, Italy.

(Figure 17). Their interconnections by road, even now, are, sinuous, even hazardous; the traditional way is indicated by the coastal footpath, though it was closed by a landslip and the threats of more to come after heavy winter rain when I was there in the spring of 2001. Amazingly, however, the villages are connected by a main railway line, a later nineteenth-century engineering feat of considerable achievement, presumably undertaken for strategic reasons rather than as a local amenity. Between the villages, it spends more of its time tunnelling through the cliffs than in the open air, thereby offering tantalising glimpses of blue-green sea, tinted houses and towering cliffs. Even modest-sized boats cannot put in at Corniglia and Riomaggiore, and the local fishing along this coast is small-scale and primarily for local consumption. So, overall, we have a short string of picturesque villages clinging to the cliffs of a surprisingly remote strip of coastland between two cities – interesting, but not of itself of World Heritage status.

The distinctive element is the dramatic, man-made terraces strung along the cliffs and what they represent (Figure 17). As we have already seen in the Philippine Corderillas, it is the combination of landscape and tenure in a difficult terrain which lifts scenery into cultural landscape. The cliffs shout of effort, not just in the creation of hectares of cultivable land where there was none but in the working of them too. Building the drystone revetments to make the terraces along kilometres of steeply sloping cliff overhanging over the sea was an enormous job; maintaining them also required long-term effort, patience and skill. This landscaping was additional to the annual task of cultivating the soil, looking after the vines – for viticulture was the primary function, though terraces were also used to grow vegetables – and collecting the grapes. All this labour had to take place before the most important task could actually begin: making wine. The 'lands' of the five villages belonged to the communes, with individuals in the community holding land by right, tradition, status – and doubtless a little bit of influence. Some of the terraces are still in cultivation, and mechanical means involving hawsers and pulleys, somewhat Heath Robinson in appearance but apparently effective, are used to ferry workers back and forth, and materials up and grapes down at harvest time.

Sadly, however, most of the terraced cliffs and valley sides have now fallen out of cultivation. Desertification, as in so many of southern Europe's difficult rural areas, has occurred and continues: people have been leaving the land for better-paid, easier lives elsewhere – shades of the Philippine Cordilleras – and there is little temptation to many of the young people in the villages now to stay and, in effect, work hard to take on Nature. Some do, but the populations are ageing: in Riomaggiore the average age is 75! So the cliffs of the Cinque Terre are well on their way to becoming an archaeological landscape, spectacular but dead – and as archaeology, they would be well worth designating as a World Heritage cultural landscape. But some local people, notably the Mayor of Riomaggiore supported by the National Park which embraces the World Heritage Site, are determined that the terraces shall not die. They have come up with some inventive ideas to bring life and money back into the area, and to keep the cultivation of the terraces going despite the demographic problems.

In particular, they have put out an appeal to people elsewhere, not for charity but offering them the chance to lease one or more terraces, provided that they accept responsibility for their cultivation. The ingenious element here is that it is not a condition that the leaseholders work the terraces themselves; and the hope is that well-off people in, say, Germany or other parts of Italy, will be attracted by the thought of having their own part of a famous vineyard (and a World Heritage Site) and will pay local people to do the work for them. In this way, so the hope is, local people will be able to earn an adequate wage through a combination of fees earned by working other peoples' terraces and the produce of their own terraces. If this succeeds, then it should not be necessary to leave purely for economic reasons, and local people should therefore be able to continue living in the villages. So far the uptake has been encouraging, and it is just possible that the early twenty-first century will see a turn-round in the economic fortunes of this World Heritage cultural landscape. Were that to happen, it would be good not only for the 'Five lands' but also extremely encouraging to others elsewhere in demonstrating that, if you can come up with the right idea appropriate to the particular landscape, then the future does not have to consist, as it has for so many places, of simply going down the tatty road of commercial tourism.

Other inscriptions

Cinque Terre was the first of the Italian cultural landscapes, inscribed in 1997; the second was Costiera Malfitana (Figure 18); third and last, for the time being, inscribed in 1998, was Cilento and the valley of the Diano National Park containing, among other archaeological delights, the temple of Paestum (Figure 19). Also inscribed that year, breaking the run of European sites, was

FIGURE 18. Another coastal World Heritage cultural landscape in Italy, Costiera Amalfitana, here with vines growing on trellises on terraces.

FIGURE 19.
Air photograph of part
of the landscape of the
World Heritage
cultural landscape of
Cilento and Vallo di
Diano National Park,
Italy, characterized
topographically by
three ridges like that
shown here and
archaeologically by
sanctuaries and
settlements along them.

the first cultural landscape from the Middle East. Superficially, it looks like many another dry, limestone valley covered with scrub (Figure 20). But a second glance takes in the multitude of small cluster of buildings and individual structures, clearly religious, dotted around the landscape and protruding through the vegetation; and the vegetation itself is not all low scrub but also contains some noble trees. These are the Cedars of Lebanon, and the site's formal name is Quadi Quadisha (the Holy Valley) and the Forest of the Cedars of God (Horsh Arz el-Rab). So the eleventh World Heritage cultural landscape not only extended the geographical distribution by putting a dot on the map between south east Asia and Europe; it also reinforced the emerging impression that a major characteristic of a World Heritage cultural landscape was holiness. Sanctity, worship and a deep respect for the landscape itself were – in very different manifestations – evident at Tongariro, Uluru, the Cordilleras, Sintra, Mont Perdu, Cilento and Quadisha. It was going to be interesting to see if this quality continued to be significant as the number of inscribed cultural landscapes doubled over the next two years (*see* Chapter 5). Meanwhile, there was much to think about.

FIGURE 20.
Cedars of Lebanon: one of the monasteries, Mar Lichaa (St Elisée) on the cliff-face above the Quadisha river, in the World Heritage cultural landscape.

CHAPTER 5

The Idea Develops, 1999–2003

In December 1998 the World Heritage Committee approved only two new cultural landscapes for inscription on the List – Cilento, Italy, and the Cedars of Lebanon (Chapter 4), bringing the total to 11. Over the next two years, 1999–2000, it approved respectively 5 and 7 inscriptions (Table 5), bringing the total to 23. In other words, the number of World Heritage cultural landscapes inscribed on the List doubled in one-third of the time, from 11 over the first six years, 1993–98, to 23 over the next two years. A further 13 were added in 2001 and 2002, maintaining this rate of about six each year. The purpose of this chapter is to look, however briefly, at some of the newly-inscribed cultural landscapes and discuss some of their features which added to the characterisation of World Heritage cultural landscapes (*cf.* Chapters 11, 12).

Table 5. Inscriptions of official World Heritage cultural landscapes, 1999–2000.

Year	Nomination number	State party	Landscape name
1999	474	Hungary	Hortobagy
	840	Cuba	Vinales
	905	Poland	Kalwaria
	932	France	St Emilion
	938	Nigeria	Sukur
2000	534	Germany	Dessau-Wörlitz
	933	France	Loire
	968	Sweden	Öland
	970	Austria	Wachau
	984	UK	Blaenavon
	994	Lithuania/Russia	Curonian Spit
	1008	Cuba	Plantations

The class of 1999–2000

Collectively these inscriptions represented a significant addition to the quality, range and interest of the World Heritage version of cultural landscape. Five are very different, major agrarian landscapes. Hortobagy National Park consists of a 'vast area of plains and wetlands in eastern Hungary' (*Brief Descriptions* 2001, the source of other quotations in this paragraph), very much part of Europe but representative more of landscapes to the east rather than the west. It was the first major pastoral landscape to be inscribed, and it was important for World Heritage that such a landscape should be recognised, precisely because it is very different from the dramatic 'Romantic' ideal of landscape typified by mountainous country.

Vinales Valley (Plate 9) is completely different again, and particularly welcome since it is in a part of the world underrepresented on the World Heritage List in general. It was the first cultural landscape from the 'New World'. It represents among other things – for better or for worse – one of the world's major crops, tobacco; its characteristics include geological interest, traditional farming techniques, and a vernacular architecture in 'farms and villages where a rich multi-ethnic society survives, illustrating the cultural development of the islands of the Caribbean.' This last phrase is an early example in World Heritage cultural landscape terms of an invisible, in effect ideological, quality being recognised in a landscape as significant and meritorious. Öland is a similar 'vernacular agrarian landscape' on limestone where over a long period people have adapted to a particular environment, but it looks rather different: it occupies the southern part of an island in the Baltic Sea, not in the sub-tropical Caribbean, it is relatively sparsely occupied and, though still farmed, it is characterised by the remains of former habitation and agriculture. Its flora, in part of an Alpine character, is also especially interesting; like the farming it reflects climatic constraints, as well as former and present land-use.

The Jurisdiction of Saint-Emilion similarly embodies a particular reaction to climate and soils over a long period – 2,000 years in this case – but its special interest in World Heritage terms is that its inscription marked the first of the 'wine' cultural landscapes. It set a precedent and at the same time represented the beginning of a policy in action which is still seeking to bring on to the List a good sample of the prime wine-producing landscapes in the world. It was followed by Alto Douro, Portugal (2001) (Figure 27), and Tokaj, Hungary (2002) (Figure 21), with others currently also being considered and a global study of the topic in hand with a view to helping further selection. Wine-growing was also an important characteristic of other landscapes nominated in 1999–2000: the Loire Valley and then Wachau, though each of those brought much else with them. Wachau landscape has considerable merit and charm, a picturesque Danubian gorge, the architecturally magnificent Meld Abbey and extremely acceptable wines which the locals wisely keep mainly to themselves; but intellectually it brought little new to the development of the idea of World Heritage cultural landscape that had not already been raised by the earlier nomination, albeit simultaneous inscription, of the Loire Valley.

The Loire Valley (Plate 10) was and is especially interesting – for its length, from Sully-sur-Loire to Chalonnes, east to west; for the diversity of land-uses contained within it, urban as well as rural, agricultural, horticultural and industrial, recreational and religious including the already-existing World Heritage Chateau and Estate of Chambord; and of course for its best-known features, its châteaux, gardens and generally ambient beauty. It was a bold and particularly sensitive nomination as a very heritage-conscious nation in effect laid a large and especially iconographic part of its *patrimoine* 'on the line' for

FIGURE 21.
Tokaj, Hungary, in its vineyard landscape, was inscribed as a World Heritage cultural landscape in 2002 as the need to rationalize the inscription of viticultural landscapes became apparent.

international approval. So there was considerable reaction when the nomination was initially pended by the World Heritage Committee, not because anyone seriously doubted the claims of it as a whole but because in the middle of the area proposed, right on the bank of the Loire, was a nuclear power station. (I discuss this particular contentious decision at some length in Chapter 9.) Doctrinal, strategic and undoubtedly political agenda were pursued in the ensuing debate which was concluded, at least as far as the nomination was concerned, with a compromise whereby the nuclear establishment had a ring drawn round it on the map to exclude it from the area proposed as a World Heritage cultural landscape. This device was, it could be argued, justified in that the proposed area then became politically acceptable and the World Heritage Committee felt able to approve inscription; but topographically, historically, conceptually and even philosophically, it was, in my opinion anyway, an ill-founded decision, a mistake by the Committee which it will one day have to acknowledge and correct.

At the time, France might well have been better-advised to take its wonderful Val de Loire away from the World Heritage table and keep its pride intact, not least because the Loire is one of these numinous areas of the world which in one sense does not need World Heritage status to provide an under-scoring of its values. More broadly, the idea of cultural landscape as conceived in World Heritage terms was, and remains, seriously scarred, for prejudices about industrial places, not just nuclear plant in particular, and about the undesirability of landscape components which are not 'beautiful' in Western, 'Romantic' mode, seem to have been activated and re-inforced. I would insert, in parentheses as it were, that quite apart from the conceptual issue here, I know I saw an aesthetically beautiful sight when I looked across from a

FIGURE 22.
Local discussion within the Sukur cultural landscape, Nigeria.

helicopter above the Loire at the cooling towers of the power station through fine drizzle high-lighted by shafts of low, slanting sunlight. Nevertheless, the good news is that, whatever the ideological issues, already the Val and its people have been able to use their World Heritage status as a trigger to initiate various economic, social and conservation moves, including a brand-new management organisation for the whole of the World Heritage cultural landscape itself. A very public symbol of such developments was a happy first Loire Festival along the quayside in Orléans during September, 2003, with an accompanying conference essentially extolling the virtues of river-based life while searching for appropriate ways of developing water-based tourism. Once again, the Loire is providing a model for the rest of the world.

Three of the other nominations also have agricultural elements but they are not their main thrust. Sukur (Figure 22) contains terraced fields but they are only a part of a landscape containing a chieftain's palace, villages, and remains of an iron industry in 'a remarkably intact physical expression of a society and its spiritual and material culture.' A small-scale vernacular iron industry is apparently acceptable in a World Heritage cultural landscape but the Swedish one which just happened to be the largest and one of the most innovative in the world in the nineteenth-twentieth centuries later proved no more acceptable than a French nuclear power station. We can see how World Heritage cultural landscape was beginning to define itself fairly distinctively well within its first decade. Almost self-defining in its title is the 'Archaeological Landscape of the First Coffee Plantations in the South-East of Cuba'. We only need add that the plantations are of the nineteenth century, providing 'unique evidence of a pioneer form of agriculture in a difficult terrain.' This landscape represents another of the world's great drinks, an idea which ought to be extended not only to other drinks, notably tea, but also to the world's staple food crops like rice, wheat and yam. The phrase 'difficult terrain' is significant in the citation here, for it has emerged that 'difficult' landscapes, in the sense of difficult to gain a livelihood from, even hostile to habitation, are meritorious in World Heritage terms. Nowhere is that better illustrated than on the Curonian Spit, an 'elongated sand dune peninsula' on the Lithuanian/Russian border. Since its early occupation in prehistory, it has been 'threatened by the natural forces of wind and waves. Its survival ... has been made possible only as a result of ceaseless human efforts to combat the erosion of the Spit, dramatically illustrated by continuing stabilisation and reforestation projects.' So here the concept of 'ceaseless struggle' is added to that of the Spit being a 'difficult' place to live in recognising it as a place of outstanding universal value.

The last two landscapes in this clutch of nominations, both in eastern Europe, gain their value from other sources. The Garden Kingdom of Dessau-Wörlitz (Plate 11, Figure 23) is 'an exceptional example of landscape design and planning in the Age of Enlightenment'; though to these English eyes, accustomed to such landscapes in their homeland, it looked like an attractive but in no way outstanding example of the type. But then, context is all, and this example lies far to the east. It also represents historic 'struggle', for it suffered

FIGURE 23.
Palace, church and
decorative water in the
Garden Kingdom of
Dessau-Wörlitz,
Category 1 cultural
landscape.

grievously during the years of Communist rule in the twentieth century and then, after admirable restoration which was itself a struggle to achieve, was disastrously affected by floods in 2002. Rather different as a created landscape is the lengthily-named 'Kalwaria Zebrzydowska: the Mannerist Architectural and Park Landscape Complex and Pilgrimage Park'. This is the odd one here, a nomination which was not followed by anything at all similar until Italy's Sacri Monti in 2003. They too share the idea of pilgrimage in the context of the sort of Christian Catholic religiosity which is at the core of Kalwaria (Calvary). But they are not singly parts of one great landscape as is the case at Kalwaria, basically natural but ornamented with religious buildings arranged in a progress on foot through the Passion of Christ and the life of the Virgin Mary. Laid out at the beginning of the seventeenth century, it is virtually unchanged and is still a place of pilgrimage.

The class of 2001

Ten cultural landscapes were nominated for inscription on the World Heritage List in 2000 and, after assessment during 2000–2001, were considered by the World Heritage Committee in December, 2001. The Committee approved five of them, referring one back to the nominating State Party for further consideration and inscribing the others on the list but not as cultural landscapes. In other words, it approved almost as many in one sitting as had been approved through the first six sessions after 1992.

Table 6. The nominations of cultural landscapes considered in 2000–2001.

Nomination number	State party	Landscape
481	**Laos**	**Vat Phou**
772	**Austria/Hungary**	**Fertö-Neu. Lake**
950	**Madagascar**	**Colline Royal**
1021	Botswana	Tsodilo
1022	Uganda	Kasubi
1026	Italy	Val d'Orcia
1027	Sweden	Falun
1030	UK	Derwent
1044	**Spain**	**Aranjuez**
1046	**Portugal**	**Douro Valley**

Those in bold were inscribed as such on the World Heritage List in 2001.

Overall 2000–2001 produced a good class of landscape. Although all the nominations contained elements already represented on the List of cultural landscapes, several were new types of landscape and thereby extended the range of the World Heritage cultural landscape portfolio. Vat Phou, for example, introduced a geometrical, religious and urban landscape.

Vat Phou

Vat Phou and Associated Ancient Settlements within the Champasak Cultural Landscape – to give it its full title – (Figure 24) lies in the Lao People's Democratic Republic. The site was planned during the second half of the first millennium AD to represent on the ground the Khmer symbolic universe, itself the Hindu view of the world. It is focussed on, to the west, the natural features of Phou Kao Mountain and, on the east, the Mekong River, used to represent respectively the sacred mountain dwelling of the god Shiva and the Ganges River or the Universal Ocean. The plain between, containing the main extent of temples and associated works, formed Kurukshestra, the Holy Land. The degree of survival of the overall topography of the Khmer landscape (c AD 600 onwards), and of many archaeological remains above and below ground, has resulted in the continued existence of evidence of the planning and utilization of the landscape over some 400 square kms during nearly a thousand years (c. fifth to fifteenth centuries AD). This is the only place in south-east Asia where such a landscape has been recognised to survive in all its essential parts.

Champasak District lies 500 km south-east of the capital, Vientiane, on the west bank of the Mekong Rover. It contains the Vat Phou Temple Complex, a major example of both early and classic Khmer architecture of the seventh to twelfth centuries AD. This complex is the focal point of a special cultural landscape centred on the Champasak Plain with temples, shrines, water tanks, water channels, quarries, historic field systems, settlement sites and an ancient road to Angkor. Shrestrapura, a planned pre-Angkorian Ancient City

FIGURE 24.
Entrance to one of the
large courtyard
buildings on the
bottom terrace of the
temple complex at Vat
Phou World Heritage
cultural landscape, Lao
PDR.

(4 hectares) on the banks of the Mekong, appears to have been replaced as the urban centre by another planned city immediately south of Vat Phou itself in the Angkor period. A probably contemporary road leads southwards from it, past quarries and other industrial works.

Many of these features exist in a carefully planned landscape laid out to reflect its sacred character, as perceived by the builders of Vat Phou. The terraced Temple Complex lies at the foot of Phou Kao Mountain, stretching from west-east to a freshwater spring on a rock terrace where the shrine was built. An axial line from the natural *lingua* (point) on the mountain summit through the shrine was used as the basis for the layout of the temple complex; it is 1,400 m long, with lakes as well as buildings to either side, bisected by an axial processional way. The use of a natural mountain-top to catch the eye (elevation 1416 m) and the relatively high degree of survival of landscape and its structural components assist modern-day appreciation of the grand concept of the original design. This was always intended to be what we now call a cultural landscape. Much of it continues in use now as shallow paddy-fields for rice.

Some of the individual buildings are of major architectural and historical significance. The Vat Phou Temple Complex itself is one of the major buildings of the pre-Angkorian and Angkorian periods, and is an example of a relatively rare form of hilltop Khmer temple planning. Much of its sculpture exemplifies high artistic standards and creativity of both the formative and classical periods of Khmer civilization.

The origins of the site lie before AD 600, at least under the city of Shrestrapura where archaeological research has produced evidence of pre-Angkorian times (up to *c.* AD 900). The development of the site as a whole, however, was intimately bound up with the origin, development and zenith of the Khmer Empire between the seventh and twelfth centuries AD. A new line of kings probably centred in the Champasak region expanded its authority from its capital at Úxxnapura from the tenth century onwards till it encompassed not only most of modern Cambodia but also considerable parts of what is now eastern Thailand. The *apogée* of the elaborate landscape at Vat Phou probably occurred during these centuries. Its historical significance lies in its role at the centre of Empire and its demonstration of Indian rather than Chinese influence in the clear evidence of Hindu religious belief.

The last major developments to the Champasak cultural landscape were in the thirteenth century just before the collapse of the Khmer Empire. There is no evidence of any maintenance of the monumental buildings since then, although various other occupations and events have occurred on the site. Vat Phou itself, in contrast to what it represented in the first millennium, was converted to Theravada Buddhism and remains a local centre of worship today. The area reverted to secondary forest which covered most of it when the first European arrived in the nineteenth century. There has been minimal conservation work to any part of the site. The process by which the Champasak landscape has passed to us in its present state is essentially one of benign neglect, natural damage and decay.

An annual three-day Vat Phou Festival demonstrates the continuing place of the site in the lives of the local community. Most of the present population live away from the main archaeological complexes. Many of the inhabited houses are traditional in form, but developmental pressures are mounting. The basically non-damaging nature of traditional agriculture (shallow paddy-fields) is changing under pressures to intensify and has recently caused considerable damage. The main road through the Ancient City is attracting constant new building and improvement of existing ones. Annual visitor numbers have more than doubled since 1997 to 14,000.

Overall, the Champasak landscape is an early designed cultural landscape, demonstrating the beginnings of urbanism in south-east Asia as well as the way in which the Khmers moulded their landscape to reflect their symbolic universe. The whole was created within a geometric framework linking man-made works with natural phenomena, notably the distinctive, pointed summit of Phou Kao. This landscape planning on the grand scale in the second half of the first millennium AD was more than an intellectual exercise or a pleasure garden but to express the Hindu relationship between the gods, nature and humanity. The sanctity of the mountain is still observed today by the people of Champasak who continue to respect and preserve the natural environment of this mountain abode of ancient gods; while, across the Mekong, the river-side temple of Tomo continues to bear witness to the cosmological template used to plan the site.

Africa

Tsodilo (Figure 25), in the Ngamiland District, in north-west Botswana was another outstanding nomination bringing forward not so much a new type of site – though it had many indiosycratic features – but a clear candidate for World Heritage status from a hitherto unrepresented part of the world. It is a major geological landmark in the Kalahari Desert. An immediate comparison with Uluṟu-Kata Tjuṯa in Australia is unavoidable. It has been called the 'Louvre of the Desert' for the quality and quantity (*c.* 4500 images) of the rock art contained in an area of only 10 square kilometres. The place combines several aspects of Earth's history with the cultural history of humankind. It shows an interplay between geological processes spanning more than a billion years and human activities, particularly those involving minerals, over tens of thousands of years. Its significance lies in its visual prominence, its geological and archaeological character as scientific resources, its use over ten of thousands of years as an area of settlement and nourishment, its outstanding rock-art and its long-term sanctity.

At Tsodilo massive quartzite rock formations rise from ancient sand dunes to the east and a dry fossil lake bed to the west. The surrounding dunes are covered with trees and open savannah vegetation. The setting and the multi-coloured rock formations combined with the large number of rock paintings immediately bestow an iconographic quality to the place. Three of the outcrops form a cluster over a 3 x 10 km rectangle; a fourth, and smallest, lies 2.1 km to the north west. Their height, shape and spatial relationships have given rise to a distinctive name for each: *Male, Female, Child* and *Grandchild*. Divuyu and Nquoma are two excavated settlements of particular significance in the first millennium AD.

Caves and shelters are one of the main attractions of the rock outcrop from the human point of view. They characteristically show a long though not necessarily continuous sequence of occupation beginning in some cases as early as *c.* 100,000 years ago (Middle Palaeolithic). They indicate repeated use thereafter by small mobile groups of people, perhaps seasonally, for example when the fruit of the mongongo tree, *Ricinodendron rautanenii*, ripens.

Most of the rock art has been executed in red ochre derived from haematite

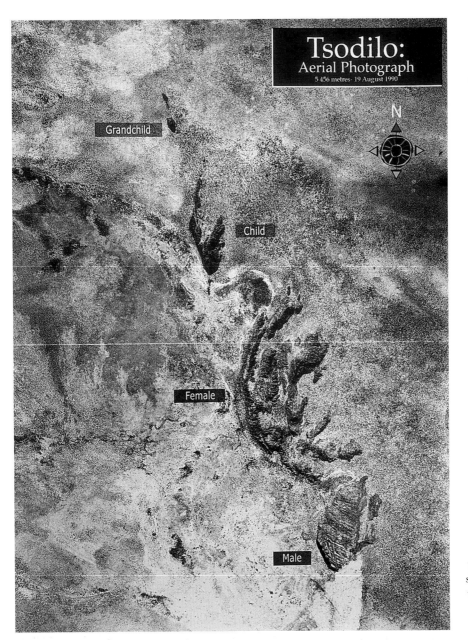

Grandchild

Child

Female

Male

FIGURE 25.
Tsodilo, Botswana: a
vertical air photograph
showing the four rocks,
with their local names,
rising above the
Kalahari Desert.

occurring in the local rock. Much of this red art is naturalistic in subject and schematic in style. Many of the graphics have been executed in fairly small, isolated panels in contrast to the large friezes elsewhere in the region. The Tsolido paintings are characterised by a variety of geometric symbols, distinctive treatment of the human figure and exaggerated body proportions of many animals. The wild animals depicted are characteristically 'big game' such as giraffe and rhinoceros until the relatively late appearance of domestic cattle. Some depictions are in outline only, others are in silhouette, differences in style which seem to relate to particular animals e.g. zebra in outline and elephant in silhouette. Human figures, or abstracts of them emphasising, for example, sexual features, are frequent. There is nevertheless a high proportion of geometric designs, frequently lines and grids enclosed in circles or ovals and in rectangles. Such apparently symbolic graphics are rare in southern African Stone Age art. A distinctive series of white paintings occurs, in some instances superimposed on the reds but never the other way round. Animals in white are rarer and include more domestic species than the reds. Human figures are common, as are geometric designs.

The art in general is not well-dated, though at least some of it could be two thousand and more years old. Pictures with cattle are regarded as *c.*AD 600–1200, following the introduction of cattle to Tsodilo after the sixth century AD. Geometric art is generally regarded as about a thousand years old. The latest paintings date to the nineteenth century on oral evidence. Some white paintings appear to be riders on horses, unknown at Tsodilo until the 1850s which possibly provides a date for the last paintings.

Cup and canoe-shaped hollows in rock, a common phenomenon throughout the continent, are particularly numerous. One group, interpreted as a trail of animal footprints, is spread over several hundred metres and is one of the largest rock pictures in the world. These hollows may have been made in the Late Stone Age about two thousand years ago.

The earliest occupants at Tsodilo were probably in the Middle Stone Age, perhaps around 100,000 years ago or earlier. Local quartz as well as exotic stone were used for tool-making in both the Middle and Late Stone Ages. The use of non-local raw material suggests that contact and some form of exchange have existed here for tens of thousands of years. Tsodilo is unique in demonstrating an extensive record of fresh-water fish exploitation in a now arid landscape where rivers formerly flowed. Barbed bone points were probably used to tip fish-spears; bone tool-making at Tsodilo may well go back 40,000 years. Sometime later the appearance of ostrich eggs in archaeological deposits indicates the development of a new strategy for acquiring a new resource for food and artefact-making. In particular, a tradition of making beads of ostrich egg-shell began then and continues today.

Until as recently as *c.* AD 600, the people of Tsodilo lived entirely by hunting, fishing and foraging for wild food. By the seventh century AD, however, the pace of change in technology, subsistence and settlement organisation increased as iron and copper metallurgy were introduced. This phase is also marked by the introduction of cattle. Copper and iron beads, bracelets and other ornaments became common. All the metal was imported – the copper probably from southern Zaire or north east South Africa, the iron perhaps from only 40 kms distant – and worked locally. Nqoma at the end of the first millennium has the richest variety of metal jewellery of any known contemporary site in southern Africa.

Domestic herding and a settled lifestyle were established as early as the seventh to eighth centuries AD at Divuyu and Nqoma. Sheep and goats augmented the few domestic cattle kept by earlier foraging communities. Cultivated crops such as sorghum and millet were added to the diet. Pottery was produced for a range of domestic purposes and personal adornment became common and often elaborate. Mining for specularite was extensive AD 800–1000, and continued into the nineteenth century. The output was enormous, doubtless contributing to the amount of jewellery and cattle owned by the Nqoma people. The rich elements of Tsodilo Iron Age culture continued well into the thirteenth century when Nqoma declined, possibly because of drought or war. No further durable exotic objects seem to have entered the Tsodilo region until the effects of the European Atlantic trade began to be felt in the eighteenth century. Tsodilo became part of the Portuguese/Kongo-Angola trade axis.

Historically, the Tsodilo area was occupied by the N/hae, who left in the mid-nineteenth century. Its first appearance on a map was in 1857, as a result of information collected by Livingstone during his explorations 1849–56. In the 1850s the earliest known horsemen, Griqua ivory hunters, passed through the region. The !Kung arrived in the area and made at least a few of the paintings, possibly some of those showing horsemen. The rock art was first sketched and brought to Western attention in 1907 by Seigfried Passarge, a German geologist.

The two, present-day local communities, Hambukushu and !Kung, arrived as recently as *c.*1860. Nevertheless, they both have creation myths associated with Tsodilo, and they both have strong traditional beliefs that involve respect for Tsodilo as a place of worship and ancestral spirits. The spirituality of the place has become best-known to non-local people through the writings of Laurens van der Post, notably his *The Lost World of the Kalahari* (1958). Today, local churches and traditional doctors travel to Tsodilo for prayers, meditation and medication, and most visitors arrive for religious reasons.

Many visitors also arrive for religious reasons at two sites, very similar in important ways, which were the first of their type on the World Heritage List. They were also the first cultural landscapes based on royal palaces in African style. The former, Colline Royale, Madagascar (no. 950), consists of a walled hill-top royal settlement and cemetery, the whole clearly influenced from the continental mainland where the Kasubi Tombs in the Kampala District, Uganda (no. 1022), represent an exceptionally well-preserved, but otherwise typical, royal hill-top complex.

The Kasubi Tombs site is situated on a hill within Kampala. It covers an area of 30 hectares, on the hill-top and down its eastern slopes. About 35 people live within it; most of the site is agricultural, farmed by traditional methods. The whole is encircled by a fence of bark cloth trees, now somewhat depleted. It consists of three main zones, all elements of the original layout of a typical example of a palace of the Baganda Kabakas:

    i. the main tomb area located at the western end of the site on top of the hill

ii. an area located behind the main tombs containing a number of buildings and graveyards

iii. a large area on the eastern side of the site used primarily for agricultural purposes

On the western border of the site is the gatehouse (*Bujjabukula*), traditionally containing guards 24 hours a day. It was constructed of wooden columns and invisible walls of fired brick supporting a thatched roof, with walls of woven reeds. Beyond is a small courtyard containing the *Ndoga-Obukaba*, a circular building containing the royal drums. Also of wooden columns and thatch, it has walls visibly constructed of fired brick. The D-shaped main courtyard (*Olugya*) lies through a gap in a reed fence. This fence encloses the courtyard and links nine buildings, five of them houses for the widows of the *Kabakas*, the other four respectively a twins' house, two tombs and a mortuary. Variously constructed of wattle-and-daub and fired brick, three have round plans, the others are square. All were originally thatched.

The courtyard itself is empty, enhancing the visual dominance on its eastern side of the large timber, reed and thatched building (*Muzibu-Azaala-Mpanga*) housing the tombs of the four *Kabakas*. This structure represents one of the most remarkable buildings using purely organic materials in the whole of sub-Saharan Africa. It is circular in plan and has a dome-like shape. Its external diameter is 31 m and internal height 7.5 m. It was built in 1898, and has both changed its profile and been significantly repaired during its century of existence. The roof catches the eye: it slopes right down to the ground and is reinforced underneath by 52 woven rings of palm fronds and spear grass, representing the 52 *Ganda* clans. The whole structure is carried by gigantic straight wooden columns wrapped in bark cloth. The building is entered through a low-wide arch flanked on both sides richly woven reeds. Its inside is partitioned with a huge bark cloth which hides the 'sacred forest' where four royal graves lie. Entrance to the 'forest' is limited to widows of *Kabakas*, the royal family, the *Nalinya*, and *Katikkiro*. The inside of the building is adorned with power insignia such as drums, spears, shields, medals, and pictures of the buried *Kabakas*. On the floor is a thick layer of lemon grass and palm leaf mats.

Beyond the *Olugya* is scattered a large number of buildings – houses, royal tombs and ones for agricultural purposes – and a royal cemetery. The whole area is sacred and is not open to visitors. It was formerly completely screened off but now moves uninterrupted into the agricultural land behind it. This land was originally occupied by homesteads but was later subdivided among the widows of the *Kabakas*. It is now rented to and farmed by members of the community; the income is used on the site. The area contains graves, two man-made mounds, medicinal plants and the trees used in making bark-cloth.

The *Baganda* belong to the Bantu-speaking people and date their political civilization from about the thirteenth century AD. Today, the *Baganda* are the major ethnic group in Uganda, their 6 million people constituting about 28 per cent of the population. The Buganda region covers about 66,350 sq kms.

From the first, legendary *Kabaka, Kintu,* to *Muteesa* I, there were 35 *Kabakas.* Precise dates, however, are known only from *Suuna* II (1836–56), who established his palace at Kasubi. He was succeeded by his son *Muteesa* I who did likewise, constructing the present Tomb structure as his palace in 1882. He became a very powerful *Kabaka,* the first to be influenced by foreign cultures. He adopted some Islamic religious practices learnt from ivory and slave traders from Zanzibar. He also showed interest in Europe after acting as host to Speke, the first European visitor in 1862. In 1875, he asked Henry Stanley, the explorer, for teachers of European learning and religion. When he died in 1884, he broke two traditions: his body was buried whole and it was buried in his palace, Kasubi, not somewhere else. This practice was followed when, in 1910, the remains of his successor, *Mwanga* II (*ob.* 1903), were brought back from the Seychelles and also buried there, establishing Kasubi as an important burial place of the *Kabakas* of Buganda. This status was reinforced when his son and successor, *Daudi Chwa* II, died in 1939 and was also buried at Kasubi. His son and successor, *Edward Muteesa* II, was first in conflict with Britain. After independence in 1962 he became President, with his own Prime Minister. Kasubi was stormed in 1966 and the President went into exile; but when he died in 1969 his remains were returned and buried at Kasubi in 1971. Four successive *Kabakas* of Buganda were therefore buried in the same tomb house at Kasubi, the building at the core of this nomination. Each prince and princess who is a descendant of the four *Kabakas* is also buried there behind the main shrine.

Between 1967–93, the site was controlled by central government, but the traditional institutions of kingship were restored in 1993. *Kabaka Ronald Mutebi* II was crowned as the *Kabaka* of Buganda and in 1997 the Kasubi tombs were returned to the Buganda kingdom. The site is now not only the most important cultural shrine for the *Baganda* but also the most attractive tourist site in the country.

During its first fifty years, 1882–1930s, the palace-cum-tomb called *Muzibu Azaala Mpanga* experienced only minor maintenance work, although in 1905 it was reduced in size to make it more maintainable. Since 1938, however, the building has suffered several processes of restoration and modification, primarily to meet threats of structural failure. It was completely reconstructed between 1938 and 1940; modern materials were introduced, such as concrete columns. During the 1990s, alterations to most of the buildings have slightly changed the architectural value of the site. The site suffers badly from rain, drainage problems and termites, with a constant threat of fire. The *Muzibu Azaala Mpanga* is structurally in good order and was re-thatched early in 2001. This event underlined the need for continuous maintenance. The traditional voluntary maintenance by the clans is, however, tending to disappear as there is no means of rewarding it; the traditional royal free meal, cooked by the widows, no longer exists.

The original reed fence around the whole site has long since disappeared;

PLATE I.
Water is a characteristic of cultural landscapes; here it is a feature of the Maori sacred
landscape of Tongariro National Park, New Zealand, the first cultural landscape to be
inscribed as such on the World Heritage List (1993). The Ketehahi Springs flow out from the
Tongariro volcano and down into the forest below. Boiling at their source, the waters cool as
they descend the mountain.

PLATE 2. The gardens of the Palace of Schönbrunn, Austria, are not officially a World Heritage cultural landscape but they nevertheless beautifully exemplify both 'a clearly defined landscape designed and created intentionally by man' and a cultural landscape on the World Heritage List.

PLATE 3. One small part of the dramatic, montane, terraced landscape for growing rice in the Cordilleras, Luzon, Philippines.

PLATE 4. An outstanding, working viticultural landscape of small plots defined by drystone lava walls arranged in a remarkable rectilinear pattern: Pico, Azores, Portugal.

PLATE 5. Shadows across the bush of a World Heritage cultural landscape as Uluṟu-Kaṯa Tjuṯa (formerly Ayer's Rock), Australia, catches the dawn sun.

PLATE 6.
Stone, slates, wood and hay present an almost tactile image of traditional domestic architecture and of the life and work of the Vall de Boí, Spain.

PLATE 7.
Sheep and shepherd high in the Odesa National Park on the southern, Spanish side of the Mont-Perdu World Heritage 'mixed site' and cultural landscape, France/Spain.

PLATE 8.
The nineteenth-century restoration of the Moorish Castle on the skyline viewed from the Palace in the Old Quarter, Sintra, Portugal, during filming for a TV 'period' drama.

PLATE 9.
The World Heritage cultural landscape of the Viñales valley, Cuba, a fine karst landscape with tobacco fields, was inscribed solely under criterion (iv) as an outstanding example of a landscape which illustrates a 'significant stage in human history', in this case the cultural development of the islands of the Caribbean and of Cuba.

PLATE 10. The River Vienne mirrors the fortified town of Chinon within the World Heritage cultural landscape of the Loire valley between Sully-sur-Loire and Chalonnes, France.

PLATE 11. Recently restored pavilion in the park at Dessau-Wörlitz, Germany, as it was in March 1998.

PLATE 12. Farmers pause in their labour on irrigated but arid fields in the Bamiyan valley, Afghanistan.

PLATE 13. Four thousand year-old Castlerigg stone circle among the mountains of the Lake District, England, United Kingdom, nominated as a World Heritage site in the 1980s (when this photograph was taken), referred for further consideration, and now in active preparation for re-nomination as a cultural landscape.

PLATE 14.
Sustainable monument
maintenance at sunset
by sheep among the
megaliths, Avebury,
England, UK. Unlike
at Stonehenge, people
can still walk among
the stones at this huge
henge monument and
entry is free. This view
is from near the centre
towards the West
Kennet Avenue,
looking out through
the southern entrance
with, to its left and
right, the outer bank
which, constructed in
the middle of the 3rd
millennium BC and
interrupted by three
other entrances,
encloses some 11.5 ha.

the living fence of bark cloth trees around the site has suffered quite badly as an obvious target in the endless search for firewood. The site has, nevertheless, to an extent been preserved out of fear and respect for its sacred and religious nature. This spiritual protection has freed the site from urban modernization in the twentieth century, despite the booming development which has occurred all around it.

The site's main qualities are intangible ones to do with belief, spirituality and identity. Simultaneously, it possesses a considerable physical presence, being visually striking and a living place of the royal dead exhibiting outstanding examples of indigenous architecture, craftsmanship and traditional organisation, methods and skills. Its overall plan also exhibits significant historical patterning. Furthermore, the site as a whole acts as a 'green lung' in an area of rapid urban expansion and is clearly of high potential in cultural and touristic terms.

The Kasubi Tombs site also presents some unique features. It is a *multiple Kabaka* burial site. It is also the cemetery of the royal family. It is bigger than most other *Baganda* tombs, and it is the best-known. Its location and status ensure that the Kasubi Tombs site will continue to be maintained for its cultural values. It has a political value for the *Buganda*. It is a unifying element in their kingdom. The site has become a landmark, not only for the *Buganda* but also for Uganda. It serves as an important symbol of the history and culture of that country and of east Africa as a whole.

Europe
There seems a certain inevitability about the rest of the cultural landscape nominations in 2000–2001 being from Europe – one each from Italy, Sweden, the UK, Spain and Portugal, with a joint, cross-frontier nomination from Austria and Hungary (Table 6). Five of them are now World Heritage sites – Val d'Orcia is the exception – but only three became World Heritage cultural landscapes. Two of those, Fertö-Neusiedler Lake, and the Douro valley, did not succeed immediately but were referred back to their nominating countries, principally for clarification of the area involved and of the proposed management plans. Indeed, those two cases and the other three refusals are, in a sense, the interesting point here. It is they, rather than Aranjuez (*below*), an outstanding but straightforward category 1 cultural landscape, which indicate how the cultural landscape concept was defining itself by a sharpening of the focus on its *desiderata*.

PLATE 15.
La porte de la marine
(*right*) and *Skala du
Port* (*left*) mark the
boundary of the World
Heritage town of
Essaouira (formerly
Mogador), Morocco,
literally overlooking the
'fishing landscape' of
harbour, fishing fleet
and the liveliness of
people and their traditional activities there.

The Fertö-Neusiedler Lake as considered in 2001 was in fact a renomination. It had previously come forward as the Natural Site and Cultural Landscape of Fertö-Neusiedler Lake (No. 772), Burgenland, Austria, and Györ-Moson-Sopron County, Hungary. The northern part of the Lake in Austria had even earlier been proposed purely as a natural site but assessors were much struck by the association of Lake and its surrounding landscape, suggesting it might be a cultural landscape. To express this concept properly, however, needed the whole Lake and its surrounds to be included, and that meant negotiating a nomination with Hungary in which the southern part of the Lake lay. This was achieved, and a joint nomination with redrawn boundaries was submitted in 2000. Its main case was centred on the natural qualities of the area and, to quote part of the justification by the State Parties, the claim that 'The present character of the landscape is the result of millennia-old land-use forms based on stock-raising and viticulture to an extent not found in other European lake areas.'

The site lies between the Alps, 70 km distant, and the lowlands in the territory of two states, Austria and Hungary. The Lake itself is in an advanced state of sedimentation with extensive reed stands. It has existed for 500 years within an active water management regime. In the nineteenth century canalisation of Hanság shut the Lake off from its freshwater marshland. Since 1912, completion of a circular dam ending at Hegykö to the south prevents flooding.

The Lake is surrounded by an inner ring of 16 settlements and an outer ring of 20 other settlements, and this is where, as it turned out, much of the problem lay with the 2000 proposal. The city of Sopron in this outer ring is the centre of the settlement pattern. Small towns or villages, all outside the proposed World Heritage cultural landscape but clearly integral to the lake and its surroundings, include Rust above all (partly in, partly out), Mörbisch, with its typical narrow lanes, Donnerkirschen, with its 'homogeneous settlement structure, walled Purbach, Breitenbrunn with its peel tower, and Fertörákos, formerly a lakeside settlement but now left high and dry as the Lake has shrunk.

Széchenyi and Fertöd Palaces are included, both in Hungary. The former is a detached ensemble of buildings in the centre of a large park, initially built in the mid-eighteenth century in place of a former manor house. It acquired some of its present form and appearance around 1800. An addition in the 1830s after English models was accompanied by sanitary novelties, while on the east were the stables for some 20 stallions and 60 mares bought by Earl Széchenyi in England as a basis for renewed horse-breeding in Hungary. The Baroque Palace garden originated in the seventeenth century. Its main avenue leads 2.6 km to the lake-shore. In the late eighteenth century an English-style landscape garden was laid out. Following fashion, major trees were added in the 1860s. They and other plants survived World War II but the building was much damaged.

Between 1769 and 1790, Joseph Haydn's compositions were first heard in the Fertöd Esterházy Palace. It was the most important 18th century palace of Hungary, built after the model of Versailles. The plan of Palace, garden and park was on geometrical lines which extended to the new village of Esterháza. There, outside the Palace settlement, were public buildings, industrial premises and residential quarters. The Palace itself is laid out around a square with rounded, internal corners. To the south is an enormous French Baroque garden; the main avenue is more than 1 km long. The garden itself has been changed several times, the present design being essentially of 1762. The garden was reconstructed in 1904 after a long period of disuse and the Baroque composition, though many of its elements require restoration, remains almost intact.

In the twentieth century, the Austro-Hungarian frontier created after World War I divided the area into two, but true isolation started only with the establishment of the 'Iron Curtain' between the Communist world and the rest of Europe after World War II. It was at Fertörákos, 'the place where the first brick was knocked out of the Berlin wall', that participants at a Pan-European Picnic tore down the barbed wire and re-opened the frontier which still crosses the Lake.

So, overall, on cultural grounds, clearly the necessary elements were present to contribute towards a World Heritage cultural landscape. But there were two problems. One was that, as already hinted, much of the cultural landscape lay outside the nominated area, suggesting the nominators may not quite have understood what was required. And secondly, although there was clear evidence of people's interaction with Nature, and despite a long list of floral and faunal species in the area, the nature conservationists' judgement was that the Lake was not quite sufficiently significant for World Heritage purposes. The Committee therefore decided to defer the nomination once again, asking the two countries to reconsider the framework of their proposal. This must have been very disappointing for those concerned, because an enormous amount of work goes into preparing such a nomination. Here it would have been doubly difficult, involving not just a trans-national border but a generation of non-contact across the 'Iron Curtain'. On the other hand, the case makes the point that World Heritage status, and perhaps particularly in this new category of cultural landscape, does not come easily. Significantly revised, the nomination was re-submitted in 2002 and the Lake and its surrounds, now convincingly presented as a cultural landscape in World Heritage terms, was duly inscribed on the List as a cultural landscape.

The Val d'Orcia nomination has not yet reached as happy a conclusion. It is still under consideration so my words have to be somewhat hedged so as not to prejudice its future; but it nonetheless provides material for a good case study of the development of the idea and practice of World Heritage cultural landscapes. The authors will not mind me saying now that the original nomination was initially found to be unfocussed, apparently unclear about its prime claims and somewhat muddled in its presentation. The flaw has been acknowledged. The area was claimed to be special in geological terms, but the dossier did not convincingly demonstrate the nature of the claim or the connection between the geology and the working of the land. That working was, it was stated, based on a 'unique' – a favourite word in World Heritage nomination dossiers – form of land tenure, but the tenurial system was not adequately explained, seemed to be similar to systems common elsewhere and did not seem to give this particular landscape a distinctive appearance. Such criticisms may seem hard on this particular dossier, but at the time (2000) such values and questions are characteristically brought into play, particularly so, it might be argued, in Europe where, given the resources, there can be little excuse for inadequacy. This nomination, profusely illustrated with stunning photographs, was not in fact markedly inadequate compared to many others and is used here merely to exemplify how the evaluation of potential World Heritage cultural landscapes was by 2000 becoming more demanding as it became more assured. In fact, Val-d'Orcia has subsequently enjoyed much thought and work as a nomination for re-submission from those who care about it in Italy.

Very different from the arcadian landscapes of the Val d'Orcia were the two other contemporary nominations which also failed to become World Heritage cultural landscapes. It is, I believe, a very great pity from the World Heritage point of view that this was so, in a way especially because both became World Heritage sites. Their official names are the Mining Area of the Great Copper Mountain in Falun, Sweden, and the Derwent valley mills in the UK; the former was originally called the Historic Cultural Landscape of the Great Copper Mountain in Falun, a reasonably clear indication, one would have thought, of how the nominating country perceived the status of the property. Both nominations are historically-outstanding industrial areas: that is their merit and was, one has to conclude, their failing in the eyes of the World Heritage Committee. Falun, a former steel-works and associated structures including its huge waste heap ('the Great Copper Mountain'), is doubtless a landscape of dereliction in many peoples' eyes, and possibly even ugly; but, aesthetics apart, it was one of the most important steelworks in the world until the middle of the twentieth century, a place where many techniques were developed. And it has left a very impressive, extremely large hole in the ground! – a monument, like an agrarian landscape, to countless, anonymous workers. The Derwent valley is another area where scenery and aesthetics are irrelevant to its world significance as the place where the factory system was invented. The product happened to be cotton. Eighteenth- and nineteenth-century factories, with much industrial infrastructure, survive, some still in use or recently restored for second uses. Each of these areas, like some other industrial landscapes, has something significant to say.

Both, in other words, possess all the qualities required of an outstanding landscape: space, integrity, authenticity, a range of components demonstrating how they functioned, and, in each case, unassailable claims for historical significance in global terms. Yet the Committee decided, quite deliberately, that they could not be cultural landscapes in World Heritage terms, apparently precisely because of their industrial nature. There seems a certain illogicality in recognising a property as possessing 'outstanding universal value', which in these cases must be 'industrial', and then denying it its appropriate status for possessing that value. Sadly, it seems fairly clear World Heritage cultural landscapes cannot be industrial because, in the opinion of the Committee, they have to be rural. Yet the year before the Committee had recognised the Blaenavon landscape, very much the product of coal-mining and iron-production (Figure 26), as a World Heritage cultural landscape. Their 2001 decisions about Falun and the Derwent valley, each of which was

FIGURE 26.
Blaenavon, Wales, UK:
above, workers' terraced
housing rising uphill
from the Workmen's
Institute, *below*, a large
building still in use,
impressive in its Neo-
Romanesque, Classical
architectural detailing.

described in, by implication, rather derogatory tones as a 'technological ensemble', smack of *post facto* horror at their Blaenavon decision, and a determination not to do the same again. It hardly needs saying that, whatever the reasons, the Falun and Derwent valley decisions were retrograde, cannot possibly be sustained intellectually, and will have to be overridden, if not actually reversed, in due course. Meanwhile, while the Committee and its agents wring their hands about a few modernist buildings, whole swathes of landscape representative of how the nineteenth and twentieth centuries actually worked cannot apparently be acknowledged for their true worth by the very mechanism that the Committee has given itself to allow it to recognise whole areas rather than individual structures. Nor is this merely a theoretical or bureaucratic matter: the status of 'cultural landscape' carries with it management implications (Chapter 10).

The marvellous landscape of Aranjuez, Spain is in many respects a one-off if ever there was one. Generically it belongs to that category (1) of planned parks and gardens (though here with a royal palace and small town). I visited the place on 5 December, 2002, an incredibly beautiful day of crisp temperature and light quality, and an almost blindingly bright sun in a cloudless, deep blue sky – ideal for photography and for walking the many walks through an almost deserted and surprisingly extensive site. Anyone can easily visit the palace but such a walk is necessary to appreciate the ingenuity of the water-management which defines and supplies different types of garden and park across the valley floor, creates the impressive waterfalls beside the palace itself, and contributes to the gridded organisation of the town plan which is so important an element in the integrity of the whole complex. And the whole is so much more than what you can see: the visual impression supports a range of iconography, from the practical science of royal horticultural experiment on reclaimed land to the concept of royalty itself, particularly as embodied in Phillip II. Unfortunately, all the undeveloped films of my visit, almost certainly containing some very good images for use here, were lost when my briefcase was stolen at Madrid airport on my way back to London.

The Alto Douro Wine Region in northern Portugal is the most illustrative of the three landscape units forming the 250,000 ha of the vast Demarcated Douro Region (Figure 27). The Region is the oldest demarcated and controlled winemaking region in the world, dating back to 1756 (earlier attempts at regulation at Chianti, 1716, and Tokaj, 1737, were not so comprehensive). The claim is made because demarcation was accompanied by mechanisms for controlling the quality of the product supported by a vast legislative framework and wine classificatory system. In many ways, the wine-making legislation here led the way for the modern legislation adopted by many wine-producing countries.

Within the Region today, 48,000 hectares are planted with vines, spreading over the hillsides that rise on either side of the River Douro and its tributaries, the Rivers Varosa, Corgo, Távora, Torto and Pinhão. They form the skeleton of the property. The boundaries correspond to identifiable natural features

FIGURE 27.
Alto Douro, Portugal:
a landscape of terraces
of three different dates,
pre-phylloxera (*left*),
post-phylloxera (*right*),
and modern (*middle
distance*).

of the landscape – watercourses, mountain ridges, roads and paths. The Site itself is of 24,600 hectares, surrounded by a buffer zone 225,400 hectares in extent. The climate, surprisingly given the location, is more Mediterranean than Atlantic. The local version is 'nine months of winter and three months of hell'.

The unique cultural landscape of the Alto Douro is, in the words of the Convention, a combined work of man and nature. It is the result of a centuries-old process of adapting specific viticultural and winemaking techniques and acumen to a poor soil, a soil endowed with the singular potential to produce the world-famous, exceptional quality wines that bear the "Porto" and "Douro" Appellations of Origin. It is a living cultural landscape in constant evolution, an exceptional example of land-use that revolves around the making of quality wines under extremely difficult environmental conditions.

The Douro landscape, with its Mediterranean-like environment, challenging topography and poor soil, presents major constraints to human settlement and development. But people have, nevertheless, completely changed the terrain and its productivity by making soil out of rock and reconfiguring the land's surface into a landscape of terraces (*socalcos* – terraces buttressed by walls of schistoid stone) from which Port Wine is produced. They have organised themselves and their tenure into a series of *quintas* (large estates) and *casais* (small landholdings). As a result, the landscape is an outstanding example of man's unique relationship with the natural environment. By adapting the natural environment to the demands of a traditional productive system, man fashioned a winemaking landscape whose unmistakable appearance provides visual drama and a visible tension between the production of the raw material for a world-class product and the forces of nature. Early in 2001, following a wet winter, heavy rain caused widespread damage to the physical fabric of the viticultural landscape. Only the creation of a unique, lucrative natural product of exceptional quality such as port wine could ever justify the superhuman effort needed to construct and maintain this collective work of landscape art.

At Alto-Douro economy-culture-landscape form an indisputable unit. The terraced vineyards have anticipated more recent concepts of sustainable land-use, and illustrate an optimal environmental solution from the viewpoint of conservation and the use of rare resources – water and soil. The people of the Douro have adapted their houses and villages to the constraints and demands of the environment and the productive process, not just of the grape but also of other Mediterranean cultivars such as the olive and the almond, as well as fruit and vegetables on more fertile alluvial soil and amongst the woodlands on high land. The concept of a continuing, organically evolved cultural landscape is well illustrated here: the results of a progressive interaction between man, a particular form of social organisation and the natural environment.

Though viticulture has been practised here since Roman times, the claims of this region on World Heritage status do not depend on the antiquity of what is visible; in fact, much of the structure in the landscape is modern. The oldest *socalcos* have low walls and narrow and irregularly-shaped surfaces – or *geios* – that sometimes only accommodate a single row of vines and which wind haphazardly around the curves of the land and rocky outcrops. These are the pre-phylloxera *socalcos*, built before the devastation of the Douro vineyards by disease during the last third of the nineteenth century. Many of these were abandoned then and today form *mortórios* – or morgues of dead vines – that have become overrun with wild shrubs. Many pre-phylloxera *socalcos* have, however, been restored and replanted and still keep their old schist retaining walls.

Other *socalcos* have tall, straight solid walls that support wide surfaces planted with four, five or more rows of vines. These are the post-phylloxera *socalcos*, most of which were built between the end of the nineteenth century and the mid-1930s, when most of the vineyards in the region underwent reconstruction. The great majority of the hundreds of kilometres of walls that we see covering the riverbanks today date from that stage in the evolution of the Douro landscape. In the 1970s, construction of *patamares* began. This operation involved scarifying the land and destroying old walls, heralding the appearance of large plots of slightly sloping, earth-banked land usually planted with two rows of vines, laid out to facilitate the mechanisation of the vineyard. Vertical planting has now gained some acceptance too.

The Alto Douro did not significantly extend the range of World Heritage cultural landscapes, for other wine-making regions have already been inscribed: Portovenere, Cinque Terre and Islands (Palmaria, Tino and Tinetto), in Italy, Le Vignoble Bordelais de Saint Émilion et son Village, in France, and Wachau in Austria. However, the Douro region is clearly worthy of inscription in its own right; it marks the continuing success of a strategy which, recognising the universal approbation and cultural significance of wine, and following an assessment of the significant grape-producing areas in the Old World, seeks to inscribe the most important viticultural regions on the World Heritage List.

Inscriptions, 2002–2003

A further 8 cultural landscapes have subsequently been added, 2 in 2002 and 6 in 2003.

Table 7. Official cultural landscapes inscribed on the World Heritage List, 2002–2003.

2002	1063	Hungary	Tokaj
	1066	Germany	Rhine valley (part)
2003	208rev	Afghanistan	Bamiyan valley
	925	India	Bhimbetka
	1068	Italy	Sacri Monti
	1099	South Africa	Mapungubwe
	1084	United Kingdom	Kew
	306rev	Zimbabwe	Matobo Hills

2002 was really just half a year since the Committee changed its meeting time from December to June; the two new inscriptions added nothing new to the development of the concept. The Rhine valley was riding on the precedents created by the Loire and Danube (the Wachau, both 2000), while the Tokaj wine landscape followed another well-beaten track. Were not political courtesies imperative at a World Heritage Committee meeting in Budapeç, the area might well have better waited for a trans-frontier nomination with Slovakia of the appropriate Tokaj region as a whole. The developmental interest lies in 2003 when, faced with a possible queue of eight cultural landscapes, the Committee rejected all bar two and inscribed in their six approvals two which were not even on the potential list a few months earlier.

The *coup*, given the international political situation, was of course to recognise the cultural landscape and archaeological remains of the Bamiyan valley: not just the famous, sadly now-residual rock-cut Buddha statues but a large area of the valley in whose side they were hewn (Plate 12). To quote the official citation, 'This site showcases the artistic and religious developments which from the first to thirteenth centuries characterized ancient Bachtria … The area contains numerous Buddhist monastic ensembles and sanctuaries, as well as fortified edifices from the Islamic period. It also bears testimony to the tragic destruction by the Taliban of the two standing Buddha statues, which shook the world in March 2001.'

This inscription represents a major triumph, intellectually to have created a World Heritage cultural landscape in such circumstances, and administratively to have done so at speed. The landscape was immediately placed on the List of Heritage in Danger – which may seem paradoxical if not pointless – but of course the two moves were to draw attention not just to the need for action but also that mechanisms were in place to take action. These could even include reconstructing at least parts of the fragmented Buddhas. Meanwhile, a clear signal was given both to and from Afghanistan about practical matters of international recognition and aid and about iconographic issues of artistic and religious values, identity, and connections between heritage and social, economic and political regeneration. It all represents a major act of commitment of resources and faith, an overt experiment in contemporary World Heritage international socio-politics if you like, and certainly something new in terms of cultural landscape in that inscription has occurred very consciously in the context of future aspiration rather than protecting past achievement for its own sake.

The Bamiyan inscription also added a welcome dot in Asia to the distribution of World Heritage cultural landscapes, and another came simultaneously with the inscription of the Rock Shelters of Bhimbetka, India. The rather curious circumstances in which this nomination suddenly appeared on the Committee's agenda need not particularly concern us; the important points are that inscription brought not only a new dot on the map in Asia but allowed the cultural landscape concept to embrace a new sort of site. The nominated area covers 1,893 ha and is surrounded by a Buffer Zone of 10,280 ha. It lies, again to quote the official citation, 'in the foothills of the Vindhyan Mountains on the southern edge of the central Indian plateau. Within massive sandstone outcrops, above comparatively dense forest, are five clusters of natural rock shelters, displaying paintings that appear to date from the Mesolithic period right through to the Historical period. The cultural traditions of the inhabitants of the 21 villages in the buffer zone bear a strong resemblance to those represented in the rock paintings.' The ICOMOS evaluation noted that 'The area has abundant natural resources – perennial water supplies, natural shelter, rich forest flora and fauna, and like similar regions of significant rock art (for example Kakadu National Park in Australia or Kondoa Irangi in Tanzania), these conditions of plenty seem to have been conducive to the development of sustainable and persistent societies and the creation of notable rock art.' Clearly there are elements here represented in other World Heritage sites – Uluṟu (Plate 5, Figure 1) as well as Kakadu (Figure 2), Australia, and the Upper Pinturas river valley, Argentina (Figures 64, 65), also have decorated, natural caves, and several other site – Tassili n'Ajer, Algeria, the Upper Azat valley, Armenia, and Matobo (*below*), for example – possess striking characteristics deriving from their geological circumstances. Nevertheless, Bhimbetka is the first official cultural landscape of its type and

FIGURE 28.
An eroded landscape of
former cultivation and
settlement, including
use of the top of the
rock on the left as a
refuge, at
Mapungubwe, South
Africa. It may not look
very striking but the
area was added to the
World Heritage List as
a cultural landscape in
2003 because, before it
was abandoned in the
fourteenth century AD,
it was central to a large
kingdom and now
contains the evidence
of social and political
development over four
centuries.

to that extent widens the range of possibilities of the category of World Heritage site.

The 2003 inscriptions of official cultural landscapes also added two properties from sub-Saharan Africa. The inclusion of Mapungubwe, South Africa (Figure 28) right on the borders of Zimbabwe and Botswana (with whom it is hoped to propose a trans-frontier extension), and the Matobo Hills in Zimbabwe, is most welcome if only because the whole continent of Africa is at the moment grossly under-represented, both on the World Heritage List and among cultural landscapes in particular. Mapungubwe Cultural Landscape is, as its citation explains, 'an open, expansive savannah landscape on the confluence of the Limpopo and Shashe. [It] developed into the largest kingdom in the sub-continent before it was abandoned in the fourteenth century ... the almost untouched remains of the palace sites and also the entire settlement area dependent upon them [survive], as well as two earlier capital sites, the whole presenting an unrivalled picture of the development of social and political structures of some 400 years.' In other words, it is primarily an archaeological landscape – a rare category 2a sort of cultural landscape – in a resource-rich setting where the history of a significant regional kingdom is represented. The quality of preservation is clearly an important factor.

Similarly on the Matobo Hills, though there preservation comes from continuing use in a category 2b landscape rather than from peaceful abandonment in a remote area. 'The area exhibits a profusion of distinctive landforms ... the large boulders provide abundant natural shelters and have been associated with human occupation from the early Stone Age right through to early historical times, and intermittently since. They also feature an outstanding collection of rock paintings ... [and] ... continue to provide a strong focus for the local community, which still uses shrines and sacred places, closely linked to traditional, social and economic activities.' Much of this description echoes that of the not too distant (by African standards!) Tsodilo site, Botswana (*above*), and the two properties are clearly comparable; yet in 2001 Tsodilo was inexplicably but deliberately not recognised as a cultural landscape whereas the Matobo Hills acquired that status in an instance where, for once in these matters, ICOMOS' advice was accepted.

The remaining two cultural landscapes of 2003 were both in Europe. The *Sacri Monti* of Piedmont and Lombardy became Italy's fourth cultural landscape, four times as many as in all the Arab States, twice the number in the whole of Latin America and the Caribbean, and the same number as in the whole of Africa. 'The nine *Sacri Monti* ('Sacred Mountains') ... are groups of chapels and other architectural features created in the late sixteenth and seventeenth centuries and dedicated to different aspects of the Christian faith. In addition to their symbolic meaning, they are of great beauty by virtue of the skill with which they have been integrated into the surrounding natural landscape of hills, forests, and lakes. They also house much important artistic material in the form of wall paintings and statuary.' This official brief summary does not exactly set the pulses racing: in practically all respects – European, Christian, Italian, religious architecture, wall paintings and statuary – the ensemble is familiar and repetitious of sites already on the World Heritage List; but oddly enough, not of cultural landscapes. In that respect, the *Sacri Monti* are different (though they share characteristics of several Chinese sacred mountains which are not official cultural landscapes). The nine separate sites are scattered over northern Italy and are not physically linked along a pilgrimage route, holy walk or heritage trail, nor do they share architects or proprietors; their commonality rests solely in the idea, common in parts of Catholic Europe at the time, of making some mountains sacred by building chapels upon them. There is perhaps something in common here with the ideas represented at Kalwaria, Poland, also an artificial creation. Overall, in what is a new, and possibly not totally convincing, type of cultural landscape in World Heritage terms, the *Sacri Monti* of Piedmont and Lombardy are held together simply by an association of just three ideas concerning Christian sanctity, chapels and mountains.

In contrast, the last of the 2003 group could hardly be more secular and scientific. The Royal Botanic Gardens, Kew, UK, contain an historic landscape garden created in 1759. It 'features elements that illustrate significant periods of the art of gardens from the 18th to the 20th century. The gardens house botanic collections (conserved plants, living plants and documents), which have been considerably enriched through the centuries ... [and] ... have made a significant and uninterrupted contribution to the study of plant diversity and botanic economics.' Obviously, I could play no part whatsoever in the evaluation of this property, but it was nevertheless gratifying to see a suggestion that it could be considered as a cultural landscape taken seriously with a joint evaluation mission containing representatives from both IUCN and ICOMOS. There was little doubt privately in my mind that the property was eligible as a category 1 'designed landscape' in its own right but I was also interested in a scientific judgement of its scientific value, both historically, including a large component of *ex situ* flora, and contemporaneously given the ambitious millennial project to build up and sustain forever a world seedbank. In that context, I had wondered whether these gardens, a monument to Darwinism if ever there was one, might not qualify under criterion (vi) – 'be ... tangibly associated with ... ideas ... of outstanding universal significance'. Instead it was inscribed under criteria (ii), (iii) and (iv): (ii) presumably recognises its role in landscape design, and (iv) presumably also recognises that it is 'an outstanding example ... of a landscape which illustrates significant stages in human history', but quite what (iii) has to do with it is difficult to decipher. Since, however, none of those criteria seem to express its scientific significance, possibly (iii)'s bearing an 'exceptional testimony to a cultural tradition' is meant to fill that gap. Anyway, the decisions meant that the UK acquired its second World Heritage cultural landscape though, it has to be said, given the range of diverse and outstanding landscapes in the UK, few would have predicted on 1 January, 2000, that within three and a half years the UK's first two World Heritage cultural landscapes would be Blaenavon and Kew! (*cf.* the next chapter, and especially Fowler 2000a which does not even mention Kew).

CHAPTER 6

Britain and Cultural Landscapes

The British, particularly the English, are not very comfortable with the word 'cultural'. On the one hand it smacks of expensive opera that is particularly good for you, as in 'cultural event', and on the other of failed, cheap centralist ideologies as in 'cultural policy'. There is nevertheless now a UK Government Department with the word 'Culture' in its title, replacing that dreadful, played-out word 'heritage'. How English, however – and the dead giveaway that the word is not being used in its anthropological sense – that the word 'culture' is then added to, giving us the Department for Culture, Media and Sport (DCMS) with a title which fails to recognise that media and sports are but part of 'culture'. Indeed, those added words imply exactly that 'culture' is what educated people do rather than what all people create – while the rest watch television and chase balls.

Elsewhere in the world, the word 'cultural' is of course commonly used in an anthropological sense. There is no problem in talking of culture meaning the lifeway, including the artefacts and art, of a group of people. Others have cultural centres; the British have folk museums. In fact, the term 'folk land-scapes' is not a bad alternative for 'cultural landscape' as a descriptive term; the essence of 'folk', as in 'folk-life', is not just people but the results of their interaction with their environment over a period of time. The vernacular cannot exist in a vacuum; tradition requires time; culture needs context: hence a landscape expressing those ideas, and its label, 'cultural landscape'.

The UK came to take World Heritage reasonably seriously during the 1990s, especially after 1997. The concept, however, still lacks legal backing. Recognition of World Heritage sites' status is, in the meantime, afforded by administrative provision, precedent, advocacy and common sense. Signal successes in protecting such sites have been gained at public and local enquiries, and management on the ground is, in general, both sensitive and sensible. Indeed, without wishing to appear chauvinistic and despite some difficulties, the stewardship of World Heritage sites in the UK is among the best in the world. To appreciate that this is the result of will and skill, not just of a relatively well-off country being able to provide the resources, compare it with the situation in France. The exception to that criticism is the World Heritage cultural landscape of the middle Loire valley where, again despite local difficulties, a conscious effort is being made to create a model structure to look after, use and enhance an immensely complicated property. Similar efforts have been under way at most UK World Heritage sites for at least a decade now – Ironbridge and Hadrian's Wall (Figure 41) spring to mind – and we look at this aspect of cultural landscapes in regard to Stonehenge and Avebury in Chapter 7.

Neither of those are, however, World Heritage cultural landscapes, a topic about which the UK has been and is, to put it mildly, ambivalent. There are in fact only two UK World Heritage cultural landscapes, Blaenavon in south Wales, inscribed as such in 2000 after ICOMOS' insistence that, despite its industrial nature, it was truly a cultural landscape (Figure 26), and the Royal Botanic Gardens, Kew (2003), again after ICOMOS advice that it was necessary for IUCN to evaluate it as well as the 'cultural' Advisory Body. Both sites were recognised as World Heritage cultural landscapes despite official Ministerial comment before their nomination that the UK needed 'further work' (Smith 1998, 17) on cultural landscapes before deciding to nominate anyway. So two 'obvious' nominations in that category, the Lake District and the New Forest, rest for the moment on the UK's revised tentative List of likely UK nominations. Though not claiming to be definitive, a first serious attempt to identify and justify possible cultural landscapes in Britain in World Heritage terms was published in 1995. It informs this chapter and indeed supplies parts of the text.

Although accustomed to the concept of '*natural* landscapes', politicians and civil servants find thoughts of culture all over the countryside, never mind the urbanscape, disturbing. Nevertheless, during the second half of the twentieth century, the science-based approaches of historical ecology, geomorphology and landscape archaeology have brought us to a different understanding of what it is that lies about us in our infancy and what it is we are about as adults. Similar thoughts in a similar time perspective were expressed at the formative Scandinavian cultural landscape conference in 1988: '... during the last 40 years, pollen analysis, plant ecology and – not least – prehistoric archaeology have contributed to the recognition of the borderline, or rather the transition zone, between uncontaminated nature and what eventually became known as the cultural landscape' (Faegri 1988, 2).

My own believe is that the loss of much folklore in the Western world in part also explains our own social insensitivity, generally-speaking, to landscape needs and values. Hence my enthusiasm for such designatory mechanisms as World Heritage and European Landscape Convention, if they lead to increased popular awareness of such things on the back of conservation management. In Britain over three-quarters of the population were rural two centuries ago; in Britain today over three-quarters of the population are now suburban or urban in their residential location, with fewer than one in twenty Britons earning their bread directly from the land. One per cent of the British workforce is in agriculture. Could a demographic divorce from rural landscape be more sudden or real? No wonder most of us now have to acquire by structured learning, formal education, those senses of seeing and valuing countryside which for so many used to come, as we wrongly said, 'naturally' from living in the country, when of course the process of our becoming versed in the countryside was actually the result of acculturation. Now, in contrast, while we may be able to explain in great detail the life-cycle and habitat sensitivities of, say, a wood anenome to a group of career-driven suburban students on a countryside management course, it is very difficult to put over, or absorb, in an educational course module what until two generations ago many people simply learnt as they grew up. In this, as in so much else, life-long learning is now an essential, not an option.

Cultural landscapes in Britain: a tour

Britain is a single archaeological site, fragmented into lots of islands. It is therefore one cultural landscape. This concept is intellectually sustainable, for Britain, Europe's offshore islands, has been extensively busy with people for a long time. They have occupied, hunted over, felled and burnt trees on, farmed in, communicated across, and extracted resources from virtually every hectare of the islands' extremely varied terrain since the final stages of the last glaciation 12,000 and more years ago. The result of this activity is the present landscape.

Of course solid, and to some extent drift, geology provide basics for cultural landscapes; but even they can be affected by what people do. Geology provides exploitable resources which people have been quick to find and use, altering in minor ways the shapes of the basics in the landscape and, much more significantly, turning inert materials into powerful agents of landscape change in the right hands. Thus flint, for example, variously used for implements from the Lower Palaeolithic onwards, was later mined and widely used to chop down trees from the fourth millennium BC onwards, iron ore was increasingly converted into strong and increasingly common tools from the mid-first millennium BC onwards, impacting on soils as ard-tips and spades, upon rocks as quarry tools and on vegetation as axe-heads. Whether felled by stone, bronze or iron, timber's uses included massive trackways which converted uninhabited fens into wet cultural landscapes from the fourth millennium BC. Timber was also used to build, for ceremony and religion, stone and organic structures of which the stones and embanked and ditched elements sometimes survive as henge monuments and other earthworks from the third millennium BC. And all this and more was happening millennia before improved Roman and medieval technology. Growing populations contributed yet more to the anthropogenically-driven evolution of landscape.

To discuss 'cultural landscapes', in the plural, immediately requires, therefore, a willingness to make subdivisions within a concept. Landscapes have to be deconstructed from landscape; identifiers have to be defined and criteria established. Or, as we propose to do, one can simply name names, on the basis of knowledge of the British landscape. In fact, there are too many individual cultural landscapes of quality within the single British one to mention them all, so the following examples are but a selection, consciously representative across a range of time and situation.

FIGURE 29.
The Isles of Scilly, England, UK, viewed from above Cromwell's Castle on Tresco: a drowned landscape, with a rich assemblage of prehistoric remains on the flooded flats between the islands.

Islands

Given Britain's insular situation and geographical nature, it seems reasonable to begin with marine and coastal contexts. In the far south west, out in the Atlantic Ocean, the Isles of Scilly embrace a superb cultural landscape, partly submarine and partly tidal as a result of long-term change in the land–sea relationship. Much of that change, with former agrarian landscapes sinking below the sea, is of the last few hundred years, though some of the landscape elements now beneath the waves date from *c.* 2000 BC. That the whole still constitutes a landscape, however, is demonstrated by the physical links, of field walls for example, from present islands down to tidal flats, and by dramatic sections in the cliffs showing long sequences of deposition intermingled with evidence of human activity (Figure 29).

Similar sequences, almost of 'vertical landscapes' if the concept be allowed, exist in many other exposures around the British Isles: on the west coast of Lindisfarne (or Holy Island) off the Northumbrian coast, for example, a stratified cliff-face looks landwards across the tidal mudflats where once what

is now the island was joined to the mainland. Lindisfarne itself is typical of many a small island around the coasts of Britain with a visible archaeology and a long history from Mesolithic microlith-users to the present clutter of the tourist economy.

On Lindisfarne, and similarly on Iona, pilgrimage and retreat are both ancient ideas very much at the heart of the contemporary Christian mission. Both ideas interestingly reflect in traditional guise two of the motivations, however secular their appearance, in contemporary cultural tourism. Both islands now enjoy, if that is the word, more visits by more 'pilgrims' than ever before. On the Farne Islands, visible from Lindisfarne, the 'active social role' of islands with no active religious foundation and no permanent residents tends now to be even more overtly, and very enjoyably, boat-trips to see seals, sea-birds and Grace Darling's *mis en scène*. Meanwhile, a significant nature conservation programme is quietly maintained, and the association with St Cuthbert respected. It could be argued that the Farnes alone justify World Heritage status on the basis of their faunal and ornithological interests – an archipelago as cultural landscape – but a much more exciting idea would be to link natural with cultural interest, joining not only the Farne Islands to Lindisfarne but both through St Cuthbert to Iona and all with Jarrow/ Monkwearmouth (on the UK Tentative List) and the Venerable Bede in an Early Christian composition imbued as much with art, learning and cultural transmission as with religious belief.

With thousands of islands just off-shore, Britain is particularly rich in insular cultural landscapes: St Kilda, out in the Atlantic west of the Outer Hebrides, is already a World Heritage Site and possesses a marvellous 'relict' cultural landscape as well as (like the Farnes) a significant wildlife interest. (It is currently being considered for re-nomination as a World Heritage cultural landscape). Many islands off the west coast of Scotland could make equally strong claims to bear outstanding cultural landscapes: examples would include the whole of Iona, mostly rocky and uninhabited but, very much like Lindisfarne and St Cuthbert, a place of deep association with a saintly missionary, Columba, and of fundamental importance in the transmission of Early Christian culture to western Europe. For different reasons, another insular claimant could well be the Machrie area of Arran, in the Firth of Clyde, with its 'megalithic landscape'. Well to the south, Anglesey, just off the north Welsh coast, is another single island with a profound, but totally different, cultural landscape.

Off the north Scottish coast, Orkney, like Scilly, is not a single island but an archipelago and also, like the Isles of Scilly, exemplifies an isolated and frag-mented land surface bearing an outstanding archaeological assemblage. Orkney's spans *c.* 3500 BC – AD 1200 in particular, bringing in a rich vein of varied cultures from those of the first farmers to that of the Norsemen, yet the monumental archaeology exists still within a 'working' agrarian landscape. This cultural landscape reflects a traditional way of life based in large part on the harvest of the sea and the joint capacity of land and long hours of daylight to produce two grass crops each year. Both landscape and lifeway are now modified of course, not least by economics and tourism, but, conditioned by the basics of climate, geology and sea, they continue to represent a distinct culture resulting from the long-term interaction of people and that particular combination of environmental factors in that particular place. In my view, a marvellous chance to place an insular UK cultural landscape on the World Heritage List, and to help develop the idea of cultural landscape in that context, was knowingly missed when those concerned in nominating Orkney chose not to put it forward in such an holistic package but merely as an assemblage of discrete monuments. It became a World Heritage site in 1999. Reasons for it being a cultural landscape have innocently been advanced since then by Colin Renfrew (2003).

Coastland

Britain also contains some outstanding coastal cultural landscapes. Some are high along cliffs; others involve estuaries, mudflats and tidal reaches. The extreme south-western end of England, West Penwith in West Cornwall, is an outstanding example of the former. Surrounded on three sides by sea, its granite cliffs edge an interior which witnesses not just many phases of different uses and lots of archaeological sites from the third millennium BC onwards; they also bound a landscape which both perpetuates in current use many old features, such as massive Cornish 'hedges' – actually large, built linear dykes – and yet at the same time is not in general despoiled by the visual crassness of much contemporary tourism. Furthermore, the more enquiry is made of this landscape, the more fulfilling appears to be its capacity to respond; whether the objective be serious scientific fieldwork on the ancient agrarian landscape, the settlement patterns of Early Christian times or the now defunct landscapes of tin-mining (now themselves under consideration for World Heritage status), or whether it be to reward a more romantic and mystery-seeking impulse. Whatever the motivation, this Penwith landscape in particular offers not just a depth of time but a range of experience, from hard-core field science to 'New Age' emotionalism. It certainly embodies remarkable archaeological landscapes; but it is 'cultural' too in being to some just as ideographic as any 'indigenous' landscape in, say, northern Australia or western North America.

Quite different visually and in nature are estuarine landscapes. One example illustrates the variety within them. Overlooking Portsmouth Harbour, more or less in the centre of the southern English coast, is a whole series of 'Defence of the Realm' installations. They range from a Roman fort at Porchester to relatively high-tech military structures of the very recent past; while out to sea are known wrecks – one, the Mary Rose, has been lifted and landed but others submerged can still be protected and are part, therefore, of a cultural landscape. Beyond to the south west is Southampton Water and the Isle of Wight, the latter with expanses of inter-tidal mudflat forming a special sort of landscape with artefacts both on it and in it. Similarly, the seemingly unattractive mud flats on the west side of the Severn estuary also conceal a well-preserved late prehistoric and Roman landscape, complete with organic survivals such as wooden structures. Single artefacts and structures do not, of course, make a landscape; but, however unappealing aesthetically such areas may look, once extents of man-made features in and below the mud are revealed and relationships in vertical and horizontal dimensions demonstrated, the essential elements of landscape created by the interaction of people and Nature would seem to exist. They deserve to be taken seriously in terms of cultural landscape.

The lowlands

We move inland now and into perhaps more familiar terrain. There are but two main divisions to our remaining discussion, lowland and upland. In British terms, a crude line between the two is at about 250–300 m. above sea level. Another, more traditional line is that between, roughly, Exeter in the south west and Lincoln in the north east, with the lowlands east of the line and the 'highland zone' to the west. A number of situations, and therefore of cultural landscape sub-types, occur throughout both zones. In the lowlands, clearly important landscapes along river valleys and across or along relatively high ground can be identified but the lack of sharp topographical distinctions calls for a certain subtlety in perception. Around the middle Thames in the area of Oxford, particularly rich and scientifically valuable areas of archaeological significance stretch not only along the higher ground, where some sites and monuments visibly survive, but also across what is visually the very ordinary-looking countryside of the gravel terraces of the river valley itself. This phenomenon is common in Britain. This is not to say that stretches of countryside with visibly surviving archaeological sites are unimportant; of course, they are, not least for their act of survival which often itself is of considerable historical interest. But what study of landscape has now brought to the fore is that, if we wish to understand, and through understanding, wish to conserve, then we should look at the workings of past landscapes. To understand and conserve and demonstrate how they evolved, we need to look at the system of which they were a part, and at its workings which produced what we now see, and not just at the bits of land where monuments survive and buildings sag in ruination.

This means in topographical terms that we need to look at 'bottom lands', to use the useful Americanism, and valley sides as well as the plateaux and hilltops. On the last two, because of their marginal nature in land-use terms since prehistoric times, archaeological structures such as burial mounds and hillforts survive. A classic example is provided by the Avebury area, already a World Heritage Site, in Wiltshire (Chapter 7). The area, already deeply studied, produced much new evidence and generated many new ideas in the late twentieth century and continues to do so. Such new information does not just fill up the landscape distributionally; much more importantly for present purposes, it helps explain the workings of a whole series of contemporary and successive landscapes in functional terms. In other words, cultural landscapes like that around Avebury do not merely contain a marked density of archaeological sites and other man-made features; they also embrace a variety of resources, natural as well as anthropogenic – 'bottom lands' and hill-tops, water and woodland, soils and stones – and the evidence of their natural and humanly-influenced interactions.

The Avebury region must represent other outstanding lowland cultural landscapes in Britain which we cannot explore here. We would be less than fair, however, if we did not even mention the Somerset Levels and the Norfolk Broads as – very different – wetland exemplars; and the New Forest and Hatfield Forest as the two outstanding examples of extensive ancient woodland with a well-documented archaeology and history making them cultural landscapes – and, thankfully, 'continuing' ones too. The New Forest is on the UK's Tentative List (see Chapter 10) specifically as a 'cultural landscape'. Its claims will presumably rest very much, not only on extent and considerable natural and archaeological interest, but rather on its continuing existence as the result of a sustainable, documented management regime over a millennium and more. Its 'universal values' must surely lie in that domain (using criteria iii, iv and/or v?).

The existing lowland heath of Thomas Hardy's 'Egdon' in Dorset is sadly-reduced and demeaned, but still in part 'continuing', a mixture of 'relict' and 'associative' landscapes; and the 'associative' landscape of John Constable in Suffolk, as the National Trust has recognised by strategic acquisitions, is important not so much for its pleasantness as for Constable's significance. The vast skies over, and high scientific value under, the flatness of the Fens characterise a sub-region not to everyone's liking by any means but it is one of the most distinctive landscapes of Britain, virtually man-created and certainly man-maintained. Its outer reaches, The Wash, are also recognised on the UK's Tentative List as a potential World Heritage site but not as a 'cultural landscape'. Land merges muddily with sea there in horizontal ambiguity, and both meet an immensity of sky, but the migrating birds moving through lord it over landscape.

On a different scale and with conscious aesthetic effect are the deliberately-created parkland landscapes sculpted and planted around some of the great English country houses such as Blenheim, Stourhead and Stowe. Parks of this type are such a feature of the English landscape that the best one thousand of them occupy 1.5% of the country's surface area. Blenheim already is a World Heritage Site (and, suitably adjusted in extent, could probably now qualify as a cultural landscape); Stourhead or Stowe would probably be the first-choice 'Parks' nomination from England as a category 1 cultural landscape (but Kew Gardens became the actual first category 1 World Heritage cultural landscape in England in 2003).

Historic gardens usually go with parks and country houses, physically and often bureaucratically too. Can a single garden be a landscape? – if it is big enough, yes. Can one constitute a cultural landscape of gardens? – again, yes. These slightly rhetorical questions serve to emphasise that gardens, within

parks or on their own, are another marked feature of the British landscape –
and 'British', not just 'English'. Some wonderful gardens flourish, for example,
in the Scottish 'Gulf Stream' counties of Dumfries and Galloway, and the
remains of one of the most ambitious of 'Picturesque' landscapes dotted with
various gardens are currently being attended to at Hafod in the Ystwyth valley,
west Wales. Indeed, it could well be argued that Britain gave gardening to the
western world and now, in England anyway, historic gardens have been cata-
logued with a view to their conservation. One, somewhere, probably ought to
be a World Heritage Site, or a composite nomination could be created from
several gardens provided they could be linked in some coherent way e.g. to
demonstrate key stages in the evolution of the English garden, or the range of
work of a significant individual like Repton or Brown.

Characteristic though gardens may be in Britain, perhaps what many visitors
come for is not one of the great landscapes on the hills or large parks in the
lowlands but just a 'typical' piece of English/Scottish/Welsh countryside. In
England it could be a quiet mosaic of lanes, village, trees and hedges, nothing
dramatic but projecting qualities of tranquillity, timelessness, permanence.
Given the dynamics of landscape, some of those qualities may be scientifically
unreal; but that which is sought and perceived, the subjective not fact, is the
significant element. It is clearly difficult to define and name such landscapes
but they would probably be in the lowland zone, a bit off the beaten track,
perhaps in Norfolk, Kent, Shropshire, Somerset or Dorset (but *see* Notes,
p. 214).

The uplands

In many respects, the uplands of Britain are very different from the lowlands.
What, after all, have the Lake District or the Scottish Highlands in common
with the flatness of the Fens or the modulated gentility of classical Stowe? To
ask the question is to fall victim to an imagined priority for visibility and to
forget the sort of criteria already discussed. Different the landscapes of the
uplands may well look but, if we are looking for evidences of time-depth,
process, interactions and evolution, then eye-catching grandeur in a cloud-
capped mountain peak is not of itself very relevant. It is diverting rather than
significant, unless our ancestors have given it 'meaning' which we wish to
respect.

By world standards, none of Britain's uplands are very high; much of even
the most mountainous countryside lies between only 1000–1300 m above sea
level whereas Europe's tallest eight mountains are all above 3300 m high. Yet,
relatively, much of the upland is high, whether it be the North Yorkshire
Moors in relation to the Tees valley, Snowdonia in contrast to the Conwy
valley, or the Grampians compared to the fertile coast of east Scotland between
Dundee and Aberdeen. In much of the mountainous area, especially in
Scotland and Wales, it is often quite difficult to detect the impact of people
on a scenery dominated by geology and harsh climate; and why should we? –
the uplands of Britain, like the Swiss Alps and Colorado Rockies (though on

FIGURE 30.
'Sheepscape' in winter
by the upper reaches of
the River Coquet in
the Northumberland
Cheviots, England,
UK.

a different scale) are sufficient unto themselves as spectacular views, with physical challenges and interesting geologies, plants and bird-life. And in truth, though people have sometimes lived in the British uplands and often passed through, searching for ore perhaps, transhuming or shepherding, the anthropogenic effects, even when detectable, have not necessarily been significant.

Many formerly important traditions of agrarian societies, like transhumance, have died in Britain, but most 'continuing' landscapes there are nevertheless to do with farming in one way or another. Possible examples for consideration might include 'shepherding landscapes' ('sheepscapes'?) such as the Cheviot Hills on the English/Scottish border (Figure 30) and the rather different livestock countryside of the 'bocage' landscape produced by the workings of the forest economy in medieval and earlier farming of the Weald of Kent and Sussex. Similar fragments of traditional practices in different fields may be discerned in England among, for example, the 'free miners' of the Forest of Dean and the withy-beds and peat-cuttings of the Somerset Levels; but such survivals are now rare in a countryside which changed visually and demographically almost out of recognition in the twentieth century. In any case, they hardly compare as 'living landscapes' at the global level with much fuller examples elsewhere where technological and social change has proceeded neither as long nor as profoundly.

In certain places in upland Britain, however, the impact of human activity has been crucial. Locally in many a now bleak upland, industry has had a major effect. It may have been shortlived, but nevertheless it attracted lots of workers and then left the landscape changed and littered with workings and waste. Stone itself has of course often been the quarry; but frequently upland industry has been out to extract the minerals in the stone. In the Lake District, over the longer term, land-clearance and stone quarrying in the fourth – third millennia BC (Plate 13), and further land-clearance and land enclosure in medieval and early modern times, both major phases of impact, have very much contributed to what we see – and value – today. But this anthropogenic dimension alone, any more than the scenery *per se*, would not qualify the Lake District as an outstanding cultural landscape. What makes it different, and of universal significance, is not what we see but the way in which we look at it. For it was here, through the eyes and then the mind, first of Wordsworth and then of Ruskin, that the revolutionary concept of the aesthetic of landscape appreciation was conceived and developed. It could indeed be argued that UNESCO's support for landscapes as World Heritage Sites goes back to what was theorised in the Lake District between one and two hundred years ago. The twentieth century's contribution has included the development of the National Trust's estate – and Peter Rabbit: truly a landscape of iconography.

Just as the Lake District meant a lot to Peter Rabbit's only begetter, Beatrix Potter, similarly, though without the literary overtones, tracts of upland in Caithness and Sutherland, north of Inverness in north Scotland, exert a strong pull on countless other, less famous people. This is the country of the 'clearances' of the nineteenth century when landlords pushed their tenants off the land to make way for sheep. The hurt of this lives on. It is perhaps worth remarking that a similar change in the Midlands of Tudor England now arouses no emotional reaction at all. Could there be a major cleft in group psychology between 400 years and 150 years ago? – if so, the point is of considerable significance in considering the designation of 'cultural landscape'.

The Highland clearances have left a characteristic landscape of low-density, rough pasture for sheep, scattered with the ruinous remains and earthworks of abandoned settlements, their fields and related features of what was a working landscape – and a home. The later twentieth century sees a steady trickle of third and fourth generation descendants of emigrants to the 'New World' returning to the field and the archive office in search of their roots. The search, for the lucky ones, leads to a bit of wall, some humps and bumps in the bracken, undistinguished features in perhaps a visually unremarkable landscape; but obviously, to the returning great-grand child, it means a very great deal. Historically, the clearances were important too, in North America and other parts of the world as well as in Scotland, and there would undoubtedly be a strong argument for designating a 'clearance landscape' as a 'cultural landscape' in World Heritage terms, perhaps, if persuasiveness could be added to bold thinking, linked to other landscapes across the seas where evicted emigrants settled and created working space anew.

Like the lowlands throughout Britain, most of the uplands are privately owned. Paradoxically, certainly in the eyes of those from countries where the national government becomes legal owner of the land in various types of Park, most of the British National Parks are in the uplands – where land values are low and competition for space is less acute than in the lowlands. One thinks by association of the vast expanses of the USA National Parks in the 'unwanted' West. The National Parks in England and Wales primarily have a twofold purpose: conservation and recreation, particularly through access. The lack of legal ownership means that Park management requires consultation and co-operation with local interests in pursuing national as well as local priorities. So three major areas of potential difficulty, perhaps even conflict, are immediately identifiable: over proprietorial rights, over national and local priorities, and over Park objectives.

A tract of upland northern England, for example, is already a World Heritage Site for cultural reasons; part of it is in a National Park. The Site consisted in 1992, largely through lack of clear definition, not just of Hadrian's Wall but a Roman military zone, some 120 kms. long and of undefined, but certainly many kilometres, width. It was the north west frontier of the Roman Empire in the early centuries AD, a frontier zone which cut across a landscape already 'old' i.e. markedly modified by people. Today the remains of the Wall, which is mostly unspectacular though partly in spectacular landscape, with its earlier and later military accoutrements, survive in a countryside deeply affected in post-Roman times by its former status as a military frontier. Visually, for example, fortified towers and defensive houses witness the continuation of the frontier role in medieval times up to the seventeenth century; and many a farmstead and kilometres of nineteenth century field wall are built of stones quarried for Hadrian's Wall and subsequently recycled into a recent agrarian landscape.

The frontier mentality, however, goes rather deeper than that. Much of the most striking landscape belongs to the National Trust which manages it as its Hadrian's Wall Estate. The whole of the Wall and much of its associated frontier archaeology is protected under Ancient Monuments legislation. In the event, it was the legally protected parts of the Wall, and only them, which became the redefined World Heritage Site when a first management plan was finally drawn up and agreed (English Heritage 1996). The landscape and its contents could hardly be more designated and it is a landscape already enjoyed by many. A few want to make it enjoyed by more; and hence a serious clash in the 1990s between conservation and recreation. A National Trail actually along the Wall (initially in parts along the top of the Wall) was proposed and eventually opened in May, 2003 (Chapter 10).

There are several other equally important upland cultural landscapes in Britain, not yet designated as of World Heritage status but of that class. Indeed, some British upland areas are of world quality as cultural landscapes. This applies to some quite remarkable landscapes of the second and first millennia BC in general, and to the five hundred years or so specifically around

1200 BC. The latter was a time of considerable upheaval throughout much of the Old World and not just on the increasingly impoverished soils of the British uplands, Bodmin Moor, Dartmoor, the Peak District, the northern Pennines, the Cheviots, and several areas in the Scottish uplands – all such display remarkable agrarian landscapes remarkably preserved and, by and large, without later, damaging intrusions. There are other, later agrarian landscapes too of similar outstanding qualities: while prehistoric elements are often present within them, it is the stone-walled fields of the 18th and 19th centuries which make the limestone landscapes of the Peak District and the Yorkshire Dales so visually attractive. But they are far more than pretty pictures because here, with important floristic, technological and land management implications, the traditional ways in which the land was worked continue in at least some degree, and can be encouraged with financial incentives through various conservation schemes.

Discussion

The topographical approach used here works in some ways but constrains thematic development. Industrial examples, for example, have been created from the Neolithic period onwards – the Neolithic flint mines at Grimes Graves in Norfolk and stone quarries in the Lake District produced a landscape of disturbance and waste heaps repeated a thousand times thereafter; while at the other extreme are the 'continuing' landscapes of the eighteenth- and nineteenth-century industries like coal-mining and ship-building which, almost completely, changed into 'relict' landscapes as their *raisons d'être* disappeared during the last two decades of the twentieth century. In the case of Smiths shipyard at Sunderland, not only did its reason for existing disappear: the place itself was broken up and its parts sold off. It no longer is.

Britain has many other cultural landscapes in various forms and of different ages, often hovering uncertainly between 'relict' and 'continuing'. Chronologically in between the two extremes just mentioned, for example, are historic industrial landscapes. The outstanding World Heritage industrial Site, Ironbridge Gorge (UNESCO 1999, no. 90) on the River Severn west of Birmingham, comes immediately to mind; it is actually a multi-period landscape, and speaks for itself (Trinder 1982). Britain already boasts three other industrial World Heritage Sites – Blaenavon, the Derwent valley and New Lanark – in addition to Ironbridge. They and their like, despite preconceptions by some naturalists and aesthetes, contain as much variety and even beauty as there is in agrarian and 'natural' landscapes – just look at some of Turner's and Spencer's work. Manufacturing, power generation, transport – they all produce different landscapes; and the landscapes of each change through time, for example as technology changes. Britain's role as world-wide generator of the 'industrial revolution' in the eighteenth century is widely recognised and, to an extent, the significance is acknowledged in designation and protection; but there are many more landscapes that could be considered, not least from very recent times. The problem, and the opportunity, here is that change is happening so fast that, before we have realised it, the familiar present has become the past.

With the deep coal-mining industry on the point of extinction in most regions of Britain, for an example, should an attempt be made to 'keep' a whole coal-mining landscape *in situ* rather than afford the future the sole option of re-creating one in a museum context? Already recently vibrant, prosperous coal-mining landscapes of but 20 years ago are fast disappearing, with villages as well as pits and pit-heaps already far-gone in physical and social decrepitude. In Co. Durham, the only existing pit-heap is a re-creation of one in Beamish North of England Museum. Should we preserve a 'motor car factory landscape' at, for example, Cowley (now too late) or Dagenham (there's just time)? And what about the power generation industry? – we can feel good about a folksy landscape of windmills in Norfolk and even wax romantic about those wonderful old gasometers outside St Pancras Station; but at what point does a redundant nuclear power station become cuddly? [not when it is in a nominated cultural landscape was the answer in 1999, *see* chapter 9]. Dounreay on the north coast of Scotland is available – and a landmark if ever there was one. I plead not for the wholesale preservation of such – that would be folly; but it is salutary to be reminded that some things are beyond the scope of conventional landscape conservation, including inscription as a World Heritage site. Nevertheless, one interesting point about all such questions dealing with recent time and items not yet in the conservationist canon is when you try to answer the question with another one: why *not*?

The word 'landscape' tends to be used only in a rural sense, though conceptually it is an umbrella word covering urban too. Cityscape and townscape are subdivisions of landscape; conversely, landscape is not a synonym for 'countryside' (which is in any case a very English concept and word). Britain of course contains some great urban landscapes, a fact acknowledged already not just by layers of national and local legislation but also by World Heritage status accorded to several outstanding examples. A characteristic of them is often the setting for the urban core. Contrast is vital, as three World Heritage Sites illustrate: the open space of Parliament Square to one side, and of the Thames beyond St. Stephen's Green, around Westminster Abbey; the similar interplay of bulky buildings and open space (which, ridiculously, is not part of the inscription) at Durham Cathedral and Castle; the vistas to the surrounding hills from the streets of Georgian Bath. Other examples spring to mind: now on the List, the contrast between the Old and New Towns and the green, railway-filled valley in between at Edinburgh; and, not on the List, the Backs at Cambridge and the 'buffer' of the green space between cathedral and the medley of houses in the Close at Salisbury. Rather different in one sense is Saltaire which was inscribed on the List in 2002. It too is of course essentially a composition of spaces and structural bulks but it was the well-preserved nature of its historical form and detail as a planned, private-enterprise, altruistic mid-nineteenth century industrial complex which brought it to the World Heritage Committee's approving attention.

Two other urban landscapes also have good claims: Liverpool's waterfront is already nominated by the UK for Committee consideration in 2004. A particularly outstanding opportunity for a 'continuing landscape' nomination in the next decade lies not among green fields but in the urban context of the Tyne bridges at Newcastle upon Tyne. With six bridges across the River Tyne in a kilometre, four of them high-level and four of them of outstanding engineering, historic and aesthetic appeal – they are all quite useful too! – surely the *ensemble* is one of the man-made wonders of the world. Conceptually, with the adjacent river banks, urban form and architecture, they form a cultural landscape rather than just a collection of monuments because they represent a repetitive response to a combination of natural circumstance and human need i.e. interaction between humans and Nature. The response has been forthcoming over two thousand years, since the first Roman bridge; the present hardware spans a century and a half as well as the Tyne. The need is of course to cross the river, on the main route north through the Wall to Scotland. A natural circumstance provides the engineering opportunity and challenge, and now the visual drama of successive challenges accepted: the Tyne valley narrows where the river originally cut through a sandstone ridge in, as at Ironbridge, a short length of gorge. It was made for bridges to be thrown across it; though they did not have to be the great works of Stephenson's double-decker High Level Bridge (road and rail), Armstrong's Swing Bridge (road), the Tyne Bridge (road) and now the elegant millennial 'Blinking Eye' (pedestrian bridge).

Urban parks, another form of green space like private country house parks but deliberately designed as such for public recreation, were virtually invented in Britain and given to the world. Obviously some of the great metropolitan ones like Hyde Park, London, belong to the international class along with Central Park, New York, and Parc du Champ de Mars, Paris. But most provincial cities have their own too, perhaps anonymous to the world in general but valued landscapes to their citizens. The first municipal park specifically laid out for public use was Birkenhead Park in 1843 by Joseph Paxton. Jesmond Dene, Newcastle upon Tyne, bought by Lord Armstrong and given to the City in 1883, is a classic, or rather 'rustic' example of the *genre*. Less mannered but equally manmade, and equally enjoyed as urban open space, are those traditional grazing areas just outside some medieval cities: Port Meadow, Oxford, Clifton Downs, Bristol, and the Town Moor, Newcastle upon Tyne, are outstanding examples.

Overall, Britain certainly contains numerous examples of potential World Heritage cultural landscapes; but common sense and a sense of fairness – after all, many countries have no World Heritage sites yet, let alone cultural landscapes – demand that selection, albeit from strength, be of the utmost rigour. One or two designed cultural landscapes could contribute to the world bank of category (i) examples: Stourhead and Stowe are outstanding in an outstanding national resource, and it would be nice to see Studley Royal re-nominated as a cultural landscape. Britain can also offer for its 'associative value' one outstanding category (iii) example, the Lake District. Undoubtedly its major contribution, however, will be in category (ii) where, especially in the relict sub-class (ii)a, it has a portfolio of global significance. From among them a selection could be made which would grace the embryonic World Heritage List of cultural landscapes. It could be further enhanced by regrading existing World Heritage sites at Stonehenge and Avebury as cultural land-scapes. The Tyne bridges at Newcastle could also be conceptualised as a cultural landscape when they are brought forward, as must be the case, for World Heritage nomination.

Such places provide not just visual stimulation and recreational space but distinctiveness, a sense of place. British people seem to like that, even to need it. Many of them think of a particular landscape as 'home', even as 'theirs' without any presumption to legal ownership. It may not be particularly distin-guished by its architecture, its history or archaeology, or even by its scenery; it just has to be recognisable in a meaningful way to a person. Sometimes that is easy: every Geordie carries an image of the Tyne Bridge around with him, just as many Australians carry a similar image from Sydney around with them. Equivalent images from elsewhere might well not be recognisable to non-locals, but that in no way diminishes the value of a particular view, a tree or a stone to someone of that place. The experts talk about the 'personality of landscape', meaning how they can categorise it scientifically; but perhaps we would do well to remember that most people have their own favourite land-scape, irrespective of its scientific qualities, and that most bits of landscape probably mean something to somebody. It would seem especially important to think of such layers and levels of perception when we look at the landscapes of a whole country with a view to evaluating them, and even more so when we presume to grapple at global level with the 'universal values' of a subtle concept labelled 'cultural landscape'.

CHAPTER 7

Landscapes of Stonehenge and Avebury

Stonehenge (Figure 31) and Avebury (Plate 14), with 'related megalithic sites', form a single World Heritage site (no. 96, 1987); but neither singly nor together are they officially a World Heritage cultural landscape. Nevertheless, each of these megalithic monuments of the third millennium BC sits in the middle of a large surrounding area of countryside which, in both cases, the World Heritage Site embraces. Each of the stone circles is therefore accompanied by its topographical context in terms of its designation. Such has always been so since building began on those sites, five thousand and more years ago.

This short chapter merely reflects on a few aspects of the two components of this World Heritage Site, places characterised in the early twenty-first century by the dynamics of change. It is not an attempt to present a comprehensive, or even cohesive, discussion of those dynamics and the sites themselves, but to reflect on some matters and issues, not always to the fore in current debate, which seem to me interesting in their context here as World Heritage sites which include a lot of landscape. The landscape incorporated in each, though not technically 'World Heritage cultural landscape', is nevertheless World Heritage landscape; and around each great megalithic site are cultural landscapes of great importance. My personal view is that Stonehenge and Avebury should be separated into two distinct World Heritage cultural landscapes. Each deserves its own inscription.

Many people will be familiar with both monuments, though perhaps not the surrounding countryside. Each archaeological monument receives hundreds of thousands of visitors annually, but relatively few venture out beyond the stones, even though much encouragement to do so is given to visitors. Each countryside contains plentiful rights of way and way-marked tracks and paths, so you do not need to get lost among the burial mounds of the ancestors (Figure 31). There are indeed many guide-books and maps, and some excellent books about the archaeology of the two areas. I do not, therefore, describe the sites in detail here but muse rather on some of the issues that they raise. Some are inevitably about management because it is difficult, and inadvisable, to separate academic knowledge and understanding from the practicalities of looking after a site and presenting it to visitors. These issues could as easily be discussed in their thematic context in Chapters 9 and 10; they could as easily arise elsewhere on official World Heritage cultural landscapes.

FIGURE 31.
Stonehenge, England, UK: a monument and its World Heritage landscape from the west, with sheep managing the sward in the foreground, visitors trailing in from the dismal entrance on the left, four thousand-year-old burial mounds on the middle distance skyline among a tree-belt damaged by storms and, on the right, a glimpse of the A303 trunk road which currently physically separates the monument from its southern landscape. Millions of pounds have recently been spent appraising this landscape. It is proposed to sink the road out of sight and sound in a tunnel which will also, when grassed over, 're-unite' Stonehenge with its southern landscape; but what about the views of monument and landscape thereby lost to road-users in the tunnel?

The two megalithic circles of Stonehenge and Avebury lie 25 km apart in Wiltshire, in central southern England. Each was in use in the third millennium BC, though activity and, almost certainly, construction was taking place on both sites before 3000 BC. Avebury's great stone circles and huge bank and ditch seem to have fallen out of use long before 2000 BC, whereas Stonehenge was still being rebuilt after that date. For World Heritage purposes, Avebury seems to have been tagged on to Stonehenge's designation as the plausible sources of Stonehenge's 'sarsen stones' – blocks of Tertiary sandstone – which make up its unique trilithons; though quite apart from the great, eponymous henge monument of bank, ditch and stone circles, the Avebury area is not entirely lacking in its own outstanding monuments, like Silbury Hill and West Kennet long barrow. They and some other monuments are specified in the World Heritage inscription. However, the areas between the monuments were included in the inscription so that the Avebury World Heritage Site is not just the great henge with other discrete humps and bumps dotted around it but a whole, roughly square and uninterrupted block of landscape. The designation differs from Orkney's in this regard. Similarly at Stonehenge: its central place in a landscape of contemporary and later monuments, particularly cemeteries of the later third and second millennia BC, was recognised in the nomination.

Both sites were in a constant state of review during the 1990s, and indeed such revisionism now seems to be a permanent feature. There is nothing new in this, for Stonehenge has attracted controversy since medieval and possibly earlier times; and it enjoyed, if that is the word, at least one major review in each of the decades I have known it throughout the second half of the twentieth century. The first decade of the twenty-first century is maintaining the track record. Fortunately, only two of the reviews, in the 1950s and 1960s, actually resulted in physical changes on site. While the intensity of its consideration has increased in each of the three succeeding decades, cerebration, bureaucracy and politics have between them limited responses to the increasingly acute issues of its management largely to reactive measures. Similarly, Avebury has excited curiosity since its 're-discovery' in the seventeenth century. Both sites and their surrounding areas now have management plans, and Avebury has recently led the way with the publication of its own Research Plan. As in the past, Stonehenge has followed in more sophisticated mode.

Typically of many archaeologists and of many other people, both monuments have played significant parts in my life, and not merely as archaeological monuments. I first visited Stonehenge in 1957 during the Atkinson/Piggott excavations when my wife-to-be was working there. I subsequently published photographs anonymously of my eldest daughter and my father at Stonehenge, and have been officially engrossed in Stonehenge affairs since my first committee meeting about it in 1962 (though I deliberately left all relevant committees and such like forty years later). I also first visited Avebury in 1957 and have experienced its change over 45 years from remote and little-known place to the better-organised and increasingly down-trodden paradox it is today. I have, therefore, known, wondered at and used both monuments and their surrounding landscapes over nearly half a century, and have seen both change almost out of all recognition, and deteriorate, under the impact of popular usage; and though I have had much to do with both professionally and officially throughout that time, now I am no longer an 'insider', privy to specialist, even confidential, information and current debate. My only connection with them now, apart from remaining a member of an informal, advisory committee at Avebury because it is enjoyable, is as a private individual and visitor.

The National Trust owns the Stonehenge Estate, and has its own management plan for it. Essentially this encompasses some 1000 acres of land around the Stones. The whole of this estate lies within the World Heritage Site and indeed constitutes a very significant part of it, both scenically and archaeologically. Of particular relevance are two facts. First, the land came to the Trust as a result of a purchase funded by public subscription (initiated by the then Prime Minister) specifically to save the environs of Stonehenge from development after some scares on this score during the First World War; and, second, that subsequently the Trust exercised its unique power under Parliamentary Act to declare the land 'inalienable'. This means that only Parliament can change the ownership or authorise significant land-use change.

The National Trust is also a major player at Avebury, and has its own management plan for its Avebury Estate (630 ha), which is different from the World Heritage Site Management Plan (English Heritage 1998). The two areas do not exactly co-incide, as at Stonehenge, and, frankly, in the Avebury case neither do the objectives and priorities of World Heritage, English Heritage and the National Trust, never mind those of the local authorities and the local community. At Avebury as at Stonehenge, a lot of people, wearing different hats – though sometimes the same person wears all the hats at once – are busily engaged in tasks which involve fairly big issues. 'Access', and 'Access to what?', for example, are issues of deep theoretical, even ethical, import as well as of immediate practical importance; and 'heritage' nowadays involves considerable sums of money, both private and public. Stonehenge, for example, generates revenue of several million pounds (sterling) per annum. At the same time, while trying to cope with a bureaucratic and organisational structure of considerable complexity, decision-makers are working with tight deadlines (for reasons that are not always apparent) – and all, of course, in the name of looking after the 'resource' better while, these days, giving more and more people a more enriching experience.

Stonehenge: a trilithon which collapsed

Stonehenge itself is in the world mega-class, truly *une destination mondiale*. Like Uluru and the Taj Mahal, in a sense it does not need World Heritage status; yet it is precisely because people, and eventually Government, have taken that status seriously that the last decade has seen increasing professional attention paid to the site and its surrounds. In some respects, notably immediately around the Stones themselves, the long process of deterioration has been arrested, but the early twenty-first century will see major tests of the site in public as plans to change access to it, the roads around it, and presentation of the Stones and their landscape are debated and, perhaps, implemented. Though a Government decision to construct a tunnel to rid the landscape near the Stones of a main road has been taken, a timetable published and planning is well-advanced, this individual at least suspends some belief that all that is in hand will actually happen. My caution stems from having heard and observed so much about 'the future of Stonehenge' when, over the last four and a half decades, little has in fact happened by managed intent. Meanwhile, many of the well-intentioned have bitten the dust. Nevertheless, the Stonehenge experience in 2010 might be very different from today; and I hope it is, provided it is an improvement. Again, Stonehenge could look to Avebury. As I write (late June, 2003), the World Heritage Committee is actually considering a report on the proposals. Why? – it has been alerted to the possibility that Stonehenge, a World Heritage site, is under threat, notably from the proposed tunnel designed to relieve it of traffic pollution. Doubtless the Committee will be re-assured but nevertheless it comes as something of a shock to realise that the result of so much well-intentioned, professional planning could be seen by the international community as the creation of a threat. What supreme irony that this should be so after such serious consideration nationally for so long of various ways of saving, and then improving, Stonehenge!

The World Heritage Site is extensive, stretching out far beyond the Stones to embrace what is scientifically a wonderful stretch of historic landscape; but most people do not want to use some 99 per cent of the inscription. Does their choice, one wonders, arise from ignorance, other priorities, time or physical constraints – or deliberate, informed choice? Whatever the reason, they all want to be at the epicentre, a monumental ruin which, like Hadrian's Wall, is as eloquent of power failure as it is of structural grandeur. People, lots of them, will go to the Stones whether we like it or not and, provided the landscape is not too obviously 'developed' with disfigurements, they will probably not worry too much about the surrounds. It is useful to remember, however, that it is visitors, *not* Stonehenge, which require a visitor centre (though some commentators would actually dispute whether such a single centre is the best way of providing for the million or so visitors a year).

No-one lives at or near Stonehenge, though the army is camped on the northern periphery of the World Heritage site, and typically economically-driven communities live to east and west and south with lots of daily criss-crossing in between. The roads, regarded as essential until recently, cut off the principal site, the cynosure of all eyes, from everything else, snipping across the landscape to hold the Stones between the blades of their noisome shears (the A303 and A344). The single most-significant Stonehenge achievement of the last decade has been to gain general agreement that the A344 should be closed; it is the trunk road to the South West, the A303, that it is proposed to put underground, though by no means everyone is agreed on this solution in principle, never mind details such as length and method of construction (tunnelling or cut and cover). It is surely inconceivable, nevertheless, that the A303 can be widened or diverted within the World Heritage site, so it seems to this author that the only options are to leave it alone (which is also unacceptable), to bury it, or to close it as a main road. The last thought is attractive, for it correctly recognises that the problem is the volume, noise and visual pollution of early twenty-first century traffic that is unacceptable, not the road *per se*. After all, marked-out ways across the Stonehenge landscape have been integral to that landscape and its development since the Avenue was first formalised some 5,000 years ago. Meanwhile, it contains a modern paradox: for many, Stonehenge is not working any more because it has lost its magic; for others now making up a prominent 'new audience' of 'worshippers' (for a host of reasons) at the Stones, the monument is now more popular than ever. All the same, it is telling us something that Avebury now seems to be taking some of the load of expectation from Stonehenge in terms of special occasions, increased numbers of visitors and a year-round visiting season.

Nevertheless, in the mid-1990s Stonehenge was graced with a great visionary plan, the Millennium Park, to address the problem and gradually restore that magic, not just visually but ambiently. It was and is a good idea, essentially restoring people to the Stonehenge landscape and presenting Stonehenge in a context to the people. But it came to be driven by political dogma and went careering off down the wrong track, in pursuit of financial objectives which were not central to the Stonehenge enigma. In 1997 the Commissioners of the Millennium Lottery Fund decided not to support a major proposal radically to change access to and the presentation of Stonehenge and its environs. A trilithon – the partnership of English Heritage, the National Trust and The Tussauds Group – aided by consultants and capital injectors, failed to deliver the Stonehenge of the future. Perhaps it was the effect on the grand vision of a particular sort of ideology which led to an incompatibility, like oil and water, perhaps it was the tri-partite organisation itself: for whatever reason, but not for the first time, a trilithon collapsed at Stonehenge.

Subsequently, the New Labour government stepped in by setting aside, on environmental grounds, enough money to built a short tunnel on the present line of the A303 south of Stonehenge. Integral to this plan was the closure of the A344 which passes even closer to the monument on the north side. The National Trust enlarged its Stonehenge estate, acquiring the land north of the A303 about 2 km east of the monument and thereby providing potential access to it from the east off public roads. The Trust also committed itself to a land management regime of pasture around the Stones: an arcadian vision of the landscape was common ground between many involved, though the practicalities of putting it in place and maintaining it are considerable. English Heritage, which all along had been frightened of losing its very considerable income from visitor entrance to the monument, committed itself to constructing an appropriate visitor centre just outside the eastern boundary of the World Heritage landscape, right beside the major road junction at Countess roundabout. Again there are practical difficulties about this, but the really significant point is that English Heritage has backed off the (absolutely wrong) idea of creating a complex at Countess roundabout primarily for commercial purposes. A number of us wasted a whole winter 1999–2000 at a series of very expensive meetings ostensibly trying to find a fit between what was appropriate for Stonehenge, its landscape and the public interest on the one hand and private sector profit on the other. Not only was such a solution undesirable on ethical and educational grounds, but the sums simply did not add up. Even I, non-mathematical and non-financial, could work that out.

In mid-summer 2003, dozens and dozens of people are working away at the future of this landscape with its monuments, sitting on committees and advisory groups, writing papers and memoranda and preparing for the next steps. These will involve public enquiries all to do with the A303 and its consequences, including the Countess Road development. The National Trust is quietly putting its land management plan into operation, but completion of the new Stonehenge landscape and its works is not now envisaged until 2010. Given the record of public works construction in recent decades, it seems unlikely that that will be achieved, even if there are no major delays from public enquiries or direct action on the ground. Fifteen years ago I wrote: 'If visitors were invited to contribute a minimum of £1 towards [putting the A303 into a tunnel or deep-cutting], the cost would probably be raised voluntarily while the Department of Transport was still shuffling its papers on such a preposterous notion; cannot English Heritage and the National Trust start such a scheme, offering to match every pound so raised' (Chippindale *et al.* 1990, 166). That did not happen, unfortunately, so we will never know whether it would have worked or not; but the 'preposterous notion' is now official government policy, on environmental grounds.

My own sense is, however, that once the public wakes up to the idea that it will have to dive into a tunnel under Salisbury Plain, opposition to the proposal will increase enormously, led by the not insignificant 'green' anti-road lobby which will object anyway. This is particularly likely to be so after the series of horrific tunnel accidents under the Alps in recent years: is a tunnel for environmental reasons beneath one of southern England's most open landscapes strictly-speaking necessary? – the question is now being asked.

Meanwhile, the landscape of the World Heritage Site, now archaeologically field-walked, mapped and digitised as no other landscape in Britain, is gradually returning to a brownish-greenish hue as it turns to grass with barrows humping upwards. I am supposed to have used the verb 'revert' there, not 'turn', for the essence of this change is 'restoration', 'reversion' to a landscape of dappled sward grazed by pastorally-picturesque sheep dotted over the swelling downs. But was it ever actually like that other than in the agricultural depression of the 1930s – and in the imagination of romantics? As the truism says, every generation creates its own Stonehenge. As we move globally towards environmental disaster, that of the early decades of the twenty-first century will be, in an anachronistic local gesture, both green and 'green'.

Avebury: a megalith which leant a bit

The Avebury World Heritage Site is also quite a big area (Figure 32). Overall, it stretches some 8 km west-east and 6 km north-south. Its size, and indeed the very nature of this World Heritage Site as a spatial entity, is one of the several reasons for uncertainty about it among local people and visitors. The idea that an archaeological site of world significance is actually approaching 50 square kilometres in area (*c.* 12,350 acres) takes some getting used to, especially in a countryside where popular perception and official designation of ancient monuments is of specific mounds and banks existing discretely in an otherwise agricultural, and (wrongly) by implication non-archaeological, landscape.

At the core of the World Heritage Site is the National Trust Avebury Estate, which has been created since World Heritage inscription in 1987. This new heritage estate, which has no historical precursor, includes the great Avebury henge monument, the West Kennet Avenue and land to either side, Silbury Hill, with the Neolithic causewayed enclosure on Windmill Hill to the north west and round barrows and other archaeological structures on Overton Hill

FIGURE 32. Ducks fly along the River Kennet, the boundary of the World Heritage site, with burial mounds of the 2nd millennium BC on the skyline of Overton Hill, Avebury, England, UK, with some of the landscape management issues indicated by the low river level, the flattened historic water-meadows in the centre ground, the intensive arable which has flattened archaeological sites on the valley slopes, the main road and its traffic, and the modern built intrusions.

to the south east. The Trust's estate also includes West Kennet Farm, not for the decayed ambience of its ruinous buildings but for the remarkable but superficially invisible late Neolithic structures beneath them. Rather more obviously, the estate embraces parts of the existing village, a settlement partly within the henge monument but whose historic core around the Saxon church lies just outside it. Avebury village consists of around 100 households and contains a population of around 250 persons. Free parking and toilets are provided in the village, with a larger car-park, also free but without toilets, on its south-western outskirts. It is indeed possible to enjoy virtually the whole site without having to pay for anything. The only formal charge is to the person wishing to experience either or both of the manor house or the great barn, both of which belong to the Trust. The barn is externally very impressive, now (2001) gloriously repaired; yet, such is the impact of a new display on its cavernous interior, it is in understated use as an almost minimalist museum. It tells of the megaliths and the landscape, and the place and some of its people.

In the Avebury area, practically every hill-top and whole stretches of surrounding downland bear the marks of former occupation, activity and structures. A Neolithic causewayed enclosure, for example, crowns Windmill Hill to the north west of the great (and much later) henge monument at Avebury itself; elongated burial mounds of *c.* 4000–3000 BC dot that landscape of early farmers, with many more burial mounds of the second millennium BC on the skylines and plateaux, while to the east of the now-derelict henge, a farming landscape was organised on the rolling downland of Fyfield and Overton Downs. These Downs are designated a National Nature Reserve for their geological interest but they also now constitute a rare tract of grassland surrounded by a sea of arable. This preserves a series of agrarian landscapes from the Neolithic up to the present, their lineaments remarkably surviving as earthworks and stone structures of settlements, fields, tracks and funerary monuments, all now designated under the Ancient Monuments Act in a remarkable act of area scheduling.

In and on what is now the plough-zone of the slopes down to and immediately around Avebury, there used to be similar survivals, some of them recorded from the sixteenth to the twentieth centuries and others into this century. To understand the evidence of land-use over the millennia, however, we have also to take into account the valley floor. Certainly the archaeology of Fyfield and Overton Downs can only be understood as the product of processes by looking down. Chance exposure in service trenches and road-widening, and archaeological excavation proper, have shown glimpses of the 'invisibles' there, for example a series of enclosures forming an elaborate complex right beside the River Kennet just to the east of Silbury Hill, *c.* 2 km south of and contemporary with Avebury itself.

The Avebury area is right on the western edge of the Marlborough Downs, an area of high chalkland that stretches to the River Thames to the north east. These Downs are designated an Area of Outstanding Natural Beauty by the Countryside Agency, yet they may well qualify, however paradoxically, as an outstanding cultural landscape. Of course, in one sense the Marlborough Downs are not even 'natural' in that their present appearance is markedly anthropogenic, not God-given. That we can see the sinuous contours of rounded chalk spurs and dry valleys is because the post-glacial tree cover has been cleared away by farmers since *c.* 5000 BC. Beautiful the countryside of the Marlborough Downs may be but 'natural' the landscape most certainly is not. But there is another objection to their being considered a high-class 'cultural landscape'. The history of the Downs and the development of their 'culture' can only be understood in relationship to what was happening around them, notably in the Thames and Kennet valleys – and around Avebury. I would argue that the environs of Avebury, embracing a range of topography, resources and archaeology, more properly constitute a 'cultural landscape' than the Marlborough Downs as a whole. The latter area is primarily a topographical one, attractive to look at and with a good archaeology, explicable perhaps as a unit in functional terms up to *c.* 3000 BC but thereafter economically and functionally fragmented and related to other places off the Downs.

The Avebury area, is also attractive, not least for its downland backdrop; it also has an impressive archaeology of a density and monumentality comparable to that of Orkney. And like that archipelago, it can be explained by looking, not just for its topographical homogeneity but for its variety. The landscape has become, in both cases, a cultural landscape; it is deep, distinctive and value-laden. A cultural landscape might indeed be defined as one which not only contains the evidence of its development but one which explains itself in eco-historical terms.

Clearly, in some ways, Avebury is far more complex than Stonehenge, and that complexity is, in some respects, increasing. Some of that increase is archaeological: our knowledge and understanding of Silbury Hill, for example, has been revolutionised in the first three years of this century. Typical of the Avebury landscape: unpredictable, except in that it characteristically puts Stonehenge in its place (as was observed by Inigo Jones nearly 350 years ago). Other facets of the increasing complexity are sociological. Hundreds of motorcyclists, for example, now routinely assemble on Thursday evenings at the Red Lion inn at the cross-roads in the centre of the henge. I do not get the impression that this great concourse, quite out of scale with the context, is occasioned by a love of scholarship or religious belief. Answers to my obviously silly question on the point included 'You know you'll meet your mates here', and 'Nice place to bring the family'. Meanwhile, a leathered male *homo sapiens sapiens* and a leathered female of the same species with young dismounted a very large bi-wheel.

The henge, and some individual stones, nevertheless, are now receiving some religious/ritual attention from genuine and would-be pagan worshippers as a spin-off from Stonehenge, where the deterioration in its ambience and the denial of access at critical times has led to many such worshippers writing it off as a usable 'temple'. A consequence is that at midsummer, 2003, Avebury village found its streets and approach roads enmeshed in double yellow lines, the device in Britain to prohibit vehicle parking along the sides of roads. This was the reaction to the place being overwhelmed by midsummer visitors in 2002, a reaction which yet again divided people. Some approved – 'Anything to stop the b*****s' – while others strongly objected, not least because the visual prohibition is apparently permanent.

Avebury is also, critically for many, in an area with a great concentration of crop circles in the surrounding fields. Along the village street, tourists, visitors and residents intermingle with independently-run enterprises like the village bookshop and the Red Lion Inn (both of which rather ham up a sort of quasi-archaeological dimension to the place). Presumably some of their use, and that of the post-office, is by inhabitants. Nevertheless, it is accepted that it is visitor spending which allows these businesses to remain viable, and it is that, and their role as employers, which has to be set against the several debits for the village community – increased traffic flows and congestion, and the air and noise pollution which they bring. Crowded streets, especially at weekends, add to villagers' discomfort in creating a situation familiar at many tourist 'hotspots' where it is difficult to deny the disturbance or the reduction in the quality of the residents' way of life. Clearly, in a way that does not apply to Stonehenge, the Avebury community can recognise a 'social cost' of its tourist-led economic viability.

These 'social costs' still need to be recognised, even if incomers should have expected them. The costs, might, incidently, include a medical one. We are not aware of any study of possible medical consequences resulting from what might be called 'tourism stress', that is the continual pressure on an indigenous population from a continuous tourist presence in its communal space, especially now that tourists come all the year round and not merely during a particular season.

The total financial cost of maintaining Avebury as heritage, including as a World Heritage site, may well be of the order of several million pounds (sterling) per year; yet when the site was voluntarily put forward by the British Government for this status, and was approved for such designation by UNESCO, probably not a single thought was given to the financial consequences, either in providing for its stewardship as a World Heritage site or in such a status being an income generator. Yet, now, there clearly is a real cost, and a not inconsiderable one. Should subscribing National Trust members, local tax payers and the community underwrite these true costs? Or should it be the visitors, the State, or an international body such as the World Heritage Fund? Or any combination of those providers? And what about the social consequences? Or, for that matter, the academic consequences?

Early in the twenty-first century, those real costs, financial and in other respects, are becoming apparent at both Avebury and Stonehenge. These sites are expensive in both capital and revenue terms. That is so with or without the World Heritage accolade; it certainly costs more with it. The argument that they should be 'earning their keep' by charging visitors might seem a strong one, but it must be resisted, on principle and in practice. There are three immediate reasons for saying so. In the first place, a developed and historic country like Britain ought to be proud to be able to look after its heritage properly from general taxation, making them freely available to its citizens and visitors, without having or choosing to treat them as commodities. Secondly, both sites generate far more economic activity than can or could be accounted for by takings at the gate. Their economic importance is much greater than the sum of potential entrance fees – in local and national jobs created, for example, and as part of the 'halo effect' which attracts foreign tourists to Britain. Thirdly, it is essential at Avebury to remember that, as in the similar if not identical situation at Stonehenge, originally the core of the National Trust Estate was given by an individual donor (Alexander Keiller), and accepted by the Trust, for the public to enjoy freely. Furthermore, the fact of the continuous living community in the village has maintained the local tradition, hallowed since the days of Aubrey and Stukeley, that anybody is free to muse among the megaliths whenever they so wish. You cannot do that at Stonehenge itself without paying (except in special circumstances) and historically the English Heritage regime continues a periodic practice of charging there which goes back two centuries. But the other 99 per cent of the Stonehenge World Heritage site is freely accessible (much of it giving splendid and even startling views of the Stones), reflecting its ownership by the National Trust and the origins of that ownership in the purchase of the land by public subscription for public benefit.

Though they would matter hardly a jot to the thousands of visitors, three points about the status and management of the Avebury area as a World Heritage site come to mind. In the first place, it should be divorced from Stonehenge as a joint World Heritage Site. Avebury should be declared a World Heritage Site in its own right. The original linkage with Stonehenge in 1987 has been superseded by a growing awareness of the difference between and distinctiveness of each Site. Each has an undeniable claim of world status, and now is the chance to recognise that fact.

Secondly, a wider Avebury World Heritage Site defined in its own right should be created as a 'cultural landscape'. Avebury meets some criteria admirably (iii and iv certainly, i, ii and vi arguably). Conversely, the World Heritage definitions of a cultural landscape include qualities which neatly embrace what Avebury and its surrounds can offer.

Thirdly, the area of the Avebury World Heritage Site should be redefined. Both major and minor adjustments could now be made to accord with modern practice and greatly improved knowledge and understanding of the landscape. Virtually all new World Heritage Sites, for example, are now surrounded by a 'buffer zone', and certainly such would be required of the Avebury site were it to be proposed now. That is something which needs attention early in the twenty-first century. On points of detail, the northern boundary could be pushed further out to provide an 'apron' in front of Windmill Hill with its extraordinarily well-preserved, five and a half thousand years old banks and ditches. To the west, the Oldbury area of magnificent, high downland, has, like so many other significant places in the Avebury landscape, come into the care of the National Trust since the first World Heritage designation. By including it in a buffer zone, or even within the Site proper, advantage could now be taken of this to acknowledge its provision of a fine view eastwards over the whole of the World Heritage Site. Further east, a small but significant adjustment on Monkton Down could include within the World Heritage Site a splendid 'portal' to it, offering to the walker along the Ridgeway fine westerly views across what was surely in some sense a 'sacred landscape' four thousand years ago.

The major opportunity to adjust to archaeological reality lies, however, on the east. There the present boundary makes little rhyme or reason in terms of anything significant in the landscape while, on the other hand, recent archaeological mapping and analysis of the landscape of Overton and Fyfield Downs presents a wonderful opportunity to adjust a boundary to take in the whole of a cultural landscape, much of it already in a National Nature Reserve and all of it a Scheduled Ancient Monument. Intelligent use can be made of improved understanding of the 'secular' landscape of sarsen stones, settlements and fields which was recognised in the initial inscription as providing the essential hinterland to the 'sacred' landscape of the henge and its mighty monuments.

Theoretically, then, Avebury's future should lie as an independent World Heritage Cultural Landscape within a redefined boundary. The reality is, however, that while there might be a real chance of altering the boundary, politics and bureaucracy are unlikely to allow the first two ideas to be implemented in the foreseeable future. Nevertheless, away from the parish pump, the sort of detail here illustrates not only the obvious fact that World Heritage Sites need to be kept under continuous review but also the profound truth that no landscape stands still; even if change may be more in the eye of the beholder than on the ground.

Think globally, act locally

The greatest medium-term threat now at many World Heritage sites, including cultural landscapes and certainly at Stonehenge and Avebury, is not the physical consequences of tourism; it is the acceptance of an expectation that designation is primarily a mechanism to promote tourism. This must be recognised and resisted for the shallow and unacceptable perversion that it is. Promoters of the conservation ethic are nevertheless awakening to the need both to argue and sustain the World Heritage case in the market place, as the ethics of the market place would daily further infiltrate our considerations. Both Stonehenge and Avebury are at crucial points in their careers. It is vital that, while taking whatever opportunity there may be in terms of *realpolitik*, we do the right thing by them as great British landscapes which Britain now looks after for the rest of the world. Both Sites are well over five thousand years into their careers, and each is strong enough in itself to last, with care, for double that time; so we can help ourselves not to take wrong decisions by refusing to be stampeded into taking decisions, right or wrong, merely because of extraneous timetables. These have nothing to do with the integrity or intrinsic quality of Stonehenge and Avebury now, nor with their well-being in the future.

In 2003, a small piece of archaeological work was carried out at Avebury beside the two remaining standing stones of what is still called, following archaic, Druidic nomenclature, 'The Cove'. The stones were leaning and, in the interests of public safety, it was necessary to know whether they were in danger of tipping over. One of the stones proved to have so much of its bulk – three metres – buried out of sight that not only is it in no danger of falling over whatsoever but it has also modestly hidden the fact that it is the longest, and heaviest, megalithic stone set up in prehistoric Britain.

CHAPTER 8

Cultural Landscape Values:
Europe and the British Isles

We are fortunate to live at a time when ideas from new areas of interdisciplinary research and activity are flourishing. This has profound implications for the concept of World Heritage which, embracing so much geographically, is nevertheless essentially both of the mind and of the soul. One of the biggest dangers it runs is of becoming intellectually outdated without realising it.

The palaeo-environmental implications of molecular biology provide an outstanding, current example of what is happening. Some of the material for the DNA analysis underpinning that research comes from geological, geomorphological and archaeological contexts of the sorts which are already in, or could be in, World Heritage landscapes. Faced with the intellectual excitements and whole new dimensions not just of knowledge but of the way we think arising from such research, to spend too much time rather pettily arguing whether one particular landscape is 'natural' or 'cultural' or 'archaeological' is to seek refuge in the familiar when opportunities exist challenging us to create and explore new paradigms.

The particular phenomenon we are privileged to discuss as part of that intellectual experience is much debated at academic conferences, and has already been perceptively defined in the outcome of the one of the World Heritage Centre's own occasions: 'A cultural landscape is a complex phenomenon with a tangible and intangible identity. The intangible component arises from ideas and interactions which have an impact on the perceptions and shaping of a landscape, such as sacred beliefs closely linked to the landscape and the way it has been perceived over time. Cultural landscapes mirror the cultures which created them' (Figure 33) (von Droste *et al.* 1995, 15). That mirror could conceivably create a mirror-image, so that in future cultures themselves might well be influenced by the cultural landscapes that we identify and protect now.

Europe is full of archaeological monuments, many of them widely regarded as among the great architectural and aesthetic creations of humankind. World Heritage is already well-represented there by such monuments, for example Classical ruins, Gothic cathedrals, military remains and the houses and grounds of the rich and well-born; equally, Europe is well-represented, some would argue over-represented, on the list of World Heritage Sites. By and large, here I ignore such heritage, a move which may seem perverse given the riches about which I could write and for which Europe is famous; but

nevertheless, and deliberately, I write of a largely non-monumental heritage, one not well-known outside some academic and scientific circles. There lies one reason for my choice, though of course one book will not change a situation that unfortunately persists despite many serious publications, and numerous attempts to popularise 'landscape archaeology' in such countries as Denmark, Holland and the UK. Another reason is a belief that, not just Europe's monumental heritage but also its landscape heritage is of considerable significance, not only for understanding the continent's past but also for realising its future. A commonality of broadly comparable agrarian experience across the whole of Europe for several millennia, as documented by Barker (1981) for example, may be as significant to a collective European psyche as supposedly unifying factors such as a largely-imagined pan-Celticism or a harking back in admiration over two millennia and more to a homophile, slave-based democracy and an imperial power sustained by military conquest.

Despite two centuries of increasingly mass industrialisation at Europe's economic core, a centre where selective decay is already a feature, this communal agrarian experience still persists not only in the memory but as a marked feature of European life. The nature of the European Community's Common Agricultural Policy indicates this. It also reflects the economic and nutritional peripherality of a significant proportion of that farming today. Both the Policy and its application to a palpable degree affect the sorts of land-

FIGURE 33.
The rock art on granite on dry land at Tanum, Bohüslan, Sweden, was recognized as a World Heritage site in 1994 and, because it is known that its nature and distribution can partly be explained by changes in former sea-levels, it could now be reconsidered as existing in a cultural landscape.

use, and therefore the landscape, which we now see. In considering 'archaeological landscapes' in Europe, we need to be conscious of the hubbub of discussion throughout the continent; revisionism is in the air about the nature of the CAP, about the nature of landscape, and about the nature of the relationships between an increasingly post-industrial continental population and the environment of its land-mass.

Landscape and Nature

'Archaeological landscape' is a phrase embraced, to all intents and purposes, within the larger concept of 'cultural landscape'; for the latter is by definition man-influenced at the very least and to some extent is therefore 'archaeological'. Conversely, since no community ever lived in a vacuum without some form of natural environment, all archaeological landscapes are the product of man and nature – which is an essential part of the definition of a cultural landscape. The term 'cultural landscape' (Chapter 2) has recently developed as a concept influenced by modern ecology, environmental archaeology and conservation and its meaning has now been modified. It is truly remarkable that, within a generation, the outcome is that the term has become an accepted part of 'management-speak' for political and bureaucratic purposes.

This reflects acceptance of the scientific recognition that the whole of the European landscape is modified by humanity and is, to a greater or lesser extent, anthropogenic. The literature behind this acceptance deals as much with humanity's relationships with Nature as with the interactions of both in the landscape; it is now vast (*see* Notes). All landscape is, therefore, in one sense cultural landscape, using that adjective to be synonymous with 'man-made' or at least 'man-modified'. What is often seen as 'natural' is usually not entirely so; but nevertheless all landscape is modified by Nature, and at least some Nature is present in all landscapes (Simmons 1989, 1997). Indeed, some of the worst man-created excrescences on the landscape, like a highly toxic slag-heap from lead smelting, can produce plant communities of considerable scientific interest where, for a time, no plant dared to go. The Alpine penny-cress (*Thlaspi alpestre*), for example, a rare plant in Britain, thrives on the 'gruffy ground' of Mendip's former lead-workings.

Rather more fundamentally, all over Europe (Birks *et al.* 1988 provides many examples) some of the scientifically most interesting landscapes are precisely that not because of their being an outstanding example of this or that particular quality, as specialist experts may believe, but because of the symbiosis that has occurred there and that is evident in the landscape today for those who are prepared to look for it. In Denmark, for example, the 'botanical layers of the Jutland fens' show that in the later Neolithic, as in much of north west Europe, clearings were not allowed to return to woodland because they were regularly grazed by large herds of cattle.

Fyfield and Overton Downs in Wiltshire, England, provide another example. They embrace an area designated a National Nature Reserve for the outstanding scientific value of its geology and lichenology in European terms; its downland flora is of national significance too, as are some of its snail communities. Yet the same area also contains one of the best archaeological landscapes in the UK, indeed in Europe, judged by criteria of typicality, integrity, study, accessibility and management. Unlike Carnac and Arles, it is not a landscape of great monuments: the landscape itself is the monument. It is the product of hundreds of thousands of largely anonymous people over thousands of years, working within Nature. Many of the blocks of Tertiary sandstone (sarsens), for example, have been moved around the landscape by farmers, quarrymen and the religiously motivated for six thousand years and more (Plate 14); lichens grow on natural stones no longer in their natural, post-glacial position; scientifically-studied snails slide slowly through the herbage growing over an abandoned late-medieval farm; and the sward produced by the grazing of millions of shepherded sheep over thousands of years is laced by lines of daisies whitening the boundaries of prehistoric fields.

No-one need have an inferiority complex about the anthropogenic being overridden by environmental science or natural history being squeezed out by cultural interests. 'Fairness' and 'balance' between the two only come into it if we have two, competing interests; and when such respected authorities as Peter Bridgewater and Theo Hooy (1995, 164) remark that 'maintaining a difference between cultural and natural heritage is clearly somewhat artificial', we are entitled to ask whether we need to keep the distinction at all. Following the advice of its Amsterdam Symposium in 1998 on that question the World Heritage Committee amalgamated its lists of cultural and natural criteria into a single list of World Heritage criteria. The crucial thing is to identify the right selection of landscapes for the benefit of the whole world and its peoples, not to worry about bureaucratic convenience already overtaken by intellectual developments in the scientific field.

Dropping the formal distinction between 'cultural' and 'natural' in identifying World Heritage Sites should have three immediate benefits:

1. it would focus attention on what matters: not whether a site is more natural than cultural or *vice versa*, but judging, after due enquiry, whether a property is or is not genuinely worthy of inscription as a World Heritage Site.

2. it would cut out one level of ambiguity, argument, doubt and bureaucracy – and a matter of fairly deep irrelevance to the public whose interest and taxes support the whole process. This is a scientists' and administrators' division, illustrating their mind-set.

3. It would remove at a stroke the clumsy and intellectually indefensible use of the UNESCO-phrase 'mixed site' as a midway grey zone of uncertainty which tends to diminish, not enhance, the status of the Site. The concept of a 'mixed site' is in any case only possible if you allow two opposing poles to exist; remove them, and all sites, all landscapes, fall into one category only

FIGURE 34.
In a fine example of natural/human interaction, the overnight tidal flooding of St Mark's Square, Venice, Italy, recedes in the early morning of 17 November, 2002.

i.e. actually or potentially worthy of World Heritage status. We could bury the phrase, ironically, because we have come to realise that, in a fundamental sense, all sites are 'mixed'. We therefore do not need the adjective: a Site is either a Site or it is not.

Our hard-won, scientific understanding of the European landscape is a product similar to that produced by intellectual enquiry in many other parts of the world. Wherever people think about and study these things, many local perceptions merge with those on a wider canvas. The basic point, fundamental in getting to grips with 'cultural landscape', is that there is nothing truly natural left on earth. Even the 'pristine' environments of the polar regions are affected by the actions of humankind. 'Cultural landscape' is a concept, not just an extent of land or a space on the ground (or map); it can seem to have the potential to say something at a global level to the peoples of an increasingly interdependent world. A key to understanding is relativism, a realisation that there is no such thing as 'a' landscape, let alone 'the' landscape, but rather a myriad of perceptions. They are to do with, not so much different abilities of eyesight but with less tangible, less mechanical processes such as acculturation, cognition, and aesthetic sensitivity. The 'genius of place' that we talk about in English resides in the human mind and, unlike a statue in a garden, it is not materially in the place itself. A cultural landscape is a place where people and Nature have interacted (figure 34), not just impacted, and the results of that interaction give the landscape in view its particular character. Cultural landscape links past and future.

Cultural landscape and World Heritage

Each of the three categories of cultural landscape as defined for World Heritage purposes raises as many issues as its definition was intended to solve (Chapter 2, Table 4). Here we can but discuss one or two aspects of each, giving scant attention to the first – 'landscapes designed and created intentionally by man' – but developing our main case study, as being of general European significance, in category 2.

FIGURE 35
The Ancient City of Sigiriya, Sri Lanka, a World Heritage site, includes this great geometrical landscape of cultural landscape category 1-type where the presence of the trees exemplifies a common management issue – to chop or not to chop, and if so, which?

FIGURE 36.
One of the nine
gardens in the World
Heritage site of the
Classical Gardens of
Suzhou, China, shown
here is part of a whole
which possesses
characteristics in design
and symbolism of both
category 1 and 3 of
cultural landscapes.

Category 1, the *clearly–defined landscape*, is self-evident (Figures 35 and 36; Plate 2). Great designed gardens and parklands are common to many cultures through time; but what seems to have been overlooked is that many ancient integrated agrarian landscapes, like that on Dartmoor in the second millennium BC or the centuriated countrysides of Roman Italy, are quite as much 'designed and created intentionally by man' as are Stowe and Stourhead. They are also rather bigger in scale. The definition of this first, 'obvious', type of cultural landscape should perhaps have concentrated more on recreation and aesthetics, which is what parks and gardens are about, rather than deliberateness.

Category 2, the *organically evolved landscape*, divides into two sub-categories, a relict or fossil landscape and a continuing landscape. The 'relict landscape' is a familiar concept, with many examples (Figures 37 and 38). Of course, in view of the marked imbalance presently existing in the whereabouts of World Heritage inscriptions in Europe compared to the rest of the world, it is neither possible nor desirable to protect them all as something special, let alone think of multiple-inscription of many British cultural landscapes; yet, from a global point of view, the British Isles possess a global resource, something of a rarity on a world scale (Chapter 6), so perhaps two or three could qualify.

Category 2 also contains the interesting concept of 'the continuing landscape'. The definition is quite clear: 'it retains an active social role in

FIGURE 38 (*left*). A genuine inland 'fishing landscape' in the cultural landscape of the Po delta, Italy, an extension to the World Heritage site of Ferrara; but restored fish-traps and renovated buildings indicate that the traditional activity has ceased and is now perpetuated as a relict landscape maintained for heritage and tourist purposes, staffed, at least for the time being, by former fishermen and fisherwomen.

Cultural Landscape Values: Europe and the British Isles

contemporary society closely associated with the traditional way of life, and in which the evolutionary process is still in progress.' Though that thought may well have been largely inspired by non-European examples, in Europe the wine-growing culture of the *vignerons* of Burgundy, for example, farming landscapes around the fortified churches of Transylvania (Figure 39), and the crofting landscapes of western Scotland, illustrate as critically as do the Banawe rice terraces in the Philippines, exactly what the definition sought to describe. The danger is that the 'evolutionary process still in progress' may well be the destroyer of the very special quality which recognition seeks to maintain. While Burgundian wine-growers may be particularly resilient in sustaining their life-style while absorbing the pressures of the international market for their product, crofting life for all its fierce independence is only maintained by a combination of hard, local endeavour and significant external support. More insidiously, the dramatic effects of Western materialism on the people of montane Luzon could well so damage the social fabric there as to turn a working landscape into just another awe-inspiring ancient monument (Chapter 3).

The world is in fact littered with 'continuing landscapes'. Les Grands Causses in southern France provide a good example (Figure 40). Interesting in themselves, with a high research profile and with a long archaeology of landscape development, the Causses can stand metaphor for many parts of rural Europe. Western Ireland in the mid-nineteenth century, and northern Scotland partly cleared of people by landlords in the nineteenth century, are

FIGURE 37 *(left)*. Statue-menhirs on the World Heritage site of Rapa Nui (Easter Island), Chile, overlooking a formerly settled and farmed area, now of cultural landscape category 2a.

FIGURE 39. Viseri, part of the World Heritage site of Villages with Fortified Churches in Transylvania, Romania, clearly a cultural landscape but not an official World Heritage one, characterized by a traditional land-use system, historic settlement pattern, medieval form of its farmsteads, and medieval churches.

historic cases in point; the high, arid country of Guadalajara, Spain, and the Cheviot country of northern England, largely emptied of people by impersonal economic forces during my own lifetime, provide contemporary examples. A better-known case is the Lake District, UK, with its fell-farming landscapes and a record of having been turned down as a World Heritage Site before the concept of cultural landscape was adopted. Certainly it is a potential World Heritage cultural *landscape*, though whether it actually needs such designation is arguable. Nevertheless, the Lake District shows plenty of evidence to demonstrate that its landscape 'exhibits significant material evidence of its evolution through time', a major precondition for consideration as a World Heritage cultural landscape. And many recognise the connection between that landscape, its associated lifeway and contemporary economics. Sheep keep the Lake District countryside going, though tourism is a very significant economic factor too; but tourists come to see a landscape which, though grand in its natural, geological splendour, is also the product of long-term agrarian regimes with a contemporary appearance maintained by sheep. Yet here too sheep-farming is dangerously vulnerable and economically threatened and so too, therefore, is the appearance of the landscape. After three months of foot-and-mouth disease early in 2001 the British government was pleading with citizens actually to go to the Lake District over Easter for economic reasons. The secret

FIGURE 40.
The generally treeless, limestone landscape of the sheep-grazed Causse Méjean, France, with the isolated village of Nivoliers typically situated at the foot of a slope surrounded by its few enclosed arable fields occupying the floor of a dry valley.

is now out: the tourist industry is economically far more important to the Lake District than farming.

We should remember, however, that though my examples come from Northern Europe, the threat or actuality of rural desertification is not merely a mid- and northern European matter. It has long been characteristic around the Mediterranean too, as the history of emigration to the United States of America in the nineteenth century illustrates; it has also been and is at work elsewhere in southern Europe. This process is creating new, fossil cultural landscapes – in parts of Galicia, for example, – and new shades of old but living landscapes. The Biferno valley in Italy, now very well explored and explained, can stand as an exemplar.

Category 3 of the World Heritage definitions is the *associative cultural landscape*, in some ways the most interesting and intellectually challenging (and difficult to photograph). It deals with intangibles and even negatives. Such a landscape has to have 'powerful religious, artistic and cultural associations of the natural element rather than material cultural evidence, which may be insignificant or even absent.' The thought here represents a sincere if cumbersome attempt to recognise that for many, many people in the world, the landscape is not only full of gods without machines but in many cases actually is the deity itself. Nature is, as it were, god and vice-versa.

Nature was certainly worshipped in one sense by the English poets of the Romantic Movement. Their, and particularly Wordsworth's, glorification of the Lake District, rather than its merits as an archaeological landscape, really drive its claim as a World Heritage cultural landscape in this third category. It is one of the very few places where its associative value is outstanding in its own right. This volume would not be couched in the way that it is, were it not for what our conservation ancestors thought and talked about there, between one and two hundred years ago (Chapter 4).

Category 3 also stipulates a 'test of authenticity', offering 'conditions of integrity' as an alternative. While such remain, consideration of nominations might well involve applying a matrix analysis – one tick and you're out, three ticks and you're in – but I hope we will also continue to keep faith with our intuition and sensitivities. 'Integrity' involves layers of historic evolution and our understanding of it that cannot be reduced to a tick. The National Trusts in Britain, following Alexander Pope, speak of 'the genius' or the 'spirit of the place'. On one of the projects where I was much involved – not yet a World Heritage Site but on the UK's Tentative List (DCMS 1998) – we have spent hours debating precisely this point in terms not just of our management but of our interpretation and presentation of it; and the word we used is 'honesty'. All these terms recognise the essential point: that a cultural landscape of World Heritage quality should have something about it – ambience, atmosphere, presence, authority, vibes – which give it a resonance many people can recognise, setting it apart. That probably results from its 'integrity', a concept more to do with ideas and the mind than with materials and completeness, more to do with how we see it rather than what we see. We may have tended to confuse, in linear Western thinking, 'authenticity' with 'original', and in particular to apply the converse e.g. unless more than 50 per cent of the original build is still there, then it is not authentic; whereas authenticity is to do with the spirit of the place.

Nelson's ship *Victory* which you can go and see at Portsmouth is now, as a result of decades of conservation, an almost complete replacement, bit by bit, of the assemblage of wood, canvas, iron and rope which triumphed at the Battle of Trafalgar in 1805; it is effectively a replica, yet no-one would doubt its authenticity. Conversely but similarly, our sheep at Bede's World are clearly not very old but, as we attempt to run a farm of about AD 700, they are 'authentic' in the sense that they are physically and genetically very close to sheep of thirteen hundred years ago. They are 'honest' sheep. They harmonise with the spirit of a place where the monastic farm supported the community of St Paul's, Jarrow, who numbered in their midst the single man, Bede, most influential in linking the learning of early medieval Europe to the knowledge of Classical, Mediterranean antiquity.

In contrast, specimens of a genuinely rare breed of Prewalski horse re-distributed to the middle of the Causse Méjean, France, are not 'authentic' in that landscape context. They have been carefully assembled from zoos around the world for breeding purposes; the stated intention is to 'return' the progeny to their native habitat in Mongolia once they have become acclimatised in a habitat believed to be verisimilitudinous to it. Now, however, they are an important part of a newly-conceptualised eco-museum promoted by the Cévennes National Park, their presence advertised as one of the attractions intended to draw tourists into an area with a low-income economy. It will be interesting to note whether, in these circumstances, they eventually depart. Meanwhile, the animals' juxtaposition with that Caussenard landscape shows not only a lack of respect for the context but also a fairly basic misunderstanding of its history and nature. Indeed, their presence there, though rather jolly but clearly not to be taken too seriously, detracts from the otherwise impeccable credentials of a landscape which is part of a draft nomination as a World Heritage cultural landscape.

The importance of values

'Outstanding universal value' is the really difficult concept, taking 'cultural landscape' far beyond mere 'archaeological landscape'. The latter, after all, could contain an excellent archaeology but be of no more than high scientific interest without at least some of the other dimensions to its significance that have been mentioned above. On the other hand, most cultural landscapes are likely to contain an archaeological component, though it may not always be visible. Kuk, Papua New Guinea, for example, is a World Heritage Site because the earliest agrarian drainage system in the world was discovered there; yet the evidence is entirely underground and invisible, though known to be extensive, buried beneath the millennial growth of a bog which, paradoxically, is also the agency of preservation. Boxgrove in Sussex, England, is a potential candidate for the UK's tentative list because it is the site of one of Europe's most important Palaeolithic discoveries; but its present appearance, a quarry, is not very attractive and we do not even know whether the site contains more evidence (DCHS 1998).

Hesitations in both cases arise surely because we have made it more difficult for ourselves over the first two decades of the World Heritage mission by judging Sites empirically, visually and scientifically rather than in abstract terms (*cf.* Pressouyre 1993). 'Universal value' itself is a very abstract concept, the meaning of which no two of us would agree about; but we probably could obtain a broad measure of agreement about at least some of a suite of themes which we regard as important to humanity, not just historically but as relevant to its future. Such concepts come to mind as reconciliation, brutality, encounter, conflict, greatness, community, religiosity, co-operation and partnership, masterpiece, permanence and continuity, frontiers, typical or representative, and now, sustainability. Do we not need to be able to look from time to time at a place and think 'So, that's what happened when people living in those circumstances did such and such. Can we learn from them?'

Landscape interpretation and cultural landscape go together, for both are about ideas and meanings, concepts and interpretations, dynamics and dialogues. For some, cultural landscape is not a matter of property in a positivist sense but is of the mind or is something to walk through or around, with the value being in the walking as experience, as participant, rather than in the visit to it as mere spectator or as receiver of others' interpretations. For some, the concept of cultural landscape has a potential beyond present arguments of definition: something new and exciting, not possible to earlier generations, something which offers us not just a new way of looking at scenery and not even a new way of looking at Nature; but a vision which could perhaps enable us to understand ourselves a little better.

CHAPTER 9

Contentious Landscapes

....

Cultural landscapes contain land – a truism, but fundamental. Indeed, whatever else they may consist of, they consist of land; and land is one of the most contentious matters known to mankind. People live on it and die for it; they will certainly contend for it. We remarked in Chapter 6 that the land in the National Parks of England and Wales is not generally in public ownership; and that this leads to three major areas of potential difficulty, perhaps even conflict, over proprietorial rights, national and local priorities, and Park objectives. The instance illustrates the generality, that attempts to designate land, however well intentioned, and then to manage and use it in a particular way, for example as a World Heritage Site, will arouse opposition and be disputed. Contentiousness can be as much about such intangibles as 'significance' and 'values' (in non-monetary senses) as about the more obvious matter of land disputes such as boundaries and land-use. The topic has come to be increasingly explored in recent years, both because disputes continually occur and make good news stories for the media and also because 'conflict' provides an attractive theme in the discourse of the embryonic academic subject called 'heritage studies'.

Three rural megalithic sites have been rather cleverly related in their management problems as heritage to current theory in crisis-management (Hayes and Patton 2001). One of them, La Houge Bie, Jersey, is a large megalithic tomb of *c.* 4000 BC, with a restored medieval chapel on top of its mound. Renewed archaeological excavations in the 1990s engaged the public to the extent that, when rumours of the chapel being in danger of falling down circulated, a crisis of confidence developed 'in which the organisations involved were criticised in the strongest possible terms by senior politicians and journalists' (*op. cit.* 49). The key factors identified *post hoc facto* as contributing to this modern storm on a tomb-top were inadequate contingency planning, failure of communication giving rise to impressions of secrecy, and a cumbersome decision-making process – all classic symptoms of much larger issues, including the designation and management of cultural landscapes. Within the discipline of management studies, however, 'there is an abundant body of literature on crisis management, disaster planning and communication strategies' (*op. cit.* 50) which can be widely applied to historic sites, including World Heritage Sites with landscape.

At the second site, Carnac in southern Brittany, France, despite the best conservation intentions the site increasingly deteriorated under tourist pressure. The authorities decided to cordon off (to allow floral regeneration) a previously openly-accessible area of stone alignments and other structures. The public opposition was vociferous and active, and even went as far as arson; but was ultimately ignored. Similarly, in the Bend of the Boyne, Ireland, another megalithic site mainly of Neolithic tombs but particularly outstanding as a collection of rock art, found itself at the centre of a nasty 'heritage storm'. Again, management proposals involving a visitor centre, re-routing access and charging for entry to a previously freely accessible, chaotically informal archaeological area were involved; again economic issues jostled with heritage ones concerning pride and access; and again ultimately government had its way with a scheme which, despite individual losers, is now judged to be a success. Whether through bad management or other causes, heritage is a very volatile and emotional area of human activity. World Heritage and cultural landscapes are bound to be, as a matter of course, in the eye of a storm from time to time.

World Heritage is inevitably involved in contention and in the theoretical debate, as is reflected in some of its own publications. One of the most contentious and long-running disputes has been, and continues to be, about Kakadu in the Northern Territory, Australia, formally a World Heritage 'mixed site' but also a cultural landscape (Figures 2, 6). The dispute, essentially about the commercial extraction of minerals in a World Heritage Site, involves many of the elements likely to be found in such incidents. Fundamentally, there is the issue of the rights of indigenous people in their own territory and the rights of a mining company in the same area. Then there is the issue of whether, as a matter of principle, World Heritage inscription takes precedence over economic priorities, and whether a nation's rights and duties to do what it wants on its own land take precedence over an international convention which it has voluntarily signed. In this case, the Australian government went to some trouble to seek international support for it to do precisely that. There are also several environmental issues at Kakadu too, for example about traffic, dumping and visual pollution.

Similar cases in Britain were relatively minor but locally significant. The Secretary of State for the Environment took World Heritage inscription into account in turning down proposals to build an inappropriate hotel on a sensitive site near Avebury (on the same skyline as the burial mounds in Figure 32) and in two cases near Hadrian's Wall in Northumberland (Figure 41). One was to drill for oil immediately south of the Wall itself; the other was to erect a tall radio mast a short distance to the north but in full view of the Wall. Neither happened; but a third threat came from elsewhere.

The landscape and its contents in this case could hardly be more designated and it is a landscape already enjoyed by many. The whole is not technically a World Heritage cultural landscape but it is certainly a cultural landscape *par excellence* (of both category 2a and 2b in World Heritage terms). Much, including parts of a National Park and several Sites of Special Scientific Interest, is contained within the very extensive buffer zone of the World

Heritage site itself. The last, after much debate, actually consists only of the principal structural elements of the Wall and its immediate appurtenances which are Scheduled as Ancient Monuments under the 1979 Ancient Monuments and Archaeological Areas Act. Some professional countryside and tourism managers, politicians and a particular recreational interest group, ostensibly wanted to give more people the chance to enjoy the Wall; and hence a serious clash in the 1990s between conservation and recreation.

The elements in this dispute over Hadrian's Wall are familiar components in management issues:

1. a programme, as part of its suite of national policies, on the part of one NGO (now the Countryside Agency) to create National Trails;

2. a duty on the part of another statutory body (the Northumberland National Park Committee) to make the National Park more accessible;

3. the conjunction of these two general functions in a proposal to

route a new Trail on, along and across the archaeology of a World Heritage Site, the statutory conservation of which is the duty of a third NGO (English Heritage);

4. a sense in some quarters that the Wall represented an under-exploited economic resource in a region struggling to maintain its share of a growing tourist industry, especially now that it enjoyed the status of being a World Heritage site (a status which barely raised a ripple of local interest on inscription in 1987);

5. a mix of land-holding, ranging in size from small tenant farms to big 'feudal-type' landed estates, and including the conservation estate of the National Trust and urban properties in and near Newcastle upon Tyne;

6. relatively high rural unemployment;

7. the availability of financial incentives from officialdom (EU, government via various channels);

8. both enthusiasm for, and serious doubts about, the desirability of doing anything to make the Wall country more attractive and accessible to more and more people;

9. various stakeholders with conflicting interests e.g. local politicians sensing opportunities to be seen bringing external funds into the region; tourism interests recognising opportunities to exploit, both in terms of local economics and their own image; elements of local 'Nimbyism' ('Not in my Back Yard' -ism); farmers' fears about damage to gates and stock; archaeologists' fears about potential damage and erosion to the best-surviving frontier of the Roman Empire and its landscape context;

10. an interested and well-informed suite of local media

One particularly interesting dimension was that it was played out on relatively remote uplands, not in the more familiar surroundings for such public controversy of more crowded lowlands. Recreation eventually won when a new National Trail was opened in May, 2003, and huge encouragement was given to the idea of 20,000 people 'walking the Wall' and benefiting the local economy. By then, however, despite objections persisting to the idea of the Wall being exploited for recreational and economic purposes, a significant improvement in management perception had occurred: the result of consultation, listening to (being made to hear?) and implementing the combined knowledge of many interested people. Certainly, the actual line of the Trail itself, originally completely unacceptable on archaeological grounds, is now sensitive to the nature of that which it would seek to bring people to and through; and it has to be of public benefit that, after much negotiation, people now have a right of way along the whole 100 km of the Wall corridor through its mosaic of tenure and variety of landscape. Some, including this author, find the accompanying litter of sign-posting and suchlike further evidence of the

FIGURE 41.
Landscape looking east along Hadrian's Wall, England, UK, near Housesteads Roman fort (behind the trees in the centre). Most of the visible Wall is a nineteenth-century rebuild. The wear-and-tear caused by walkers, and the steps for them, existed before the creation of a National Trail beside the Wall in 2003.

sad suburbanisation of the landscape, in this case a relatively wild and rugged landscape – a process which characterises this age of access and leisure in the countryside (at least in the UK). Concerns also remain about the infrastructure necessary for the long-term maintenance of that which has now been inserted into, through and alongside a World Heritage site. Nevertheless, it is a World Heritage site which was the first in the UK to have a professionally written management plan after extensive, and often hot-blooded, public consultation; and it is a plan, now in its second edition, which is constantly monitored and formally reviewed every five years.

Several other key contentious issues can be identified. We illustrate some by looking first at a brief, international spat about World Heritage cultural landscapes themselves in 2000, the World Heritage nomination in 1999 that triggered it, and at some of the general points that emerged from the subsequent discussions. We then look at three other recent nominations of cultural landscapes which, in different ways, are also contentious or at the very least raised some interesting issues.

As we have seen (Chapter 5), after several years' preparation, France submitted its nomination of the central part of the Loire valley as a cultural landscape to the World Heritage Centre in 1999 (Plate 10; Figures 42–44).

FIGURE 42.
Roofscape at Tours, a city in the Loire valley World Heritage cultural landscape, France, looking eastwards from the *Tour Charlemagne* towards the *Cathédrale St-Galien.*

FIGURE 43.
An arrangement of
embankment and
ramps down to water
level constituting a
typical 'port' in the
cultural landscape of
the River Loire,
France.

Conceptually, it was a bold nomination, both for its size and in its willingness to submit to others' evaluation a particular part of France which is at the very core of the French idea of its own *patrimoine*. The Loire exudes identity, nationality, linguistic purity, and a not entirely unacceptable pre-Revolutionary history of relatively rare military success, royalty, lavish courtliness, and sheer style in the intellectual life as witnessed by accomplishment in the arts and humanities. This would include, for this writer at least, a distinctive viticulture epitomised by Chinon's mighty *caves*, formerly quarries. Now, tourism is important too, but long lengths of the nominated littoral are not particularly affected by it, and even in the seasonably crowded areas somehow the *chateaux* and their grounds seem to stand a little aloof from the fraternising equality of their liberated visitors.

The basin of the River Loire occupies a huge area in central and western France, stretching from the southern part of the Massif Central to an estuary on the Atlantic coast. Some 200 km of the central part of the main river valley were the subject of the nomination, stretching from Sully east of Orléans to the junction of the Rivers Loire and Maine near Angers in the west. Essentially this is the 'new' Loire, for the river originally drained north eastwards into the Paris basin. This length now lies in two Regions, Centre and Pays de la Loire, and four Départments. The complexity of local government is a characteristic of linear World Heritage sites, as along canals, routes and Hadrian's Wall, UK. The valley runs almost exclusively east-north-east to west-south-west along the length of the World Heritage cultural landscape proposed in 1999, and is much affected by the prevailing south-westerly wind. The Loire itself is fed directly by two long tributaries running off the Massif Central some 350 kms to the south; numerous tributaries, all from the south and including the Cher, Indre and Vienne, enter the Loire in the length proposed for inscription. They mostly drain areas of limestone, clays and sands, producing significant deposits in the valleys. Along the Loire between Orléans and Angers, the valley is characterised by low cliffs of tufa and limestone and a flood plain dissected by old channels. The river itself contains many islands and gravel and sand banks; it also fluctuates significantly in depth and width from season to season and year to year. Some of the flood plain is regularly under water in winter, a phenomenon welcomed as refreshment for the soil rather than a hazard. The valley has, however, a long history of periodic catastrophic flooding – 'les crues', carefully recorded as stone-cut water levels at numerous places along it – and even today its inhabitants live perennially under threat of severe inundation. There was far more to the nomination than placid manicured gardens alongside a well-mannered river as perceived by the summer day-visitor – and now that the Loire is a World Heritage cultural landscape there is far more to the realities of management.

Much of contemporary river management is concerned to minimise the flood risk. For most of its length in the proposed area the Loire is confined within dykes – *levées* or *digues* – representing a massive investment in water control from at least the twelfth century onwards. Obvious consequences affect the depth, width, flow and extent of the Loire, the permanence or otherwise of the many river islands, and land-use behind the dykes. In a fairly major sense, then, neither the river itself nor its immediate environs can be 'natural': both have been man-managed for centuries, a process continuing today with ever-increasing intensity and sophistication. Nevertheless, the river itself is undoubtedly the personality of the landscape, particularly when it is in impressive and near-flood mode. In this state it flows at considerable speed and the whole extent between the river banks can be under water, giving the river a wide aspect as it flows over many islands, sand-banks and, in many places, recreational areas and access points. In several places, extensive areas behind the banks can also be under water, one of several phenomena linking river and surrounding landscape in time and land-use. Yet, in most years during the summer much of the river-bed is dry and indeed, historically, an inadequate depth and flow of water have characteristically been a severe handicap to the otherwise thriving use of the river as a major trade and communication route between the Atlantic and the Paris Basin.

The banks of the Loire are punctuated at intervals of only a few kilometres by a series of villages, small towns and cities, notable among the urban settlements being (from north east to south west) Sully, Orléans, Blois, Amboise,

FIGURE 44
The ICOMOS mission
evaluating the
nomination of the
Loire valley, France,
here examines
particulars of the
irrigation system near
the river with officials
and water engineers.

Tours, Saumur and Angers. Land-use is extremely varied: urban areas, (Figure 42) through intensive horticulture, vineyards (some reliant on flooding) and hunting forest are all present. In general, the economy of the region is buoyant, only in part based on a tourist industry primarily concerned to extol a quality of life associated with the heritage in general and the *chateaux* in particular.

Essentially, the notable features of the valley's history particularly relevant to the nomination were:

1. a long prehistory and considerable Roman impact on the landscape which still today strongly influences (especially urban) settlement location and form, and road communications. Undoubtedly the Loire was in use at an early date;

2. a period either side of *c.* 1000 AD when seigneurial power and Christianity developed, leaving *inter alia* a tradition of feudalism, castles and some early medieval religious centres with buildings which have survived;

3. the Hundred Years War (1337–1453) and Joan of Arc, which left

France in the hands of the French and a permanent memory of a war-leader whose statue graces many a market place along the Loire;

4. in the sixteenth century: the Renaissance along the Loire valley – universities, art and architecture, the Royal presence, accompanying wealth, large *chateaux* for pleasure and show;

5. the seventeenth and eighteenth centuries: the development of a secular, commercial economy based on industry, crafts, trade, shipping, rivers and towns;

6. late eighteenth century – mid-twentieth century: water-management and wars: in the wake of major floods in 1846 and 1856, in 1860 the first of many official reports proposed measures to alleviate the threat of flooding; the French Revolution, the 1870–71 war, and both the First and Second World Wars all played out significant episodes along the Loire and each has left its mark. Tours, for example, was severely damaged in 1940 and in 1944 – and it still shows.

Essentially the Loire valley is a landscape which displays the 'interchange of human values, over a span of time ... on developments in architecture [and] technology (flood control, canal engineering, nuclear energy), monumental arts, town-planning [and] landscape design' (quoted from this author's report to ICOMOS). All these are within this particular landscape, giving it particular distinction. The Loire valley also contains many buildings which both individually (like Chambord, already a World Heritage site) and as a truly remarkable ensemble 'illustrate significant stages in human history', in this case late and post-Renaissance ideals in West European thought and design. The definition in *Guidelines* Paragraph 36 could have been written with the Loire valley in mind: 'combined works of nature and of man ... illustrative of the evolution of human society and settlement over time, under the influence of the physical constraints and opportunities presented by their natural environment and of successive social, economic and cultural forces ...'. The Loire valley is all those things, embracing (Paragraph 37) 'a diversity of manifestations of the interaction between humankind and its natural environment.' This quality of being able to demonstrate a diversity of interactions was in fact the key to validating the Loire's nomination.

Of the three main categories of cultural landscape (*Guidelines*, Paragraph 39; Chapter 2, Table 4), the Loire valley proposal obviously included examples of category (i), notably Chambord Parc, but its main claim rests on category (ii) as an 'organically evolved landscape'. Since it is evolving still, it clearly belongs to the second sub-category as 'a continuing landscape ... which retains an active social role in contemporary society closely associated with the traditional way of life', here a rich mix of rural life of great estates, market gardening, fruit-growing, viticulture, hunting and fishing intermeshed with 2,000-year-old urban living. Both countryside and town are long-versed in catering for visitors, formerly royalty and its train, now tourists in their hundreds of thousands. A major change is that the Loire itself has ceased to be a great artery of trade, its maritime history now confined to museum displays and some restored quays at ports along its banks (Figure 43).

Finally, the Loire valley – some would say *par excellence* – exhibits elements of being an 'associative' cultural landscape by virtue of its 'artistic and cultural associations' (category iii), in this case partly by its contributions to the very ideas of 'landscape' and 'garden' and partly because of the inspiration it has provided to scholars, artists and writers, prominent among whom are Gregory of Tours, Descartes, Turner, Rabelais and Balzac.

Yet the World Heritage Committee did not accept the nomination. It did not reject it absolutely but it referred it back for further consideration. The problem was the nuclear power station, aggravated by the fact that it was not fully discussed in the Committee papers. This led to the suspicion that the French had tried to cover it up, a quite unfair suspicion because the assessors had been taken there and also flew over it. I was one of the assessors and the fault was mine in that, failing to perceive that the presence of a nuclear installation was contentious, I simply did not make an issue of it in my report. I saw it simply as the latest stage in the use of the Loire as a source of power: exactly the same in principle as such undoubted parts of our heritage in late-twentieth-century minds as, for example, the eighteenth- and nineteenth-century watermills which lie along the Loire. That is a perspective I am happy to live with. As I wrote in my evaluation for ICOMOS: 'Debate should not . . . be so much about the "naturalness" or otherwise of the river but rather about the degree to which the very conscious relationship between river and human beings in the context of "control" has added to the interest of the river landscape. To grasp one particular example which some may find difficult in a World Heritage context, the site of the first (now redundant) nuclear reactor at St Laurent-Nouan was effectively if unconsciously created by the building of a medieval dyke to divert the Loire southwards. This eventually left on the landscape the exact twentieth-century counterpart – a machine to create energy – of the many water-mills from earlier centuries already gracing, as we now see them, an interesting and eloquent landscape.'

The Committee's initial decision was, in my view, misguided and its subsequent decision indefensible; but in such a committee there are clearly forces at work other than the pure light of reason, and I was politically naïve in not recognising this fact. A year later, in December, 2000, the Loire sailed through the Committee and is now a World Heritage cultural landscape. French face has been saved to a certain extent. For me, however, – and I know for many others – the inscription of the Val de Loire is not quite the 'noble, global concept' that, of all places, it should have been. Geographically right in the centre of this landscape as inscribed on the World Heritage List is a small gap, a hole in the middle of the map, where the power station was, is and will continue to be. This is intellectually an indefensible result which has quite seriously demeaned the concept of World Heritage, and particularly of cultural landscape. The questions remain: does this decision mean that modern structures cannot be contained within the concept of World Heritage? Or is it just mid-twentieth century structures? Or just industrial structures? Or just nuclear structures? Or is it that there are special, unstated criteria for cultural landscapes? The only slight consolation is that the World Heritage Committee will have to revisit its decisions in due course, it will come both to regret and override it.

The nomination of the Vall de Boí, in Catalonia, Spain, was specifically of it as a cultural landscape (Plate 6; Figures 45a and b). There was no fall-back position; numerous other nominations cite a 'natural' or 'mixed' site which might also be a cultural landscape. Its claim was that either it was a cultural landscape or it was not. In one sense, it was an 'obvious' case for approval, for it consisted of beautiful Romanesque churches in a dramatic east Pyrénéan mountainscape; but it proved contentious too, this time basically for theoretical reasons with a major practical implication.

The full title of the nomination was 'The Romanesque Catalan Cultural Landscape of the Vall de Boí'. The Vall de Boí is situated in the high Pyrenees in the Alta Ribagorça region, some 120 km due north of Lleida and north west of Barcelona. Above it is rocky mountainside, though with small plateaux of summer pasture; the deep valley is screened by the high peaks of the Beciberri/Punta Alta massif. The valley floor scenery is one of woodland and

FIGURE 45a.
The isolated Church of the Assumption of St Mary, dated to 1110 by an excavated foundation inscription, remains in use outside its village of Cóll in the World Heritage site of Catalan Romanesque Churches of the Vall de Boí, Spain.

meadows, adjoining and surrounding the small villages with their Romanesque churches characteristically slightly up-slope. The tall church-towers which are such a characteristic feature of the valley served both to house bells and to act as lookouts. Alongside each of them is the walled village cemetery.

Only at Boí itself has the medieval gateway been preserved; fragments of

FIGURE 45b.
Architectural detailing typical of the Romanesque churches. St Climent, Taüll.

wall survive too. The layouts of the villages follow the feudal pattern of individual houses grouped around a main central building (church or castle) or main road (usually on Roman roads). Each has a small open space for meetings and festivals, their shape being determined by the alignments of the buildings that form them. Some of the villages rise steeply up the mountainsides (*pujadors*). The streets are paved with stone slabs or cobbles, their settings varying according to the local topography. Water is brought to the villages by means of channels linked with mountain streams and terminating in the central open spaces. Here it is available in drinking troughs for humans and domestic animals.

The traditional houses consist of the central residential portion, rectangular in plan, but considerably modified over the centuries by additional of outbuildings, stables and storage sheds (Plate 6). They form interior yards, closed by the buildings and by high stone walls. The doorways on the ground floors of the older buildings are in stone, their rounded arches being formed using voussoirs. They normally have double wooden doors. Window-frames are also in stone; those at the lowest level are small, resembling loopholes, to prevent access by humans or animals. Other common features are cellars for storing food and wine, elevated granaries, hay and straw barns, and exterior stone bread ovens. The severe winter climate has resulted in the creation of covered passages between the different buildings of a single property, at first-floor level.

There is little industry, though there are small quarries adjacent to each of the villages. The sulphur and mineral content of the waters of the area is the source of the small thermal establishments in the valley. Outside the villages are to be found animal houses built on the steep mountainsides. These are at two levels, each with its own entrance. The lower one was for sheltering animals and the upper for storing straw. Scattered across the landscape are small huts used by shepherds. These are simple structures built of stone, using a mortar of earth and straw. They are usually to be found alongside an enclosure formed of small drystone walls.

The history of the place is, perhaps surprisingly given its remoteness, complex and eventful. The Arab invasion and occupation of the Iberian peninsula never penetrated the valleys of the high Pyrenees. Despite their inaccessibility, these valleys were nevertheless exposed around the beginning of the second millennium AD to ideas and cultural influences, brought there by merchants, by itinerant monks, and by Christian pilgrims travelling to Jerusalem and Santiago de Compostela. In the eleventh century Ramon Borrell II established the hegemony of Barcelona and created a dynasty which survived until the early fifteenth century. New cultural styles were brought into Catalonia from Italy, particularly Lombardy, but this cultural movement was late in reaching the remote Vall de Boí. The exceptional number of Romanesque churches in the valley, which has supported a relatively low population since the end of the Middle Ages, is attributed to the fact that large quantities of silver came into the region, especially in the first decades of the twelfth century. The profits of the local counts of Erill were in part spent embellishing their villages with handsome churches in the new style (Figure 45b).

The claim of the Vall de Boí for World Heritage status as a cultural landscape was as 'the largest concentration of Romanesque art in Europe'. The group of nine exceptionally well preserved rural churches constitute a unique example of the cultural tradition which flourished in twelfth-century Catalonia. The Romanesque churches and the villages in which they are located 'form an excellent example of a cultural landscape which bloomed in a harmonious way in a natural setting in which the wealth of the environment has remained intact.' (quotations from the nomination document). Following the language of the World Heritage *Guidelines* (criterion i), 'The nine Romanesque churches of the Vall de Boí are a masterpiece of their period and result from the human creative faculty. The[ir] Lombard Romanesque style ... took on an indigenous form of expression in which the rural spirit manifests itself in remarkable ways, such as the chain of elegant bell-towers which stretch throughout the valley.' Furthermore, 'The churches of Sant Climent de Taüll, Santa Maria de Taüll, Sant Joan de Boí, Santa Eulàlia d'Etill la Vall, La Nativitat de Durro, Santa Maria de Cardet, and Santa Maria de Cóll have remained open for religious use since they were consecrated during the eleventh and twelfth centuries.'

Then could be added, 'In addition'; but perhaps the more appropriate word is 'However'. Most of the mural art which once decorated the churches has either been lost or is saved in the National Museum of Catalan Art in Barcelona. Wall paintings from Sant Climent de Taüll, Santa Maria de Taüll, and Sant Joan de Boí were moved there in the 1920s in the face of increasing desecration, something difficult to inhibit in such a remote and relatively inaccessible mountain valley. Either way, though no-one disputes its splendour or artistic significance, the art is no longer *in situ*, and that is quite a serious issue for an international convention much concerned with 'authenticity' and 'integrity'.

Critically for present purposes, as a cultural landscape under criterion iv, it was claimed that 'the Vall de Boí illustrates the continuous occupation of an area of land. The churches were built in the Middle Ages at the instigation of a single family, as a sign of affirmation and geographical settlement at the time that historical Catalonia was created.' An immediate reaction would be that such a reason was perhaps not sufficiently strong, not least for its apparent lack of 'universal value'. I happened to be the assessor who visited this nomination for ICOMOS, and wrestled with the issue, philosophical rather than visual or practical, not so much as to whether or not the area as a whole containing the villages and churches met the criteria for being a World Heritage cultural landscape but whether it was a cultural landscape in the World Heritage sense at all.

That it was a cultural landscape was not, however, in doubt, for clearly people and nature had interacted here for thousands of years in a process visible in different ways to local inhabitants, visitors and specialists. The villages themselves were witness to this; the churches were an outstanding and sudden, short-lived manifestation of the process, similar in nature to the extraordinary artistic florescence around AD 700 in north east England which gave rise to the idea of the 'Golden Age of Northumbria'. Yet, in the end, my recommendation – which ICOMOS and the World Heritage Committee accepted – was that the Vall de Boí was not a cultural landscape in the World Heritage sense. The three main reasons for so concluding were that, as a land-scape, it was difficult to see its 'universal value'; that there was no direct historical linkage between, on the one hand, the landscape itself and the way it was worked, and, on the other, the area's outstanding characteristic, the churches, for they did not own the lands, which were administered from a distance. The Church was never a local landowner and the land came by its present appearance through secular, seigneurial workings; I also suspected, fuelled by my visit to Mont Perdu (Chapter 4), that, striking mountain scenery though the Vall was, it and its traditional pastoral regime were neither outstanding nor extraordinary. But the hesitation was only about the Val as a cultural landscape of World Heritage quality; that its main features, the churches and villages, were of sufficient merit to be of World Heritage quality in themselves seemed not in doubt, and happily the recommendation that they be inscribed on the World Heritage List as nine separate monuments making up one Site was accepted by both Spain and the World Heritage Committee.

Underlying the consideration of this intellectually challenging case was, however, the fact that the individuals and bodies concerned had no means of rationally assessing in global terms the Vall as a montane agricultural landscape in Europe. The need for a thematic study of 'ordinary' agricultural landscapes was obvious and urgent. This was something others had already thought about and to which I had already drawn attention in general and continue to do so (Chapter 10).

Completely different issues were raised by the nomination of Central Sikhote-Alin in the extreme east of Asia, overlooking the Sea of Japan, a nomination which eventually resulted in inscription on natural grounds alone. The interest lies in the journey to that decision. A huge area of land was involved in five blocks, in all 1,549,179 ha extending over Ternejski, Krasnoarmejski, Dalnegorski, and Pozharski Districts in the Primorski Region of the Russian Federation. It is a unique region with locally dominant wood-land such as virgin, broad-leaved Korean pine forests to the north-west and, to the south in the Sikhote-Alin Nature Reserve and along the coast, discrete areas of larch and Japanese oak. Overall, the environment is remarkably stable and unpolluted. A small indigenous population continues to live within a sustainable hunter-gatherer economy which, as well as keeping people alive, maintains the natural diversity of flora and fauna. This hitherto sustainable process could well, however, succumb to the early twenty-first century.

The original World Heritage nomination was deferred over matters of boundary, legal protection and the (non-) involvement of local government, all fairly contentious issues in themselves and not at all uncommon in initial submissions. A reconsideration was invited, and the nomination returned to the World Heritage Committee in 2000 as a mixed site (*see* Chapter 1). One of its justifications stemmed directly from the property's geographical location: naturally and culturally, it occupies a key location in the study of the interface between Eurasia and further east including, ultimately, North America.

The critical issues revolve around the presence of no more than 2,000 indigenous people, forming a very low density population even by the standards of eastern Siberia. The traditions, language, and material culture of the present-day Udege and their ancestors have been preserved and are respected. Hunting and fishing are their traditional and basic activities, combined with collecting fern, berries, mushrooms, and seeds. The Udege's ability to manage the game animals and the habitat by the effective use of non-wood resources is critical to their survival. A particular habitat of outstanding importance and fragility is in the middle and upper reaches of the Iman River, where the species range from ginseng to the Amur tiger in association with 122 people of the Iman group of the Udege. Special words are in use for various types of building: for example, *kumirni*, used as both birthing huts and mortuaries. Traditional clothes are retained for ceremonies, festivals, and ritual occasions. Nevertheless, a basic question in World Heritage terms was whether the nature and influence of the human presence are sufficient to stand alongside the undoubted natural qualities to merit inscription in that rather intellectually messy category of 'mixed site' or whether, as ICOMOS suspected, the anthropogenic impact, though slight, was sufficiently significant to make it a cultural landscape.

Historically, the Mukri developed here under Mongol and Turkish influence. In the mid-nineteenth century, the Ussuri region became part of Russia, and thereafter various Western influences affected local culture to some degree. Despite the remoteness, traditional clothing materials, for example, were replaced by woven cloths in the nineteenth century for everyday use. About 1900 Chinese migrants brought with them naive Taoism to mix with Udege paganism. A further addition was given to local culture by the arrival of Russian Old Believers, devout ultra-orthodox Christians fleeing persecution and seeking refuge in the remote valleys and mountains which were the hunting and collecting territories of the indigenous peoples. The process of collectivization reached even as far east as Central Sikhote-Alin. In the later 1930s the population in the nominated area was brought together in just two settlements, one of which, Krasny Yar, continues as the main settlement today (population 700). In 1993, the Sikhote-Alin Ethnic Territory was formalized around the concept of man in relation to the taiga (pine forest) environment, itself representative of the principle of reasonable and sparing use of the natural resources.

The small size of the population and external influence now inhibit continuation of the indigenous way of life. A locally-produced *Biodiversity Conservation Strategy for the Sikhote-Alin* (2000) is concerned with natural aspects, but part of its purpose is to provide for indigenous peoples

(Chapter 12). It may, however, already be too late. The traditional way of life in the area is now under considerable threat of collapse. Its reinforcement presents a task probably more important than simply ensuring the physical protection of the nominated territory. Faced by all the negative influences from man and nature, the existence, even rebirth, of a strong ethnic-cultural complex is a more reliable mechanism for integrated management of people and nature than all the laws that government can provide. The future of the people is unresolved; the nomination resulted (2001) in inscription solely as a natural site under criterion iv. While that outcome was justified scientifically, it avoided a fundamental issue for the operation of the World Heritage Convention: is its role to preserve people and their way of life as well as monuments, nature and landscapes? Nor is the question merely rhetorical or theoretical. In this case, it is virtually certain that unless the low-level but crucial human use of the environment continues, the natural interest of the environment will change. So here it is not merely a matter of keeping a lifeway going, as is very much the concern of numerous organisations such as 'Survival' campaigning for political recognition of the need to maintain human diversity; it is a matter of social, human viability in order to sustain a very special environment of high scientific value. In fact, the issue was implicitly recognised in conceptualising 'cultural landscape' in World Heritage terms; but it was not specifically articulated.

Paragraph 37 of the *Guidelines* states that a cultural landscape 'embraces a diversity of manifestations of the interaction between humankind and its natural environment', and Paragraph 38 then goes on to note that they 'reflect specific techniques of sustainable land-use', a phenomenon clearly in operation in Central Sikhote-Alin. It continues with the key sentences in this particular case: 'Protection of cultural landscapes can contribute to modern techniques of sustainable land-use and can maintain or enhance natural values in the landscape'. This clearly implies that, provided sustainable land-use even if managed by modern techniques is in operation, the twin objectives of protecting a cultural landscape as a physical entity and maintaining natural values can be met. Maintaining the traditional lifeway of land-users as such, even though they may originally have created the circumstances of sustainable land-use and high natural value, does not appear to be a priority. Yet, this paragraph contains a contradiction for it continues by immediately remarking that 'The continued existence of traditional forms of land-use supports biological diversity ... The protection of traditional cultural landscapes is therefore helpful in maintaining biological diversity.' So, even though their role is to support nature rather than anthropogenic for its own sake, local indigenous people clearly have to continue living and working *in situ* in order that cultural landscapes can continue to contribute to biological diversity.

The muddled thinking here probably represents nothing more than a lack of adequate intellectual rigour on a wet afternoon in a mock Alsatian castle in 1992 (Chapter 2). The important matter now is to think this one through properly, for the issue is not going to go away. Indeed it is likely to become more pressing as the lifeway of small groups of remote peoples develops further as a political issue. In the future, various parts of the developing world are likely to bring forward more of their own cultural landscapes, many of them of great natural interest and with minute populations, for consideration as potential World Heritage. Furthermore, that World Heritage in concept and practice is as much to do with people as with sites was explicitly recognised at the 30 Year Conference at Venice in November, 2002.

In this chapter we have looked at only four cases and mentioned a few others. The range of issues, all contentious to some degree, is nevertheless wide, though by no means comprehensive. Our sample touches on various aspects of land, landscape and indigenous peoples, politics at international and national, inter-institutional and intra-committee levels, management, criteria, assessment, research, ethics and presentation. Heritage hits hard at those involved in such matters; but then it was never an easy option. With land and landscape in association, contention is the norm. That said, however, the good news is that, in practice, in World Heritage terms most contentiousness over cultural landscapes has so far been successfully, even amicably, resolved.

CHAPTER 10

Conserving Cultural Landscapes

....

The early twenty-first century bears witness to a paradox. On the one hand, as we have remarked, countries are queuing up with their lists of properties to gain new inscriptions on the World Heritage List (and to extend existing sites) while, on the other, in reality the acute problem for World Heritage throughout the world is in looking after the 754 properties already inscribed. In all 45 sites were considered for nomination in one form or another at the World Heritage Committee's meeting in early July, 2003, and already another 46 are in line for consideration in 2004. Yet the problem of inadequate conservation, indeed inadequate management in general, exists as much in developed countries, like France and Italy, as in developing parts of the world where acute economic and social priorities might well be justifications for conservation shortfalls. Places like Arles in southern France are simply a disgrace in terms of what is to be expected of a World Heritage site, especially in a 'first world country'. The sheer amount of high-quality architectural heritage requiring repair and maintenance in the towns and villages of Italy is overwhelming: it alone would absorb the resources of the richest treasury in even the most well-disposed and professionally-equipped country. This is Italy's heritage, not its fault: it tries to cope.

We do not intend or attempt to write a manual of cultural landscape management in this one short chapter, mainly because it is already written. Furthermore, other volumes already exist about the management of World Heritage sites specifically and rural landscapes in general (*see* Notes). Such a minimalist approach here, however, is in no way to minimise the basic importance of managing World Heritage sites and cultural landscapes in particular. The future, indeed in many cases the continued survival, of sites and landscapes depends not just on management but on high-quality management. The management needs of World Heritage sites are spelt out in *Guidelines* (1999), Paragraph 24 (b) (ii), here reproduced (almost) in full since the matter is so important:

> '[Each property nominated should] have adequate legal and/or traditional protection and management mechanisms to ensure the conservation of the nominated ... cultural landscapes. The existence of protective legislation at the national, provincial or municipal level and/or a well-established contractual or traditional protection as well as of adequate management and/or planning control mechanisms is therefore essential and ... must be stated clearly on the

nomination form. Assurances of the effective implementation of these laws and/or contractual and/or traditional protection as well as of these management mechanisms are also expected. Furthermore, in order to preserve the integrity of cultural sites, particularly those open to large numbers of visitors, the State Party concerned should be able to provide evidence of suitable administrative arrangements to cover the management of the property, its conservation and its accessibility to the public.'

In terms of conservation, inscription of a site on the World Heritage List is part of a process, not an isolated event. It should be preceded and followed by steps in an evolving continuum conceptualised as a very long-term commitment. All properties need continuous maintenance as the very minimum; many, almost certainly the majority, are either not being conserved properly or appropriately or are actually in need of repair. Among the reasons for this are misunderstandings of what is required by a World Heritage site in terms of conservation and management. Professional incompetence and ignorance, and sheer lack of resources, are major issues. Sadly, however understandably, many an inscription is nowadays seen by the nominating country primarily as an economic meal-ticket to promote tourism rather than as an opportunity to contribute to the conservation of a primary global resource.

Perhaps such strictures about World Heritage sites in general do not apply quite so distressingly to cultural landscapes in particular. This could be partly because even the oldest is not more than a decade old as a World Heritage site and has therefore not had very long to decline from the reasonably satisfactory state that it should have been in when approved for inscription. Note, nevertheless, that the Cordilleras landscape (Plate 3) has gone from nomination, through inscription on the World Heritage List (1995) to entry on the World Heritage in Danger List (2002) in less than a decade. And 2003 saw a new development when Bamiyan valley in Afghanistan, minus the great carved figures blown up by the Taliban, was nevertheless inscribed on the World Heritage List as an emergency move (and, let us acknowledge, as a political gesture) and, immediately afterwards, placed on the List of World Heritage in Danger. However admirable the move and lofty the motivation, this step raises interesting questions, about integrity for example, which will remain to be pondered even if its conservation objective is achieved.

Cultural landscapes are rather special in both their nature and in their conservation requirements; they are very complex in some respects yet, not least on account of their extent, not quite so dramatically vulnerable to adversity as a single building or an architectural complex. Yet such landscapes often contain one or more such complexes which, as Bamiyan itself all too violently illustrates, can be subject to threat, damage and destruction. The drama of sudden landscape destruction was all too clearly exemplified by the flooding at Dessau-Wörlitz, Germany, in 2002. This heart-breaking event – for an enormous effort had been going into bringing the place back from the grave of dereliction before the 1990s – emphasises the need for continuous effort to control that most attractive of elements so characteristic of World Heritage cultural landscapes, water (Chapter 11). The sad case of the Cordilleras emphasises the need for sophisticated management in dealing with large areas, special farming practices and fragile local communities. Conservation, however, and the management regime of which it should be a part, do not begin after inscription: both should start long beforehand, both to provide the framework within which local management can occur and to work out the details of managing a particular site.

At a meeting of international experts on "Cultural Landscapes of Outstanding Universal Value" at Schorfheide, Germany, in 1993, for example, an *Action Plan for the Future* was prepared, which was adopted by the Committee in December, 1993. It recommended that regional expert meetings be held to assist with comparative studies of cultural landscapes and that thematic frameworks be developed for the evaluation of cultural landscapes to assist the World Heritage Committee in its decision-making concerning cultural landscapes. The Action Plan also asked for 'an exchange of information, case studies and management experiences on the level of regional and local communities for the protection of cultural landscapes between State Parties'.

In 1994 another meeting examined the representative nature of the World Heritage List and the methodology for its definition and implementation. The meeting was organized in response to perceived imbalances in the types of heritage included on the List and its regional representivity. A Global Strategy for a representative and credible World Heritage List was proposed at the meeting, and subsequently adopted by the World Heritage Committee in December, 1994. The Global Strategy is both a conceptual framework and a pragmatic and operational methodology for implementing the *World Heritage Convention*. It relies on regional and thematic definitions of categories of heritage which have outstanding universal value, to ensure a more balanced and representative World Heritage List by encouraging countries to become States Parties to the *Convention*, to prepare tentative lists, and to prepare nominations of properties from categories and regions currently not well represented on the World Heritage List.

Between 1992 and 2003 a number of regional and thematic Global Strategy meetings were organised by the World Heritage Centre, among them a number of global and regional expert meetings on cultural landscapes. Australia, Austria, Canada, France, Germany, Kenya, The Netherlands, Peru, the Philippines, Poland and Spain have hosted meetings which have considered themes such as 'associative' cultural landscapes (of which more anon), canals, rice terraces and routes and regions such as Africa, the Andes and eastern Europe. The management of such landscapes has become an increasingly overt concern. These meetings have certainly helped bring forward nominations and encouraged people in many parts of the world, particularly those working in less favoured areas, to acquire the skills, resources and support necessary to stake an appropriate claim on World Heritage attention.

The Caribbean is a case in point: a workshop there in September, 2001, attempted to share with local professionals skills and experience gained elsewhere, particularly among members of staff and consultants of the World Heritage Centre and the Advisory Bodies.

Management planning begins at the latest with the preparation for nomination, but it should have been under way long before that. Indeed, nomination and inscription should be encompassed as part of the *process* of management, not thought of as events, and certainly not as events only after which management has to be taken seriously. This was often the case in the 1980s on, for example, Hadrian's Wall, and unfortunately still is in many places such as France (though no longer in the UK where every World Heritage site now has its management plan). Natural sites are excluded from that generalization because, by and large, nature conservation has developed in a rational and professional manner which has included formulating long-term plans. In any case, many natural World Heritage sites are National Parks and the like and it is now common practice world-wide for such major designations to be managed according to plans. Not so, at least until very recently, with cultural sites, where again very broadly a different tradition of looking after monuments has tended to respond *ad hoc* to identified need rather than pro-actively to create long-term strategies. Few cultural sites, archaeological monuments in the care of public bodies, for example, enjoyed the privilege of having the question asked of them: 'What state do we want this to be in fifty years from now and how are we going to bring that about?'. This field has been changing rapidly, however, and continues to improve in line with generally accepted professional principles world-wide. Specifically in World Heritage matters, two major mechanisms, the management plan and periodic review, are now in place to circumvent short-termism, reactive thinking and conservation isolation. We briefly look at both, but first a word on a preliminary management mechanism, described in pure UNESCO-speak as a 'Tentative List'.

Tentative Lists

As an encouragement towards processual rather than events-led thinking, each signatory of the Convention is supposed to have lodged with the World Heritage Centre a Tentative List of possible forthcoming nominations. More and more countries are now in fact producing such lists because, strictly-speaking, all places nominated have to be on such a list to be considered by the World Heritage Committee. On the basis of data available in 2002, it was estimated that up to about 200 cultural landscapes could well be on the Tentative Lists overall (Table 10; Fowler 2003b, 47; Annexe E); and nowadays each such site should have a management plan at this early stage (though many have not). This Tentative List and its requirements help in all sorts of ways, locally in encouraging initiatives, for example, logistically in international liaison, and from the Centre to States Parties in offering assistance, for example professional advice with a management plan or in preparing a nomination. Initial discussions can also take place, as opportunity offers, with Centre staff and representatives of the Advisory Bodies who might well be in the region on occasion on other business. Henry Cleere and I, for example, when in Australia for other purposes, were invited by ICOMOS Australia to an informal discussion about Sydney Opera House as a possible World Heritage site. Such informal but informed meetings are in train all the time, often leading to more formal embassies later.

Nomination

Nomination is part of the process of site management; in itself, it is quite a difficult and complex task, particularly if it is done properly. It should be quite a drawn-out process – three to four years is not unreasonable – to allow time for critical site assessment, professional advice, public consultation and 'getting everyone on board'. The *Guidelines*, Paragraphs 7–21, provide much advice specifically on what is expected of a nomination. It is imperative that those concerned use the new *Guidelines* as soon as they are available (?in 2004). The work can be broken down into several stages, though they are not necessarily entirely sequential. Public consultation, for example, can be occurring throughout.

Analysis: the site, its resources and the evaluation

Before starting the technical tasks of completing a nomination dossier, it is good practice to carry out some sort of evaluation or systematic analysis of the property concerned. One or more of several methods can be used but a simple and effective one, used in many fields and now almost routine, is the 'SWOT analysis'. This involves setting down as objectively as possible the Strengths and Weaknesses of a site, and of the potential nomination. The Opportunities presented by the site and its possible inscription on the World Heritage List are then systematically identified, followed by a similar review of the Threats that exist or could exist to the site now and in the future. This last is in fact the beginnings of risk analysis (*below*).

Nomination dossiers

The *Guidelines* provide a form to fill in and a fairly detailed description of what is required. Actually working up a dossier to an adequate standard, however, these days involves far more than filling in a form. Once decisions about the format, style and content of the dossier itself have been taken, its scope might well include the following (not necessarily in this order):

* identification of the site being nominated, with GIS co-ordinates;
* cartographic location at different scales with maps also

indicating buffer zones and extents and varieties of legal protection, other relevant conservation designations;

* the World Heritage criteria under which the site is being proposed;

* statements about the extent of property and its legal status;

* a statement of significance;

* a statement about the authenticity and integrity of the proposed site;

* a description of the state of and provision for conservation;

* detail, with cartographic or other illustrative presentation, of components such as geology, topography, archaeology, history, population, demography, resources, communication networks, house types etc;

* character analysis: economic factors, land-use and settlement patterns, vegetational distributions, visitor facilities etc;

* research, carried out and potential; scientific, historical; and published;

* aesthetic, literary and artistic achievements and significance; the 'famous visitors/local worthies' dimension;

* a comparative study, if appropriate on a world-wide scale, of the proposed site in relation to analogous sites elsewhere;

* participation and consultation undertaken in preparing the nomination;

* a management plan;

* copy of the 'popular' booklet published as a spin-off from the work undertaken in preparing the dossier;

* copies of any major publications about the area.

Many nomination dossiers, especially ones from the mid-1990s onwards, are highly professional and elaborate creations. Some of them consist of numerous volumes; the best, whatever their bulk, are works which have taken a long time to prepare, not only in themselves but also in creating the circumstances in which it was possible to move forward with their preparation. Certainly the acceptable standard now is a high one; many early nomination dossiers would not now be acceptable. This is tough on countries with scarce resources and no or little experience in such matters, bringing their nominations forward for the first time: it is certainly more difficult to present a nomination now than it was even a decade ago. But help is available (*below*). It is against the currency of the situation in the early twenty-first century that the following character-istics of dossiers submitted in recent years were noted, as a result of critical examination. Many were criticised as:

* too hastily prepared;

* too brief or too elaborate;

* applying a formula but lacking understanding;

* not providing a statement of significance;

* on location:

   † not giving a precise location;

   † not defining boundaries;

   † not defining buffer zone;

   † providing inadequate maps;

   † offering poor or non-existent cartographic analysis;

* insufficiently rigorous intellectually;

* deficient in research, especially in comparative studies;

* on criteria:

   † failing to name those under which site is being nominated;

   † failing to justify the criteria quoted;

   † misunderstanding the criteria;

   † listing too many criteria;

* lacking evidence of public participation;

* deficient in one or more technical requirements e.g. using a language other than the five UN-recognised ones, missing the signature of the properly responsible person, failing to supply a sufficient number of sets of colour transparencies;

* arriving late.

Clearly, the point of publishing this list here is that it provides a check-list of characteristics to be avoided in their dossier by would-be nominators. If such faults are present, they will become apparent during the desk evaluations at the WHC and by IUCN and/or ICOMOS following submission of the dossier. Similarly, merits of the landscape itself will be assessed, and strengths as well as faults in the relation between the dossier and the landscape, and in the management of the site, will become apparent during the few days of intensive examination on the ground by a mission from one or both of the Advisory Bodies (Figure 44).

Consequences of inscription

This sub-topic is one to which very little attention seems to have been given by those preparing a nomination. 'What happens afterwards?' is in fact a pertinent question, one to which there are now a number of answers. Some are bureaucratic e.g. the State Party will be formally accountable for the Site to the World Heritage Committee every six years (*see* below); others are practical e.g. tourists will almost certainly be attracted to the Site. In one way and another, inscription almost inevitably also seems to involve a lot of money – expenditure, investment, income generation – yet until recently nomination procedures seldom seem to have taken a financial view of the consequences of inscription. There is furthermore almost certainly a need for an environmental audit in many cases. We can summarise the consequences of inscription under a number of headings:

A public resource:

* Inscription attracts attention to the new World Heritage Site which will move into the public gaze.

* World Heritage site stories make for good journalism because of the prestige attached to WH status.

* In countries where there is a conservation lobby and an alert press, the inscription will not be allowed to be forgotten and pressures to make it mean something will develop.

* A disadvantage of inscription from the State's point of view, but of benefit from the conservationists', is that if things go wrong, the immediate consequences will become known fairly quickly (even if unofficially) to those who need to know, and will become common knowledge soon thereafter.

* Whether or not there is public interest, diplomatic moves within UNESCO are likely in the event of an apparent contravention of the Convention.

* Local pride may also be demanding of action and enhancement and may indeed take initiatives itself.

Management and the management plan

* The newly inscribed Site must have a management plan in existence before inscription. After inscription, management and the World Heritage site are open to appraisal, by visitors, professionals (official or otherwise), and in formal inspections. Therefore:

* Management quality has to be manifestly high and appropriate to the particular World Heritage site.

* Management must manifestly operate within the published global guidelines.

* Management must satisfy, in a form of practical peer review, the considerable practical experience which now exists

centrally in the World Heritage Centre and among the Advisory Bodies.

* Presentation of the Site should be changed with the intention of improving it to meet the status of the Site and the expectations of visitors; but such changes can characteristically be deleterious to the Site, the visitor experience or both.

* Management is often as likely to threaten aspects of the Site's values, particularly ecological and structural ones, as is greater wear and tear on the Site by visitors following inscription.

* Not least because of the range of expectations from a range of stakeholders, management will be criticised whatever it does, often with justification.

Visitors and tourism

* Visitors will come even if there is no national, local or commercial promotion of a new WH Site.

* New inscriptions are publicised by UNESCO itself, not least on the web, and there are always travellers looking for new destinations.

* The successful nominating State will probably use the new inscription to promote tourism.

* Such increased economic activity may benefit some local interests financially, but not necessarily so.

* Such activity can lead to inappropriate commercial development and behaviour.

* Visitors, in their numbers and behaviour, can start to affect adversely the quality of local life e.g. traffic congestion, overburdening of facilities.

* Pressures to develop an infrastructure to cope with and attract more visitors will become very strong and can tend to be incompatible with the values of the original inscription.

* Overall, tourism, at World Heritage Sites as well as others, can impact physically, socially, environmentally and economically on far more than just the site itself.

The site

* The site maintenance requirement will rise according to a formula consisting of:

* (inevitable, natural site deterioration e.g. decay of original materials, effects of climate, weather, flora, flooding etc.) + (human-induced deterioration e.g. pollution, dehydration,

erosion, visitor wear etc.) + rising expectations of interested parties + annual and medium-term resource availability – management competence = increasing costs.

* Presentation of the site in terms of what it and its World Heritage status deserve can deteriorate under political and populist pressure.

* If the WH Site is bombed, shelled, storm-damaged, flooded, vulcanised or otherwise damaged, it will attract the attention of the world media in a way which would not have happened before or without inscription.

* Inscription itself may attract violent action as a means, for example, of making a political point.

International assistance

Financial international assistance is available in relatively small amounts both before and after inscription in specific circumstances spelt out in the *Convention* Paragraphs 19–26 and *Guidelines* Section IV (all available on the web). One of the web summaries (http://whc.unesco.org/kit-ratification.htm) states:

> 'It is the States Parties' responsibility to provide adequate protection and management for their (World Heritage) sites … a key benefit of ratification, particularly for developing countries, is access to the World Heritage Fund (which can make grants), mainly to Least Developed Countries and Low Income Countries, to finance technical assistance and training projects, as well as (for help) to prepare … nomination proposals or to develop conservation projects. Emergency assistance may also be made available for urgent action to repair damage caused by human-made or natural disasters. Inscription … may also open the way for financial assistance from a variety of (other) sources. In the case of sites included on the List of World Heritage in Danger, the attention, and the funds, of both the national and international community would be focused on the conservation needs of these particularly threatened sites with the common aim of preserving or restoring them.'

The emergency inscription in 2003 on both Lists of the Bamiyan Valley in Afghanistan is a good example of many of the facets touched on here. Heritage management in the twenty-first century clearly has as much to do with finance in one form or another as it does with professional expertises in conserving the heritage itself.

But what if nothing happens after inscription?

* Inscription on the World Heritage List can simply be ignored, as was the case politically with some early inscriptions, and unfortunately remains the case on-site in numerous instances.

* eventually lack of care could lead to the placing of a Site on
  the World Heritage in Danger List and, theoretically, removal
  of World Heritage status from the Site by the World Heritage
  Committee (though this has never actually been done).

And what if none, some or all of the foregoing happens?
Irrespective of events, at the moment of inscription of a Site on to the World
Heritage list, the State Party accepts a requirement to look after the Site
appropriately. This means it must:

* safeguard and present it as one of significance to the peoples
  of the world and not just of the country in which it is
  situated.

* monitor its condition and take appropriate action to maintain
  its values as a World Heritage site.

* submit to the discipline of Periodic Reporting in which the
  State Party has to report every six years on the general state of
  its heritage provision and on the particular condition of each
  World Heritage Site.

Monitoring and periodic reporting

Monitoring the condition of any heritage property is an essential and normal
part of good site management, regardless of whether or not the site is a World
Heritage site. Those responsible for the site – the site manager, a government
department, an NGO – need to know how it is changing, in response to
climatic factors perhaps or as a result of the pressures of tourism. They need
to know what is causing the changes, the speed at which they are occurring,
and their consequences. Such information is a pre-requisite of well-informed
management, especially in the medium and long-term. So sound management
will involve the installation of a system of checks – they can take various forms
– throughout the site, to test for specific changes, for example in masonry, in
water levels, in vegetational growth or decay, in aerial pollution, and in the
site's contribution to the local economy in terms of number of jobs.

Of particular importance in World Heritage terms is whether or not the
values for which the site was inscribed are being maintained over time.
Deterioration of fabric or flora through over-visiting, for example, are fairly
obvious effects but as important, if more subtle, are changes such as the loss
of 'a sense of place'. That a site has lost something of its special quality may
only be realised through an accumulation of monitoring data over a period of
time. So there is no point in checks, however regular, without a systematic,
periodic making and keeping of records at various time-scales. These may be
short-term, perhaps only a matter of days, or very long-term, over decades.
And the results of such monitoring will be systematically assessed – otherwise

what is the point of the activity? – and reported periodically too, perhaps to a committee, perhaps also to an academic audience or to the scientific world.

Monitoring requires a rigorous approach and the application of a range of techniques: the use, for example and as appropriate, of air photography (for details of roofscape and the layout of architectural ensembles as well as landscape morphology and archaeological and floral patterning), a geographical information system, documentary research, archaeological mitigation, digitised imaging technology, various photographic, graphic and verbal recording procedures, systematic measurement of meteorological, hydrological, biological and structural conditions, and a sound documentation/archival system, accessible to interested parties as well as staff.

'Risk preparedness', though not a technique in itself, should also be an important element in the management attitude towards a site. It embraces not only such practical matters as emergency exit arrangements from a site for visitors and staff but longer-term thinking about such matters as erosion, earthquakes, flooding and armed conflict (the 'T' in a SWOT analysis).

Although monitoring techniques may require adaptation to particular local circumstances or needs, in general they are well-known and routine in their use. Monitoring using such techniques should be part of normal management anyway, to evaluate the impacts of change and external forces on a site, to evaluate the state of conservation of a site, and to evaluate the effectiveness of actions taken on sites. Monitoring is not something to be hastily applied as a site becomes caught up in the needs of World Heritage re-active monitoring or periodic reporting. In sending specialist missions to check out specific situations, in asking for periodic reports on World Heritage sites, the World Heritage Committee is merely exercising its responsibility through a management technique, monitoring, that is already well-established in the conservation world. The particular forms of monitoring in World Heritage contexts, reactive monitoring and periodic reporting, with their own terms and formats, should not obscure this fact.

Reactive monitoring (*Guidelines*, Paragraph 75) involves the carrying out of a check on a World Heritage property in response to a complaint or complaints or to information that all is not well at the site e.g. in its management or state of conservation. A report is the usual outcome, a document which can be critical in the management of a site. The World Heritage Committee may decide that no further action is required, recommend specific measures to the State Party, request the Secretariat and/or the Advisory Bodies to undertake specific actions, or decide to inscribe the property on the List of World Heritage in Danger and adopt a programme of corrective action. The scope of such a report is exemplified by the list of contents of one prepared by ICOMOS and IUCN about a cultural landscape (which, suitably adapted, may well serve as a model in other circumstances):

Contents

An example of a good, recent report on a reactive monitoring mission is that on Islamic Cairo, Egypt (2001). The occasion for it was the expression of considerable concern about the ambition, management and standards of a large programme of restoration work being carried out in Islamic Cairo. Its structure was essentially similar to that of the Sintra report detailed above although, being entirely concerned with an urban context and work on individual monuments, its concepts and language were a little different e.g. 'Integrated urban conservation' and 'The open-air museum project' were sub-heads. It also made 'Recommendations for international assistance', a characteristic outcome of such reactive reports.

Periodic reporting

Periodic reporting is formally explained in *Guidelines* Paragraphs 69–76. It is also explained and discussed in a World Heritage Centre booklet (WHC–99/WS/4) and in an illustrated, coloured pamphlet published by the same organisation. The format for a periodic report is set out in *Guidelines* Paragraph 78 and in the booklet, covering both types of report (generally and site specific). The latter document also contains 13 pages of explanatory notes. The official explanation of the need for a questionnaire to acquire the necessary information is: 'The information collected in this way will help the States Parties to assess their own strengths and weaknesses concerning the implementation of the World Heritage Convention, putting them in a position to (re)define policies and to request assistance in order to finance projects and / or training. On the other hand it allows the World Heritage Committee to collect information needed to devise Regional Action Plans, give well-informed advice to States Parties and to focus funds as well as attention on the region(s), States Parties and/or properties that need the collective support of the international community.'

The periodical reporting exercise is a voluntary contribution of the States Parties to the 1972 Convention carried out upon the Committee's request. The first paragraph of Article 29 reads: 'The States Parties ... shall, in the reports which they submit to the General Conference of [UNESCO] on dates and in a manner to be determined by it, give information on the legislative and administrative provisions which they have adopted and other action which they have taken in this fields for the application of this Convention, together with details of the experience acquired in this field.'

In 1997 the General Conference of UNESCO invited 'the States Parties to the Convention ... to submit to it in accordance with Article 29 of the Convention ... reports on the legislative and administrative provisions they have adopted and other actions which they have taken for the application of the Convention, *including the state of conservation of the World Heritage properties located on their territories*' (author's italics). A world-wide review of World Heritage sites has subsequently been initiated. Officially, the periodic reports prepared by the States Parties serve three purposes:

* to assess the current state of all World Heritage related issues in a State Party;

* to help focus the Committee's as well as the State Party's future activities and funds;

    *   to strengthen sub-regional and regional co-operation between States Parties.

Essentially, under the first bullet point above, each State Party is invited to submit a report on two aspects of its custody of World Heritage. It has to report on:

    *   the general state of heritage provision within its territory;
    *   and the state of conservation of each WH Site in its territory.

Periodic reporting now has to be carried out by each State Party on a regional basis every six years. The current cycle is:

1999–2000: Arab States: 46 sites inscribed up to end of 1992;
2000–2001: Africa: 40 sites / end 1993;
2001–2002: Asia and Pacific: 96 sites/end 1994;
2002–2003: Latin America and the Caribbean: 62 sites/end 1995;
2004–2005: Europe and North America: 243 sites/end 1996.

The Committee is very conscious of sensitivities on the principle of State sovereignty in the whole process, and it is now contemplating the synthetic reviews of the results arising from the first periodic reports. These can have major effects. One of the early follow-up workshops has recognised that, such is the poor state of conservation documented by the reports, the Committee's prime concern for the foreseeable future should be to look after existing World Heritage properties rather than accept the nominations of new ones. Both on the part of the World Heritage Committee looking at the whole of its port-folio, and of signatories to the *Convention* looking at their own sites, a reporting exercise has a number of management objectives:

    *   to assess the application of the World Heritage Convention by the State Party;
    *   to assess whether the World Heritage values on the basis of which a site was inscribed on the World Heritage list are being maintained over time;
    *   to update information about World Heritage properties in the territory of a State Party to record changing circumstances and state of conservation of the properties;
    *   to promote regional co-operation and exchange of information and experience.

Current thoughts on management

An expert meeting on vineyard landscapes at Tokaj in 2001 typically made eleven recommendations, six of which were overtly or indirectly about management (WHC 2002b, 78–79). Recommendation 6 in particular speaks of the need for 'regulatory preservation' and ways of ensuring:

* 'the continuation of economic activities that sustains the site;

* the provision of economic benefits for site maintenance;

* the sharing of site know-how among stakeholders and their [sic – 'its'] transmission to future generations;

* the acceptance of a common culture and identity by all stakeholders'.

The last one might well be considered contentious, and even misconceived – rural conservatism rules OK? – but the general thrust towards continuing, real-life use with a local, living community, as distinct from a museum land-scape of nine-till-five peasants, is well-made and common to most cultural landscapes, not just vineyard (*cf.* Figure 22). Similarly of wide application, 'Community participation and development' should be in place at the time of nomination, with an 'effective cultural landscape conservation strategy ... in force which involves all stakeholders' (Recommendation 8). And certainly relevant to all cultural landscapes – for this is a dimension in which they are particularly vulnerable – is Recommendation 9. It stresses 'the importance of effective tourism management planning', not to fossilize the landscape as a museum piece, not to spoil people's fun, but 'to avoid the potential degrada-tion of the cultural values for which [the site has been] inscribed on the World Heritage List.' That precisely expresses the point of management of World Heritage cultural landscapes. Less precisely, I would personally like to see 'cultural values' expanded to include natural ones and those which lie at the core of the concept of cultural landscape, that is those expressing the interac-tion through time of natural and cultural processes which have created the particular qualities and values of the landscape in question.

Two other recent sources provide thoughts on the management of World Heritage cultural landscapes. Of my own twelve recommendations (Fowler 2003b, 64), four directly concern management. I urge the World Heritage Committee to insist that nominated properties' outstanding universal values are spelt out and that the proposed management regime of nominated prop-erties is both appropriate in style and appropriately resourced in order to conserve them. Recognising that the management of World Heritage cultural landscapes is neither God-given nor self-evident, and that knowledge of what to do and how to do it is unevenly distributed, I look to the Committee posi-tively to encourage ideas and practice about appropriate and effective ways of managing them. Given that no management regime can encompass every-thing, I recommend that the Committee encourage countries to emphasize, from a range of options, the scientific and educational potential of their cultural landscapes. And, in common with the thoughts of many others in these matters, I re-emphasize that 'co-operation in the management of cultural landscapes is particularly needed and should everywhere be sought, always with local people and wherever appropriate with other [conservation] programmes ...'.

The other source of current thoughts on the management of World Heritage sites lies with the reports of the international workshops in several Italian towns which preceded, and reported to, the Thirty Year World Heritage Conference in Venice, November, 2002 (WHC 2003b). The workshop in Trieste on 'Partnerships to conserve nature and biodiversity' recognised *inter alia* that it is as important to ensure 'that the sites already designated as World Heritage are protected and managed at internationally acceptable standards' as it is to expand the List; that conservation of World Heritage sites should be linked to local aspirations in the fields of education, information and economic well-being; and that partnerships at international through to local levels were essential in developing management for conservation purposes in their widest sense. Clearly the thrust of the workshop applies very much to cultural sites and landscapes too. The report, however, contained nothing on cultural landscapes as such, being solely concerned with nature conservation in isolation as if it were not an integral part of cultural landscape management and *vice versa*. We still have some way to go.

'World Heritage site management' was the concern of a workshop at Padua. Selecting points from its much more generally relevant deliberations, we can note the human dimension not recorded at Trieste: 'Diverse, changing and widening understanding of societal values makes management sites and areas in their context more complex' (than would otherwise be the case) – an observation applicable whether the site is 'cultural', 'natural' or a symbiosis of both in a cultural landscape. The human dimension is developed in two more successive observations: 'Wider social involvement in the process of managing heritage leads to sustainability and strengthens its role in the process of human development'; and 'In planning and managing heritage sites and areas, it is important to give due consideration and respect to beliefs, practices, traditions, and needs of owners and local communities'. And then, in a formal observation which I had already unconsciously echoed *below* in writing my penultimate paragraph of this chapter before inserting this summary of the pre-Venice workshops, the Padua participants remarked that 'The process by which stakeholders, including the local communities, are involved in planning and decision-making for successful and sustainable management of heritage sites and areas is as important, if not more important, than the actual management documents which are produced.' Bureaucrats who would never find themselves in such front-line situations, and others unfavourably disposed towards management plans through principle or prejudice, would do well to mark that observation and draw the correct conclusion.

Other observations from Padua must await the publication of the proceedings; many are pertinent to our discussion even if they were not developed specifically for cultural landscapes. Similarly, the fifteen recommendations, though at first sight unexceptional, appear so because they accurately reflect some of the broad principles and policies already being followed – or at least advocated, since implementation in all this is the weakness. They are in any case without exception relevant to cultural landscapes. Nevertheless, the issues and points they raise have all been mentioned either in this chapter or elsewhere in this book. Seven of the recommendations are concerned with on-site matters, and eight deal in one way or another with the context in which site management takes place, that is issues such as international co-operation and funding, capacity-building at (UNESCO) regional level, training, and information flows between signatories of the Convention and between site managers. It is so important in all this, however, to remember always that the objective is to sustain the site or landscape and enhance people's enjoyment of it: management plans and other such mechanisms are of course important but as means to an end, not an end in themselves (though they tend to take on a life of their own).

A synchronous workshop at Ferrara was specifically concerned with 'Cultural landscapes – the challenges of conservation.' It identified a number of challenges, all essentially ones of management, which had emerged in the first decade of the concept's implementation:

* insufficient co-operation between countries;

* limited implementation of the Global Strategy for a balanced World Heritage List;

* regional imbalances: 21 of the [then] 30 official cultural landscapes are in Europe;

* lack of capacity to bring forward credible nominations of cultural landscapes;

* restricted resources and weak institutions for effective management;

* difficulties in sustaining traditional forms of land-use, which give rise to cultural landscapes, in circumstances of rapid socio-economic change and limited capacities to deal with tourism;

* the need to strengthen linkages between the cultural landscape concept and other designation systems, notably IUCN Category V protected area (protected landscapes/seascapes) and the UNESCO Biosphere Reserve network.

The last four of those points are central to the future and management of cultural landscapes as World Heritage sites. The identification of an incapacity among many Convention signatories to prepare a credible nomination of a cultural landscape is realistic and honest but of real concern. It is probably a weakness intellectually as well as in practical respects. There is a danger that the cultural landscape concept might well founder as a global concept on

exactly this issue. It is indeed difficult to bring a successful cultural landscape nomination forward, not least if widespread consultation is attempted beforehand. Well-oiled government mechanisms with close links to the relevant academic and research communities in rich countries like Canada, Australia and the UK can be expected to propose a steady stream of appropriate properties; but that is not what World Heritage is supposed to be about. It is specifically what cultural landscape was supposed not so much to counter as to run in parallel with, as countries with non-monumental heritages were conceptually enabled to bring their particular heritage sites to the world's heritage table. It would be unacceptable if, through a particular management incapacity, the implementation of cultural landscape as a World heritage concept gradually withered and died. The answer is obvious: every encouragement and practical help possible must be made available to those developing countries with potential World Heritage cultural landscapes who simply lack the means to deliver a successful nomination – which, let us remind ourselves, must now be accompanied by a credible and sustainable management plan.

Such incapacity will almost certainly reflect 'restricted resources and weak institutions'. Though failure to secure inscription for want of a convincing nomination can be disappointing to the proposer, it is as well for World Heritage, the State Party and not least the site itself to have such systematic weakness exposed early on rather than through inevitable ineffective management

FIGURE 46.
The difficulties and
moralities of
maintaining indigenous
ways of life on the land
are epitomized by this
photograph of
traditional cultivation
taken, for its scientific
interest, with
permission, near Mejji,
Morocco – reasonably
remote but beside the
main road to
Marrakesh. One
problem is that the
young ploughman is
planting sunflower
seeds. Another is that
an ugly and bitter
altercation occurred at
the roadside when the
photographer failed, in
the eyes of the
ploughman, to pay a
sufficiently large
'facility fee'. No
arcadian simplicity this.

thereafter. Systems can, after all, be strengthened; people can be trained; public interest can be cultivated. The whole contemporary context within which a cultural landscape exists can be improved by deferring inscription for future appraisal; and in the interval the foundations of better management can be laid by more critical assessment of the landscape's actual values, public consultation, a review of management structure, improving resource provision including the legal framework, and by recruitment and training of personnel.

The penultimate point – 'difficulties in sustaining traditional forms of land-use ... in circumstances of rapid socio-economic change' – is particularly distinctive of cultural landscapes (Figure 46, 47). This expression of the 'challenge' reflects a great deal of experience in numerous places throughout the world. It is illustrated, and briefly discussed, throughout this book; but there is no easy solution, and solutions, themselves characteristically complex, involve far more than conventional heritage management across fields as diverse as local politics to international, inter-agency co-operation. The latter aspect is reflected in the last 'challenge' noted at Ferrara, 'the need to strengthen linkages between the cultural landscape concept and other designation systems, notably IUCN Category V protected areas (protected landscapes/seascapes) and the UNESCO Biosphere Reserve network.' The point reflects the fact that different agencies with different schemes often find themselves homing in on the same area of land. Perhaps the question to ask is why this should be so; and the answer, fairly obviously, is that, whatever various special-interest groups may call them, such areas are cultural landscapes in one or more of the holistic senses defined in Chapter 2.

In July, 2003, for example, the World Heritage Committee inscribed the Three Parallel Rivers of Yunman Protected Areas, China, and Uvs Nuur Basin, Mongolia/Russian Federation, on the World Heritage List, both solely as natural sites. Yet the former is noted in the Committee's own draft Report as having experienced 'thousands of years of human habitation' and the latter as 'inhabited and ... used for nomadic pastoralism for thousands of years'. Both smack of cultural landscape, whatever their outstanding natural values; and is not their evidence of interaction between the human and natural worlds itself a value to be identified and maintained? It seems unreal to pretend that such places are only of 'natural' value, indeed have only managed to hang on to that value 'despite' (the word used in the draft Report) human activity. Nor is this merely a theoretical or debating point. Without recognition, conceptual as well as empirical, of the values of a place, of its significances, fully appropriate management cannot be developed; so that, in these two examples, if management proceeds purely in accord with the precepts of nature conservation alone, then the landscape, never mind the people and their culture, will suffer in the long run. Though both inscriptions are picked out as examples merely because they are current, it would nevertheless be interesting to check them out in ten years' time to see how the people are faring who, perhaps to their surprise, now find themselves not only living in but contributing to the interest of huge nature reserves. The issue broadens, of course, as it relates to

the previous challenge about 'difficulties in sustaining traditional forms of land-use'.

Though I was not to know this when I used the above example, the major issue in it came to the fore at the IUCN World Parks Congress in Durban, South Africa, in September 2003. This was the fifth such Congress at which, every ten years, many of those involved world-wide with nature conservation meet – some 3,000 delegates from international bodies, NGOs, governments and national organisations including National Parks, and from the funding and voluntary sectors. Essentially, delegates from the developing world rose during the conference in a common protest at so many of its peoples now either having been removed from their homelands in the name of nature conservation or, still living on their land in what has now become a protected area, actually being or at least feeling that they were of secondary importance to conservation interests. This was certainly the aspect that the world's press took up, probably to the detriment of other issues, and it seemed to come to dominate proceedings. It says much for the success of the nature conservation movement over the last century, and in particular in the later twentieth century, that a sufficient amount of land in the world has been affected for the issue of how it is used to become of global concern. In fact, some 10 per cent of the world's surface is protected in some 100,000 designated conservation sites. It has, therefore, according to your point of view, been expropriated, properly recognised, or at least defined for management with a priority for faunal and/or floral conservation.

FIGURE 47.
The fragility of traditional ways of life, and of maintaining them, are symbolised by this image of a nomad encampment, with its lorries, genuinely far into the Arabian desert, near Asraq, Jordan, but actually photographed from a bus on the Amman–Baghdad highway.

Clearly, in a conservation world inevitably so far dominated by First World history, concepts and interests, attitudes struck over this issue can reflect a political agenda as well as genuine concern and even injustice. Nevertheless, a contrast is all too clear over the Durban occasion between what interested the media on the one hand and, on the other, official presentation of the Congress. The latter understandably deals with a much wider menu. This single but major issue of resident people's experience of protected areas, expressed here in rather abrupt and crude terms – reflecting media interest – was not so specifically represented in the material released officially at the end of the Congress. A media release quotes the South African Minister of Environmental Affairs and Tourism's reference to 'sustainable livelihoods' and the Africa Protected Areas Initiative is described as 'a major programme ... that will meet the environmental *and social* (author's italics) needs of the continent' but that is about it in that document.

Three 'Level One Outputs', however, obliquely acknowledge the debate, and together represent a significant development of nature conservation thinking away from a 'less human presence, the better' paradigm towards a more holistic and realistic approach which is inclusive of people. The 'Durban Accord' 'celebrates ... new participatory management strategies emphasizing the role of local communities to share in protected area benefits and decision-making. The first of three broad themes reflected in the 32 Recommendations of the Congress is 'The importance of engaging with the broad array of people who reside near and around protected areas to ensure that their interests and needs are understood and considered in the management of these areas.' And the second of three 'essential requirements' identified in the message from the Congress to the Conference in 2004 of the Parties signatory to the Convention on Biological Diversity is 'The need to put in place mechanisms to ensure necessary participation and equitable sharing of the benefits of protected area, particularly with indigenous and mobile peoples, as well as local communities.'

This theoretical – one might also say theological – shift to recognise humanity in nature conservation is of great significance, not just for people everywhere and nature conservation itself but also for the recognition, designation and management of cultural landscapes. People have always been present in the thinking behind the World Heritage Convention (1972). They appear centre stage in paragraph one of the *Operational Guidelines*. When World Heritage cultural landscapes were defined in 1992, right from the start they were conceptualised, using a phrase from Article 1 of the Convention, as 'combined works of nature and man'. Involvement with local people was also envisaged at the initial 1992 meeting, appearing in the *Guidelines*, Paragraph 41, as 'The nominations should be prepared in collaboration with and the full approval of local communities.' Unfortunately, no equivalent recognition of people appears in the provisions for 'natural' World Heritage sites, the 'populations' referred to being floral and faunal. Indeed, people are specifically excluded: for example, '... to protect the site's (natural) heritage values from direct effects of human encroachment and impacts of resource use …'. So there has been a sort of barrier between natural and cultural expectations of World Heritage sites, carrying over perhaps even into consideration and management of sites which, whatever their name, enjoy values in both fields of interest. But, of course, the essence of cultural landscape is that it carries not merely interests of both natural and cultural sorts but that it bears witness too, is indeed the product of, something new and different, that is the interaction of natural and cultural processes. It is therefore extremely timely, not least for World Heritage in general and its cultural landscape concept in particular, that the human factor in protected landscape, and specifically its management, is now so clearly and unambiguously recognised in nature conservation by the Durban deliberations. The future looks more positive in several respects as a result.

The Ferrara workshop identified ways of progressing the concept of World Heritage cultural landscape and outlined a vision for the next ten years. Many of the points are scattered throughout this text but it is important to emphasise here some of those which relate to management. A basic assertion was 'As World heritage cultural landscapes provide models of stewardship for landscapes as a whole, a particularly well informed and sensitive management is required. This management needs to take into account not only cultural and natural values, but also their interaction, and the presentation of this process to the public'. A most important observation, unknowingly echoing Padua, was that 'Many forms of traditional resource management, often supported by customary law, have been recognized in cultural landscapes and found relevant for the management of other types of properties and other contexts.'

The participants at Ferrara concluded that their 'vision for the next ten years' lay in:

* preparing thematic studies e.g. on agricultural landscapes, the better to encourage and assess cultural landscape nominations;

* seeking 'new approaches in international co-operation', not least with imaginative linear-type nominations such as trade and pilgrimage routes;

* strengthening 'co-operation between natural and cultural heritage institutions', especially in working partnerships in landscape conservation and management to support 'an integrated and holistic management approach';

* supporting 'social structures, traditional knowledge and indigenous practices';

* recognizing 'the crucial role of intangible and spiritual values';

* preparing 'guidelines for national legislation for cultural landscapes';

* re-assessing 'cultural and natural sites already on the World

FIGURE 48.
A sense of place and local tradition on the Causse du Larzac in 2000, expressed in the wake of an anti-capitalist protest at MacDonalds, Millau, France.

Heritage List, to ensure that cultural landscape potential is recognized through re-nomination if appropriate';

* extending 'the concept of cultural landscapes from its present rural focus to include other landscapes, including cityscapes, seascapes and industrial landscapes;

* 'demonstrating how the recognition of cultural landscapes can generate economic development and sustainable livelihoods within the site and beyond';

* 'developing a stronger system to ensure rapid intervention and mobilizing resources for cultural landscapes under threat';

* 'addressing as a priority for advice and assistance the specific challenges of agricultural change and tourism pressures within cultural landscapes'. (Plates 3, 4, 12; Figures 5, 8, 9, 12, 15, 27, 32, 40, 41, 46, 47, 50, 55, 57)

That list picks out the points bearing directly or indirectly on management, so it is not comprehensive. The workshop finally addressed the question 'What are cultural landscapes for?'; and, possibly with tongue in cheek, expressed its appreciation for the food products of such landscapes.

A conservation case study

A choice could be made from many examples so I simply take one from my own experience, picking out some aspects of its management and not attempting to discuss the site as a whole. The area is not a World Heritage cultural landscape, though it is certainly a cultural landscape and is in part within an area now nominated as a World Heritage cultural landscape.

Le Causse Méjean, Languedoc (France) (Figures 40, 48, 49)
How do you explain this? In a part of the world – it happens to be deeply rural France – where ox-ploughing continued until fifty years ago, most of the local population still lives on as well as off the land, in this case by shepherding. Le Causse Méjean is a classic case of a 'montane limestone sweat-and-grief marginal farming landscape'. Almost all of it is part of a UNESCO Biosphere Reserve and it is immediately adjacent to a Natural Regional Park; much of the area is in a National Park and its buffer zone; and it has recently been nominated as an addition to French World Heritage Sites as a cultural landscape. The whole is of great natural diversity. Yet the area is experiencing a process of impoverishment of its landscape, perhaps imperceptible to the casual visitor but very obvious in the form of six trends noted over a decade (*see* Notes). Individually and collectively they are detrimental; yet this is a landscape massively researched in terms of its scientific and socio-economic characteristics, it is designated up to the eyeballs, and it has a local population directly working the land. How can landscape quality be going so wrong in these circumstances? – my question, though a real one in other contexts, here is rhetorical, for my purpose is primarily to stimulate thought by using the Causse Méjean as a real-life metaphor. My guess is that most areas with 'special' or protected landscapes are experiencing two or more of these trends in any one of several combinations. An explanation in the Caussenard case might have something to do with the paradox that the 'culture' part of this particular cultural landscape is expressing itself in a drawn-out process of landscape degradation. Now, there is something for theorists as well as practitioners to ponder.

One sort of result of a process such as this we can readily see now in much of Europe's montane landscape – and indeed further afield too – although much of it, in one way or another, is designated and even highly-managed (Plates 7, 13; Figures 12, 13, 27, 30, 41). All too characteristically, traditional lifeways have often disappeared, or been severely compromised as living elements among the majority of rural society by subsidy and technical innovation. Whether their time will come again remains to be seen but meanwhile climatic change has arrived. It alone could render nugatory much of what we do and propose. Has anyone yet paused to think through at European or world level the implications of global warming for our landscapes, not in agricultural, botanical or economic terms, but in cultural terms? We have some idea what will happen around our coasts but what about the changes in

FIGURE 49.
Fire is a considerable hazard in heritage management, not least in the landscape. Here fire rages through pine-forest on the Causse Méjean, Languedoc, France, on 4 August 2003.

prospect for those montane landscapes, so rich in their humanity, land at 500m and more above sea-level, when the mean annual temperature is two degrees Celsius higher than now?

Among the many things needed to address such major issues is 'partnership', not just a politically correct word that was flavour of the Congress at Venice in November, 2002, but a real practical choice. Practicality and partnership go together: the former strengthens the latter. The fact that Hadrian's Wall, despite my strictures, is actually well-managed is of course due to there being a good management plan but that itself, and its implementation, is in large part due to the experience of those involved in drafting the first version in the early 1990s. Then not only were the issues outlined in Chapter 9 brought into the open around the *cause célèbre* of the Hadrian's Wall Trail but those holding divergent views actually had to argue their corner across the table with others, now peers, who perhaps had not previously been considered as having views of any merit. Having been through that steering experience myself – thank goodness! – I became an advocate of the need for World Heritage management plans, not on principle, not necessarily for their contents, but to provide the experience of tackling the issues and reaching pragmatic solutions to all those going to be involved in looking after a World Heritage site. This seems to me an essential component in the process of preparing a nomination – obviously in different forms in different parts of the world – and I am deeply suspicious of nominations which have not benefited from such an experience. There are always going to be difficulties in managing a World Heritage site, and if they are not recognised, confronted and solved beforehand, it is likely that their emergence after inscription will guarantee a difficult early phase of life as a World Heritage site.

In the meantime desertion and decrepitude are now on the agenda as possible threats to cultural landscapes quite as much as development. Tourism can be a mixed blessing in such circumstances, but nevertheless it is one mechanism for preserving and managing cultural landscape, of both associative and relic varieties, by giving it a non-agrarian but contemporary function. And surely that points a way forward? Landscape may be identified as 'cultural' but its future, as a continuing dynamic entity attracting funds and sympathetic management, must lie in it also being able to serve several purposes over and above its historic, ideographic and aesthetic values. It could, for example, meet various needs in tourism, education, recreation and nature conservation. With many countries now emerging, like Britain, as a world tourist destination, visited as much for the variety and beauty of their landscape as for specific monuments or for activities like shopping, perhaps cultural landscape does have a role to play; but the concept it embodies will have to be presented to both its indigenous and foreign audiences quite as carefully as is now the norm in presenting the nomination of a particular area to the World Heritage Committee. Management of course primarily concerns properly looking after the property and its set of 'outstanding universal values' in the case of World Heritage sites and landscapes; but good management in the twenty-first century will as expertly include excellent presentation, whether it be through various media externally or on-site in interpreting the place and its spirit to welcome visitors. How can they be 'Landscapes for the world' if, in parallel with the priority of long-term conservation, management does not tell people about them?

CHAPTER II

Reviewing the Achievement:
World Heritage Cultural Landscapes,
1992–2003

No World Heritage cultural landscapes existed in 1992; on 3 July, 2003, there were officially 36 (Table 2). There are, however, many other World Heritage Sites which are cultural landscapes, and many cultural landscapes which are not on the World Heritage List (Fowler 2003b, chapter 4; Cleere 2003). Some existing World Heritage properties might have been inscribed as cultural landscapes if such nominations had been possible prior to 1992, especially some of the great designed gardens like Versailles, France, and extensive archaeological landscapes like those around Stonehenge, Avebury and Hadrian's Wall, UK. They could certainly be inscribed as cultural landscapes were they nominated for the first time now or if they are re-nominated in the future.

Precedents have been set by Tongariro, New Zealand, and Uluṟu, Australia, previously inscribed as 'natural' World Heritage sites and re-nominated and re-inscribed as cultural landscapes in the 1990s. A similar example, St Kilda, UK, is currently being considered. Doubtless other sites inscribed under natural criteria may also merit consideration as cultural landscapes; Lorentz National Park, Indonesia, inscribed in 1999 under natural criteria, has been inhabited for 25,000 years and is today home to eight indigenous groups, living largely by subsistence agriculture, hunting and fishing. These 36 places are neither exclusive in quality nor finite in number. The World Heritage concept is one of humanity's saner ideas, and the mechanism of inscription is becoming increasingly better known.

This is now particularly relevant as many people, recognising humanity's near all-pervasive environmental influence, are coming to see much of the world's terrestial surface as, to a greater or lesser extent, 'cultural landscape'. At best, World Heritage cultural landscapes are but tiny, carefully-selected samples from that global phenomenon, even including the hundred or so cultural landscapes on the World Heritage List (Fowler 2003b) as an enlargement of the list of 36 official ones.

This chapter attempts an analysis of World Heritage cultural landscapes, 1992–2003. We first of all take note of how well the 'blue skies' proposal made at La Petite Pierre in 1992 to recognise three categories of World Heritage cultural landscape has worked in practice. We link that in Table 8 with an analysis of which of the Convention's criteria have been used, and how often, in inscribing the 36 official World Heritage cultural landscapes.

We then attempt to characterise how those 36 cultural landscapes have in effect gone some way to defining in practice what a World Heritage cultural landscape is. The 29 columns in Table 9 may appear daunting but they represent one simple way of presenting this analysis. An explanation of the column heads follows immediately in a key to Table 9. Aspects of this analysis are then discussed in prose.

We then break away from the limitations of the 36 official World Heritage cultural landscapes and briefly explore the proposition that there are in fact about 100 cultural landscapes on the World Heritage List. They have simply not hitherto been recognised as such. This somewhat contentious issue is documented more fully in Fowler 2003b, Chapter 4 and Annexes C and D, of which the version here is little more than a summary without the supporting data. Table 10 provides a sample of it, showing, in addition to five official cultural landscapes, 11 other World Heritage sites all of which are probably cultural landscapes too. Table 11 summarises the situation, showing a continuing 2:1 ratio of category 2b cultural landscapes over category 3 among the 100 sites as with the 36; but also showing much less of a numerical difference among the 100 as compared to the 36 between the three most popular categories, 1, 2a and 2b. The last remains the most popular but is comparatively less dominant.

We then look at the global distribution of both the 36 and 100 lists (Figures 53, 54). This throws up some interesting differences, notably in China, with some pointers to the future perhaps in Africa, Asia and the Latin America/Caribbean regions.

Finally in this chapter, we note the existence of Tentative Lists of possible forthcoming nominations and, drawing heavily on and summarising the results of analyses published in detail in Fowler 2003b, Tables 10–13, predict that, from about 100 cultural landscapes on the World Heritage List in 2002, the total will have risen to 200 or more before 2020. The number of official cultural landscapes is likely to have increased in the same period, at an average rate of about six per annum, to rather more than one hundred.

Categories

The three categories of cultural landscape (Table 4) have so far stood up well to ten years' use. There has been no great demand to change them, nor any apparent need. Almost certainly this is because they are conceptual rather than functional categories, dealing with the nature of landscapes rather than the uses which made them what they are. Discussions about whether they are agricultural, industrial or urban are therefore dealing with second order issues, for all or none such descriptors can fit inside one or more of 'designed', 'organically evolved' or 'associative' models. Although in practice many cultural landscapes have characteristics of more than one of the World Heritage categories, each can without much difficulty be ascribed to a principal category. The principal characteristic is taken in each case in Table 8, and was also used in categorising the one hundred possible cultural landscapes already existing on the World Heritage List (Fowler 2003b, Table 8. The same 100 sites appear in Cleere 2003). Here, all the category 1 ascriptions, and most of those to category 3, seem well-founded. In other words, both now with 36 World Heritage landscapes, and with one hundred cultural landscapes on the World Heritage List, the 1992 categorisation works well with a much larger order of numbers than previously attempted. The distribution of the 36 official cultural landscapes is shown in column three of Table 8.

World Heritage cultural landscapes

The use of cultural criteria (i)–(vi) for the inscription of cultural landscapes is tabulated alphabetically by State Party in Table 8.

No standard use of the six World Heritage criteria (Table 8, Columns 4–9) characterises the inscription of the thirty six official cultural landscapes. Of the criteria by which cultural landscapes have been chosen, number (iv) is used almost twice as much as any other criterion. This is rather surprising in two senses. In the first place, many of the early architectural and monumental Sites were inscribed on this criterion, which is looking for a Site to be 'an outstanding example of a type of building or architectural or technological ensemble or landscape which illustrates (a) significant stage(s) in human history.' So here a 'new' type of World Heritage site is, at least initially, adhering to a commonly-used criterion for conventional sites.

In the second place, the phrase '(a) significant stage(s) in human history' is often misunderstood. The 'value' represented by the phrase is not an option in using this criterion: a site has to be, not 'might also be', able to demonstrate its role in one or more significant stages in human history *as well as* be an 'outstanding example' of a type. Assuming 'human history' means 'the history of humanity', not some event or development of only local significance, criterion iv is often wrongly claimed and has perhaps even been mistakenly applied in inscribing World Heritage Sites. On reflection, it might well be that half a dozen, if not more, of the 28 official cultural landscapes using criterion iv are not actually qualified in that respect, however 'outstanding' they may or may not be. It could well be, then, that while criterion iv is certainly popular, its numerical disparity with criteria iii and v is not quite so justified as the figures would suggest. It is striking that until 2003 not a single official cultural landscape required more than three criteria for inscription and that three found one criterion sufficient. The average number of criteria used was 2.3 until 2002. It was lifted to 2.4 by the average 3.1 apparently found necessary in 2003 when two sites required five and four criteria respectively.

Table 8. Analysis of categories and cultural criteria used in inscribing official World Heritage cultural landscapes, 1993–2003

Category 1 ('designed'): 5;   Category 2a ('organic – relict'): 4
Category 2b ('organic – continuing'): 18;   Category 3 ('associative'): 9

State Party	Site	Category 1, 2a, 2b, 3	i	ii	iii	iv	v	vi	Total
Afghanistan	Bamiyan	3	+	+	+	+		+	5
Australia	Uluru	3					+	+	2 [a]
Austria	Hallstatt	2b			+	+			2
	Wachau	2b		+		+			2
Cuba	Viñales	2b			+	+			2
	Plantations	2a			+	+			2
Czech Rep.	Lednice	1	+	+		+			3
France	St Emilion	2b			+	+			2
	Loire	2b	+	+		+			3
and Spain	Mont Perdu	2b			+	+	+		3 [b]
Germany	Dessau	1		+		+			2
	Rhine	2b		+		+	+		3
Hungary	Hortobágy	2b				+	+		2
	Tokaj	2b			+		+		2
and Austria	Fertö-Neu.	2b					+		1
India	Bhimbetka	2a			+		+		2
Italy	Amalfitana	2b		+		+	+		3
	Cinque Terre	2b		+		+	+		3
	Cilento	2b			+	+			2
	Sacri Monti	3		+		+			2
Laos DPR	Vat Phou	3			+	+		+	3
Lebanon	Quadisha	3			+	+			2
Lithuania/Russia	Curonian Spit	2b					+		1
Madagascar	Ambohimanga	3			+	+		+	3
New Zealand	Tongariro	3						+	1 [c]
Nigeria	Sukur	3			+		+	+	3
Philippines	Cordilleras	2b			+	+	+		3 [d]
Poland	Kalwaria	3		+		+			2 [e]
Portugal	Sintra	1		+		+	+		3
	Alto Douro	2b		+		+	+		3
South Africa	Mapungubwe	2a		+	+	+	+		4
Spain	Aranjuez	1		+		+			2
Sweden	Öland	2b				+	+		2
UK	Blaenavon	2a			+	+			2
	Kew	1		+	+	+			3
Zimbabwe	Matobo	2b			+		+	+	3
Totals: 21 States Parties	36 sites	1–5 2b–18 2a–4 3–9	3	15	18	28	17	7	88

[a] Plus natural criteria ii and iii;   [b] Plus natural criteria i and iii;
[c] Plus natural criteria ii and iii;   [d] Could have justifiably used i also;
[e] Could have justifiably used vi also.

Table 9. World Heritage Cultural Landscapes 1992–2003: an analysis

The following table lists, and attempts to characterise, the cultural landscapes inscribed as such on the World Heritage List between the decision of the World Heritage Committee to recognise such a type of Site in December 1992 and its inscription of the 36th World Heritage cultural landscape in July 2003.

Key to the columns in Table 9 (following page)

Year: year of inscription on the World Heritage List

No.:   the number of the Site on the World Heritage List

State: the State Party which, being signatory to the World Heritage Convention (1972), nominated the Site for inscription

Name: the name of the Site (perhaps shortened) as printed in *Properties inscribed on the World Heritage List* (WHC 2000/3, Jan. 2000)

A–W   identify a number of characteristics which seem to be significant in the nature and management of World Heritage cultural landscapes; but the list is subjective and neither inclusive nor definitive:

A: aesthetic quality is significant on the Site

B: buildings, often large buildings, are present

C: continuity of lifeway/landuse is an important element

F: farming/agriculture is/was a major element in the nature of the landscape

G: the landscape is, or contains as a major element, ornamental garden(s)/park(s)

I: primarily an industrial Site

L: the landscape is, or contains elements which are significant in one or more forms of group identity such as for a nation, a tribe, or a local community

M: a mountain or mountains is/are an integral part of the landscape

N: the landscape contains, or is entirely, a National Park, or other primary form of national conservation designation.

P: a locally-resident population is a significant part of (the management of) the landscape

R: the landscape possesses an important dimension of religiosity/sanctity/holiness

S: survival is a significant theme in the landscape, physically as of ancient field systems and archaeological monuments, and/or socially, as of a group of people in a hostile environment

T: towns, and/or villages, are within the inscribed landscape

W: water is an integral, or at least significant, part of the landscape (see last column for Wi, Wl, Wr, Ws)

other: the last column lists by initials less common characteristics of cultural landscapes which are nevertheless significant for that particular Site:

Jf: jungle/forest/woodland environment

Ra: rock art

Wi: irrigation, or other form of functional water management

Wl: a lake or lakes is/are an integral part of the landscape

Wr: as last, for river(s)

Ws: as last, for sea

Table 9.

Year	No.	State	Name	A	B	C	F	G	I	L	M	P	R	S	T	W	Other
1993	421	NZ	Tongariro	+	+			+	+	+	+	+					Jf
1994	447	AUSL	Uluru	+	+					+	+	+					Ra
1995	722	PHIL	Cordil'ras	+		+	+			+	+	+	+	+	+		Jf/Wi
	723	PORT	Sintra	+	+	+		+			+	+			+	+	Jf/Wl
1996	763	CZECH	Lednice	+	+			+							+		
1997	773	FR/SP	Perdu	+		+	+			+	+		+	+			
	806	AUSTRIA	Hallstatt							+	+				+	+	Wl
	826	ITAL	Portov'ere			+	+			+	+			+	+	+	Wi/Wr/Ws
	830	ITAL	Am'lft'na	+	+	+				+	+		+		+	+	Jf/Wi/Ws
1998	842	ITAL	Cilento		+	+		+			+			+	+	+	Wr/Ws
	850	LEBAN	Quadisha		+	+							+	+			
1999	474	HUNG	Hortobagy	+	+	+	+							+			
	840	CUBA	Vinales	+	+	+	+			+		+		+			
	905	POLAN	Kalwaria	+	+			+			+		+	+			Jf
	932	FR	St Emilion		+	+	+				+		+	+	+		Wr
	938	NIGER	Sukur	+		+	+					+		+			
2000	534	GERM	Dessau-	+	+			+							+	+	Wl
	933	FR	Loire	+	+	+	+	+		+					+	+	Wr
	968	SWED	Öland		+		+				+		+	+	+	+	Ws
	970	AUSTRIA	Wachau		+		+	+				+			+	+	Wr
	984	UK	Blaenavon		+				+	+	+	+			+	+	Wi
	994	LITHUANIA/ RUSSIA	Curonian Spit		+	+				+		+	+	+	+	+	Ws
	1008	CUBA	Pl'tations		+		+				+		+	+	+		Wi
2001	481	LAOS	Vat Phou	+	+		+	+		+	+	+	+		+		Wi/Wl/Wr
	772	AUSTRIA/ HUNG	Fertö- Neuseidler Lake			+	+	+		+		+			+	+	Wl
	950	MADAG	Ambohimanga		+	+				+		+					
	1044	SP	Aranjuez	+	+	+	+	+		+					+	+	Wi/Wl/Wr
	1046	PORT	Alto Douro	+	+	+	+			+		+			+	+	Wi/Wl
2002	1063	HUNG	Tokaj		+	+	+			+		+		+	+		
	1066	GERM	Middle Rhine	+	+	+	+			+		+	+	+	+	+	Wr
2003	208	AFGHANIS	Bamiyan	+		+	+			+	+	+	+	+	+		Wi
	306	ZIMBABWE	Matobo	+	+					+	+		+				Ra
	925	INDIA	Bhimbetka	+	+					+	+		+				Jf, Ra
	1068	ITALY	Sacri Monti	+	+						+		+				Jf
	1084	UK	Kew		+	+		+								+	Wi
	1099	S AFRICA	Mapungubwe				+			+			+				
Total 36		25	36	21	24	24	20	11	2	21	17	16	15	15	24	21	Jf–7 Ra–3 Wi–9 Wl–7 Wr–8 Ws–5

Year	No.	State	Name	A	B	C	F	G	I	L	M	P	R	S	T	W	Other
				21	24	24	20	11	2	21	17	16	15	15	24	21	

182

The characteristics of World Heritage cultural landscapes: discussion of Table 9

The definitions attached to letters A–W in the Key to Table 9 indicate the emergence of certain trends, and how, by 2003, World Heritage cultural landscapes are beginning to define themselves. Negatively, I have dropped one column, N, from this version of Table 9 compared to earlier published versions of it (Fowler 2003a, and 2003b, Table 7) since whether a World Heritage cultural landscape is or is not a National Park is a management issue rather than a defining characteristic. In any case, information on the point is defective and furthermore, by definition all World Heritage sites have to be protected by some form of national provision and many cultural landscapes in particular are also covered, in part at least, by one or more international designations e.g. by another UNESCO programme involving Man and the Biosphere areas. Nevertheless, there is an area of fact-finding here which would be worth pursuing.

On the positive side, the analysis brings out some points clearly. The four natural criteria, for example, were only used in the first five years of inscription. The six cultural criteria are used in three clumps of numbers: criteria (i) and (vi), as expected and intended, minimally on only three and seven occasions respectively, criteria (ii), (iii) and (v) in the mid-'teens (respectively 15, 18 and 16 times), and criterion (iv) almost twice as many times as them (29) and four times as often as criterion (vi). In large part this reflects the 18 category 2b landscapes (Table 8).

The most common characteristic is the presence of towns and villages within the designated area. This may be a surprise. Cultural landscapes are clearly not so far mainly about the world's wildernesses. Perhaps more than expected, cultural landscapes are often about living people as much as living landscapes; they may sometimes be remote but in general they are not deserted places. They are characteristically areas where people are continuing to try to gain a livelihood.

Sometimes that involves managing water. Water (Plate 1), and a variety of its manifestations, is characteristic: as sea, as river(s), as waterfalls, as lake(s), natural and artificial, and in some managed form, usually irrigation (Figure 50) and sometimes as a food source. It is present naturally but managed to aesthetic and functional ends at Sintra with its sub-tropical vegetation, and supremely so at Aranjuez, Spain, where the River Tagus has itself been modified. Water is used decoratively and more formally in great ornamental landscapes, most of which on the World Heritage List are not officially cultural landscapes but notably in the one which is, The Garden Kingdom of Dessau-Wörlitz, Germany (Figure 23). There, however, it found itself truly under water in August 2002. Water is or was often used, in cultural landscapes as elsewhere, for transport and delight, as along the Loire for example (Figures 43, 36). It, and particularly the sea, is also significantly present environmentally, at Portovenere (Figure 15) on the north western Italian coast, for

FIGURE 50.
The waters of the
Minjiiang River are
controlled by the
Dujiangyan irrigation
system, part of a World
Heritage site with
Mount Qingcheng,
China, which began to
be constructed in the
third century BC.

example, and menacingly along the Curonian Spit on the borders of Lithuania and Russia.

Water has not so far emerged, however, as particularly significant in a religious or sacred sense in cultural landscapes; but religiosity itself has begun to appear strongly as a feature of cultural landscapes (Rössler 2000Ib). Its presence is unambiguous at Tongariro, Uluṟu, Kalwaria, Poland, and Sukur, Nigeria, and such is the strength and flexibility of the World Heritage concept, that the same bureaucratic device can as readily embrace the great abbey at Melk in the Wachau landscape and the resonantly Biblical cedars of Lebanon at Horsh Arz el-Rab, the Bamiyan valley, the Rock Shelters of Bhimbetka, India, and the Matobo Hills of Zimbabwe.

Another topographical feature emerging as not uncommon is a mountain. Seventeen Sites claim a mountain, or mountains, as significant. The range includes a holy mountain at Mont Perdu, an outcrop mountain with rock art in the desert at Uluṟu, and another oddity in the mountain above Hallstatt village, made of rock-salt, mined since the Bronze Age and constantly changing shape within (Plate 5; Figures 7, 14, 25, 50, 55).

Continuity itself has also already appeared as a recurring factor, both as a lifeway and a form of landuse. It is present in 23 of the 36 Sites. There is obviously a cross-link here with criterion (v), a criterion looking for traditional human settlement or land-use and used in thirteen of the inscriptions. This heavy embryonic emphasis on continuity and tradition in landscape and lifeway is good in the sense that, apart from anything else, attention is being drawn to places and peoples of considerable scientific and historic interest. Such places might well also be good examples of Phillips' (1995, 381) 'living models of sustainable use of land and natural resources.' Such models need not be in easy places to live: difficult landscapes exist, both on and outside the World Heritage List, and one of their repetitive but admirable qualities is that, almost by definition, they show environmental and technological adaptability e.g. in the High Atlas of Morocco (Figures 51 and 52). On the other hand, particularly where life is not quite so markedly on the margins, sustainability can become a matter of traditional routine and almost unthinking manual application, with the social culture fossilizing around the precept of 'Nothing must change'. It would surely be undesirable for the World Heritage List to become the refuge of only conservative societies and a shrine to landscapes of inertia. There must be room for innovation and change too, for disruption as well as continuity; they too are 'good' and have their place in any world-wide selection of cultural landscapes expressing the human experience.

FIGURE 51.
Telouèt and its irrigated valley in winter in the High Atlas, Morocco.

Aesthetics were also showing as an important element by 2003. Nor is this dimension confined to landscapes like Lednice-Valtice where an aesthetic effect was deliberately sought, as category (i) allows; the aesthetic of the unintentional is as marked in the laborious landscapes of the Cordilleras rice terraces (Plate 33) and among the port-producing terraces of the Alto Douro in Portugal (Figure 27). What has not happened, however, is for the portfolio of cultural landscapes to become dominated by sites of category (i). That might have happened given the obviousness of parks and gardens in the European heritage, their widespread influence beyond Europe, and the desire to organise landscape systematically in other cultural traditions (Plate 2; Figures 35, 36) Furthermore, there is a strong aesthetic, architectural and art historical point of view within the conservation world. So far, such parks and gardens with their palaces have tended to continue being nominated in modes other than cultural landscapes, with only five of the Sites in Table 8 being in category (i) in their own right as designed landscapes.

FIGURE 52.
Irrigated fields in the valley of the Asif Mellah through the High Atlas, Morocco.

A wider view

Table 10 here is a small extract from Fowler 2003b, Table 8. Looking at the whole list, the number of potential cultural landscapes not nominated for cultural landscape status in the twenty years 1972–92 (when it was not an option) more than doubled in the decade 1992–2002 (when it was). Twenty six of the 36 formal CLs were nominated as cultural landscapes; 10 were not. Seventy seven of the 100 possible cultural landscapes were not put forward as cultural landscapes in the period 1993–2002. These figures suggest that the cultural landscape category, far from being a liberating mechanism, has actually been avoided. Particularly striking is the case of China (Figure 50) but even in Europe, with 51 possible cultural landscape nominations in the decade, 30 were not put forward as cultural landscapes.

Table 10. Cultural landscapes on the World Heritage List: properties identified in Europe as a sample of the whole. Properties in bold are official World Heritage cultural landscapes.

UNESCO region	State Party	Site (short name)	Year inscribed	CL Category
Europe	Netherlands	Schokland	1995	2b
		Kinderdijk	1997	2b
		Beemster Polder	1999	2b
	Poland	**Kalwaria**	1999	3
	Portugal	**Sintra**	1995	1
		Alto Douro	2001	2b
	Spain	Granada	1994	1
		Santiago Route	1993	2b
		Las Médulas	1997	2a
		Elche	2000	2b
		Aranjuez	2001	1
	Sweden	Drottningholm	1991	1
		Tanum	1994	2a
		Skogskyrkogarden	1994	1
		Laponian Area	1996	2b
		Southern Öland	2000	2b

Perhaps this reluctance to use the category has something to do with a perception that it is more challenging to put together a successful World Heritage cultural landscape nomination dossier than one for an 'ordinary' cultural or natural site. When both natural and cultural values are obviously involved, it may well seem easier to go for a 'mixed site'. The latter is certainly not the case, for in it both sets of values have to be 'of outstanding universal value'; but it may well be the case that, at least intellectually, a successful nomination of a cultural landscape is indeed challenging.

Analysis of the whole tabulation of cultural landscapes, actual or potential, on the World Heritage List produces the following figures:

Table 11. Analysis of the first tabulation of potential cultural landscapes on the World Heritage List (to June 2002).

UNESCO region	State Party	Cultural landscapes	Inscription period	CL Category
5	43	100	1978–2002	1: 25 sites
				2a: 23 sites
				2b: 35 sites
				3: 17 sites

Only 30 of these 100 sites have been officially inscribed as cultural landscapes, and only 17 of them seem to qualify for category 3. For whatever reason, then, in a numerical sense the Committee's and originators' hopes for the popular success of the cultural landscape concept as a mechanism for the inscription on the World Heritage List of sites of a non-monumental nature were not realised in its first decade.

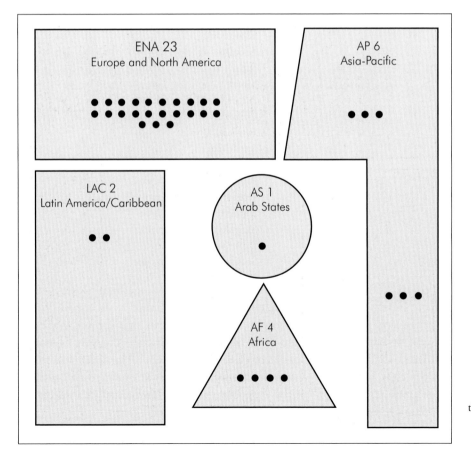

FIGURE 53. Map: global distribution of the thirty-six official World Heritage cultural landscapes.

Reviewing the
Achievement:
World Heritage
Cultural
Landscapes,
1992–2003

Distribution

The geographical distribution of official cultural landscapes, 65 per cent in Europe, 35 per cent in the rest of the world, mirrors the lop-sided distribution of Sites on the World Heritage List as a whole (Rössler 2001a) (Figures 53 and 54). The idea of cultural landscape of itself is not, it would already appear, going to change that numerical unevenness. The hope was and is that the existence of this type of Site will encourage nominations from parts of the world which express their culture in ways other than the 'monumentality' towards which the Convention is itself unconsciously biased. Yet, though the 10 possible cultural landscapes identified here in China represent a very welcome florescence of the phenomenon in the East, the fact is that China did not, presumably deliberately, nominate them as cultural landscapes. Meanwhile, in the West, in addition to leading the field with officially-recognised cultural landscapes (Table 2), France, Germany, Italy, Spain, Sweden and the UK apparently contain 40 (= 40%) of my unofficial list of potential cultural landscapes already on the World Heritage List.

The two schematic distribution maps are based on the five UNESCO regions by which World Heritage is administered (ENA: Europe and North

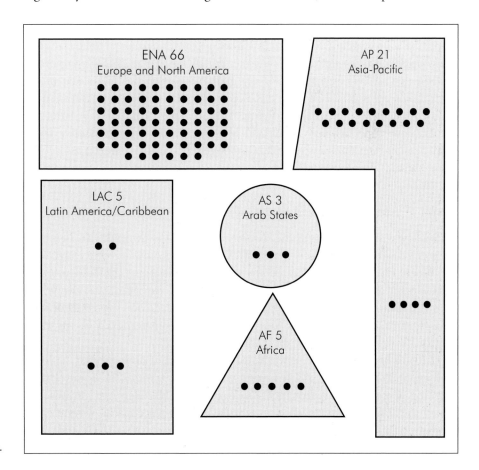

FIGURE 54.
Map: global
distribution of 100
potential cultural
landscapes on the
World Heritage List.

America; LAC: Latin America and the Caribbean; AP: Asia and the Pacific; AS: the Arab States; Af: Africa). Figure 53 shows the distribution of the thirty six official World Heritage cultural landscapes as at 3 July, 2003. They are clustered heavily in Europe (23 out of 36 = 64%), with the remaining 13 (36%) scattered as 2 in LAC (both in Cuba), 6 in AP, 1 in AS and 4 in Africa (2 inscribed 2001, 2 in 2003). Clearly the geographical impact is negligible except in (largely western) Europe, though the thin scatter elsewhere does not at all represent the impact of the *idea* of cultural landscape world-wide.

Figure 54 takes into account the other 70 possible cultural landscapes on the World Heritage List as it was in June 2002 when the analysis was done. It heavily reinforces Europe's predominance (66 out of 100), though in percentage terms (66 per cent) Europe's share has fallen from earlier times and in 2003 continues to do so. This is, however, mainly because the 2002 list of 100 possible sites incorporates a rise from nil to 13 sites in the Sino-Japanese area of the Asia-Pacific Region, the only major change in the map distributionally compared to Figure 53.

All bar one of the Chinese sites on Figure 54 have been inscribed since 1992, and not a single one of them is on the official list of World Heritage cultural landscapes. This remains true in 2003 when another natural site with an historic human presence was inscribed (Chapter 2). Yet without exception the Chinese landscapes on the '100' list are clear-cut World Heritage cultural landscapes by any standards, most as category 1 (gardens/parks; Table 4). Their presence makes a considerable difference, not so much numerically, important though that is, but as distributionally giving due recognition to one of the outstanding areas of the world for the creation of man-made landscapes interacting with nature in spiritual mode. Some of the point of inventing the cultural landscape category for World Heritage purposes is obviated without such outstanding landscapes on the list of official cultural landscapes as well as the World Heritage List.

World Heritage and cultural landscapes: Tentative Lists as indicators

Another way of approaching the future in this field is through the Tentative Lists of possible nominations which all States Parties now have to lodge with the World Heritage Centre before any of their nominations can be considered (Titchen and Rössler 1995). Three electronic searches carried out on the World Heritage Centre Database of Tentative Lists produced four tables: three with data from the searches, and a fourth listing each site retrieved in the three previous searches (Fowler 2003b, Tables 10–13).

The purpose of the exercise was to gain some idea of how strongly 'cultural landscape' as a concept was featuring in the preparations of States Parties thinking about future nominations to the World Heritage List. It was also hoped to gain some figures which might be used, in the context of the Global Strategy, to estimate the number and location of potential cultural landscapes which could be coming forward in, say, the next decade. The data-base was interrogated with three different questions but of course the data behind the analyses were incomplete, in part inaccurate and not necessarily up-to-date (*see* Fowler 2003b, Table 13). All the same, from them it was possible to identify 174 properties from 58 States Parties.

These numbers would suggest that over, say, the decade 2003–2012, some two hundred nominations of properties which are, or contain, cultural landscapes is very probably the maximum that can be conceived. My suggestion would be that in reality something like *c.* 75 official cultural landscapes will be inscribed over the next decade or so. That 6 were inscribed in 2003 after making these calculations is spot on! The actual number of cultural landscapes on the World Heritage List, extrapolating from the data here on top of the hundred such properties already on it and including the *c.* 75 official ones already predicted, is therefore likely to be above two hundred well before the first two decades of the twenty-first century have passed.

CHAPTER 12

'A Noble, Global Concept'?

Whatever individual countries have in mind for the future, it is important that we are clear what, collectively, we are doing. Either we leave the future of cultural landscapes to individual, political choice and see what we end up with; or at least some central encouragement can be looked for to take their future in particular directions. The roles of the World Heritage Committee and the World Heritage Centre are clearly crucial here, and it is to be hoped that their thinking and actions will continue to develop along the strategic lines already in evidence.

Thematic and comparative studies

Strategically, it would be appropriate if the idea behind the 'targeting' of European wine-producing areas could be extended to other major world culinary products. We all depend, after all, on food and drink, so the 'universal significance' of such potential cultural landscapes cannot be in much doubt; and in many parts of the world academic studies of ethnographic and agrarian matters exist which can give pointers to the significance in such landscapes. Another drink already represented on the List is coffee, underpinning the cultural landscape of Cuban plantations. Almost certainly there ought to be an equivalent nomination of an outstanding 'tea cultural landscape'. But which one or ones?

Evaluation of nominations has already become increasingly difficult where no comparative study exists; conversely, evaluation is significantly improved where a comparative study has already been carried out, whether at local, state, regional or global level. The outstanding need is for a comparative study of agricultural landscapes, ideally worldwide and synchronously; but certainly to include Europe at an early stage. This would be not because Europe is more important than other places but because it enjoys an extraordinary variety of farmed landscapes. It is in no-one's interest to encourage nominations of, let alone inscribe as of 'outstanding universal value', an endless repetition of European 'agrarian' cultural landscapes. The point has already been raised by consideration of Vall de Boí (Chapter 9; recommendations to address the issue are in both Cleere 2003 and Fowler 2003b).

Probably the best way of tackling the issue further afield is also on a continental or regional basis since, after all, the world is full of farming landscapes. Selecting from them for World Heritage purposes is a considerable task and

FIGURE 55. Modern terraces constructed over a recent lava flow on the slopes of Mount Etna, Sicily.

systematic, academic study on a geographical basis without prejudice to what States Parties may already have in mind would in the long run be a sound way of proceeding.

Another thematic approach, already implicit in what has been inscribed, is that of the 'functional landscape'. Blaenavon, Falun and the Derwent valley are industrial landscapes. Öland and the Cuban plantations were working agricultural landscapes; Amalfitana, Cinque Terre (in part anyway), the Cordilleras, the Douro valley, the Loire valley and Wachau still are. Some refinement of such broad functional categories is required to prevent endless repetition of similar 'industrial' and 'agrarian' cultural landscapes. It is also desirable to provide some pointers as to whether development of the World Heritage List of such landscapes is to be, without being exclusively so, in particular directions. We have mentioned the 'functional' approach, which can also be applied in subdivisions of 'agrarian', as in wine-growing, rice-growing and pasture. Pointers could favour, or otherwise, other directions such as

FIGURE 56.
Parallel, axial walls,
with short cross-walls,
forming small
rectangular plots in
which to grow vines in
cracks in the solid lava
on Pico, Azores,
Portugal.

'scientific' e.g. geomorphological, as with the Val d'Orcia where the landscape is on a particular geomorphological subsoil; as at Alto Douro where the cultivated soil is created from schist; or as in Sicily (Figure 55), and the Azores (Figure 56) and Hawaii Island where farming is carried out on recent soils in volcanic areas. Alternatively, should the assemblage of cultural landscapes be seeking to cover a world range of geographical/topographical variety e.g. montane pasture, as at Mont Perdu (Plate 7; Figures 12, 13), or flooded valley, as along the Loire (Plate 10)? If so, does it matter if one such variety is on the List as a Site but not a cultural landscape e.g. reclaimed wetlands, as at Schokland, The Netherlands?

Thematic studies could also be used to *anticipate* and *encourage* new nominations. In thinking about this sort of strategic approach, one significant theme which might be considered is provided by the world's staple food crops. World Heritage cultural landscapes already represent montane rice-growing in the Cordilleras (Plate 3); a lowland equivalent, with flat paddy-fields counterbalancing steep terraces, is needed. And so too, along this line of thought, would be outstanding examples of landscapes producing potatoes (South America? Ireland?), yam (central Africa?), maize (terraces in the Andes?),

FIGURE 57.
Taro planted in a plot
in an irrigated system
of paddy fields on
Kauai, Hawaiian
Islands, USA.

cereals (Russian Federation? central Canada/USA?) and taro (south east Asia? Hawaii? Figure 57).

With critical parts of the human diet also coming from domesticated animals, other landscapes which might be sought could include a 'sheepscape' (Figures 5, 30, 40, 58) (New Zealand? The Cévennes, Cheviot, UK), a non-European (Hortobagy, Hungary, is already inscribed), animal-grazed extensive landscape as on the steppes of Asia (the Orkhon valley, Mongolia (Figure 59), was nominated for 2003), and a cattle-ranching landscape (Argentina? USA?). A 'fishing landscape' or a 'cultural seascape' might be more difficult to define on the ground and in water but it can be done (Plate 15; Figure 60) – and indeed at least one is part of a cultural landscape, the Po Delta in north eastern Italy, added to the existing World Heritage site of Ferrara (Figure 38).

Whatever emerges as responses to such theoretical but real issues, a very practical matter is already with the concept of World Heritage early in the twenty-first century. What should we do about the twentieth century, which already seems in another age? World Heritage already contains some outstanding examples of earlier twentieth century architecture, notably in modernist mode, and it is now considering 'post-modernist architecture.'

Cultural landscape has the same challenge: what can we already identify as significant in landscape terms from the twentieth century? 'Landscapes of nuclear power' is one clear answer among several others which might well include 'communications landscapes', 'landscapes of the war dead' and 'landscapes of exploration'. The last might well include an example from one of humanity's last terrestial frontiers, Antarctica, a continent – the only one – currently with no World Heritage Site at all.

Another awkward issue, especially for landscape, is war. We have recently witnessed the direct relationship between fighting and heritage looting, between war and historic landscape, in Iraq. In a broader perspective, we can already see that truly global warfare was one of the significant features of the twentieth century, and significant battlefields and their cemeteries must in due course come into consideration as World Heritage landscapes. Sadly, there are plenty of candidates, even though my priority here is landscape, not just a place where a perhaps militarily significant encounter occurred. In a west European's eyes, fairly obvious war landscapes exist in northern France but other perspectives will suggest equivalent places elsewhere. World Heritage will come to be diminished if it does not develop sufficiently robustly to take such matters aboard – after all, it does so already for the nineteenth and eighteenth centuries, and earlier, in the way of fortifications, urban defences and naval ports e.g. the Dacian fortresses of the Orastie Mountains, Romania, the naval

FIGURE 58.
The Cévennes National Park, France, began to organize an annual transhumance festival in the 1990s, in memory of local tradition and as a tourist attraction, about a generation after the practice died out in terms of huge numbers of sheep walking up from the Mediterranean to montane pastures in late May/June (they now travel in lorries). Here a large and colourful flock symbolically leaves Esperou during the 2001 festival.

port of Karlskrona, Sweden and the Defence Line of Amsterdam, The Netherlands. The World Heritage Defences of Amsterdam were started somewhat tardily around 1890 as a Dutch response to one of the obvious lessons for The Netherlands of the Franco-German war of 1870–71. Although they proved redundant in the First World War, 1914–18, they were used in the Second (by the Germans!) and remained in part in commission until the later twentieth century. So they are not exactly very ancient. They provide a useful precedent, even if they should have been recognised as a cultural landscape upon inscription, for potential World Heritage sites which are military, recent and unpretty. The centenary of the First World War will be with us before long and it is important that the concept of World Heritage is strong enough, and ready with practical arrangements, to take aboard a few appropriate sites and landscapes.

FIGURE 59.
Erdene Zuu monastery in the Orkhon valley surrounded by the steppic landscape of Mongolia, a type of landscape over a huge area of the world's surface not yet adequately represented on the World Heritage List.

The fort illustrated here, Fort Nigtevecht (Figures 61 and 62), south east of Amsterdam, almost incidentally touches on three other contemporary and significant aspects of World Heritage early in the twenty-first century. They are emphasised by the somewhat grim purpose and present aspect of what might well be regarded merely as bits of modern dereliction. In the first place, as I was assured by the Mayor, the fort really is regarded as 'heritage' by the local community: they regard it as 'theirs', they are proud of it, and they certainly want to see it preserved. Such are of course common and admirable feelings about local heritage, but the military nature of the 'heritage' in this

case, frankly not very attractive in itself and unconvincingly 'of universal value', led me to ask the questions which produced these positive answers. Secondly, although it is proving difficult to maintain the many kilometres of earthwork and other defences between the forts, elements of the Defence Lines, and particularly some forts, attract the attention of bodies prepared to fund conservation work. This is particularly so where this can involve the care and effort of volunteers, notably on the artificial island of Pampus in the Zuyder Zee where they have first sensibly made the place habitable – and hospitable – again in order to address the very considerable challenges of maintenance and restoration. Fort Nigtevecht itself is now the centre of a successful social inclusion and skills development scheme for unemployed young people. They have made the place usable once more, if not for military purposes then at least as a work-base and as a show-case for the Defence Line of Amsterdam. It provides an example of heritage re-cycled in a way which is acceptable, dynamic and socially useful.

Religion is in some respects similar to war as one of the world's great themes expressed in terms of monuments, ruins and landscapes. The great world religions have largely come to be represented on the World Heritage List by an architectural approach so far. Cleere (2003, 2.1.1.9), however, considers 'Religious Properties' as a category 'based on function'. Three aspects of this field need to be considered further. Does the List adequately represent the rich

FIGURE 60.
Forming a unity prompting thoughts about the possibility of a 'cultural seascape', Cabrits Fort, Dominica, overlooks Portsmouth and its bay where many ships rested after early transatlantic crossings to obtain fresh water at a place which changed hands between France, Spain and Britain several times in the seventeenth–nineteenth centuries.

FIGURE 61.
Disguised as a natural knoll, the late 19th century Fort Nigtevecht is buried in the top of this rise above wetland beside the Rhine canal, part of the World Heritage site of the Defence Line of Amsterdam, The Netherlands.

FIGURE 62.
A loaded canal boat marks the line of the canal as viewed from the fort lookout, just visible on the top of the mound in Figure 61, at Fort Nigtevecht, Defence Line of Amsterdam, The Netherlands.

diversity of religious belief in the world, past and present? Is the range of sites, monuments and places associated with at least the main religions adequately represented (as distinct from yet more monasteries, temples and the like)? And are we adequately searching out the great religious landscapes of the world, irrespective of architectural mass and regardless of particular creeds? Tongariro, New Zealand (Plate 1), set the standard for a deeply religious, but entirely non-monumental, landscape; Uluru followed (Plate 5). There should be a select number of other such landscapes and their variants – some in China are on the longer list – and both the concept and mechanism of cultural landscape should encourage people to think positively and boldly about religion in land-scape terms. Mountains and water – often key components of sacred landscapes – come in here.

Another issue directly concerns heritage – the initial concern of the Convention – and small communities of people as 'survivors', an aspect of heritage which was not embraced by the Convention's original concept. It was emphasised by the nomination and consideration in 2001 of the Central Sikhote-Alin region in the far east of the Russian Federation (Chapter 9). The need is apparently to consider in a global perspective whether or not 'preserving' small, essentially non-Westernized indigenous populations in their 'natural' habitats is the proper business of the World Heritage Convention. Given that it was devised to protect natural and artefactual heritage, including landscape, it would be a significant move were emphasis to shift to people too. The celebratory 30 years of World Heritage Conference at Venice, November, 2002, witnessed a palpable movement in this direction. The World Heritage Committee knows in any case that the best way at most properties to secure the future of that which we wish to maintain is to involve the residents and other local people and organisations. Conversely, it would follow in many case logically that if we sustain the people first – something which many would in any case regard as the priority – then we have secured the best means of main-taining the heritage which we wish to perpetuate. That applies particularly to landscape (as exemplified at the places illustrated in Figures 7, 8, 15, 22, 25, 26, 27, 32, 38, 41, 56, 61).

Landscape and World Heritage

One of the most important long-term benefits of the inclusion of cultural landscapes under the World Heritage Convention is that it should help promote everywhere greater awareness of landscape issues generally, and of cultural landscapes in particular. And, though the task is never-ending, that is happening.

'Cultural landscape' is a phrase characteristically used to mean 'rural land-scape'. This is a particularly World Heritage concept, and a narrow one, for it seemingly excludes *urban* landscape. In fact, many a real-world cultural landscape contains whole or significant extents of urban settlement. Towns are indeed a marked characteristic of World Heritage cultural landscapes in

FIGURE 63. Relict industrial landscape created by Roman gold-mining at the World Heritage site of Las Médulas, Spain.

practice (Plates 8, 10; Figures 10, 14, 26, 42), so the apparent World Heritage stance of excluding urbanscape from cultural landscape is logically unsustainable. Furthermore, different ideas of 'city' and 'town' exist in different cultures; the Western concept of *urbanitas*, deriving from Mediterranean models in the Classical cultures of Greece and Rome, is indeed now widespread but does not everywhere prevail. Many a 'city' in Africa, for example, would not qualify as such within that Western concept, but who is to say that it is not indeed a 'city'? Equally, the 'city' of the desert nomad is not quite the same settlement form as Tokio or Detroit (though if you want to see a minimalist American 'city', try Everglades City, Florida). Furthermore, theoretically an urban landscape can be *par excellence* a cultural landscape. Indeed, arguably cultural landscape is at its most sophisticated in certain cityscapes e.g. the historic centres of Rome and Paris, and downtown New York – all, be it noted, closely related to water. In ecological terms, as I understand them, these cities are the climax at the end of a succession. The concept of World Heritage cultural landscape ought to explore the idea of natural climax in its consideration of cultural affairs, and allow, if only in the interests of its own credibility, the inclusion of urban landscapes, not just within cultural landscapes but as cultural landscape.

Similarly, industrial landscape, the idea and the reality, should be

encouraged as worthy of World Heritage status (Figure 63). Agreed, redundant industrial structures tend to be removed from sight as well as site; and in potential World Heritage cultural landscapes, in industrial properties as with rural, a range of features as well as good integrity is to be looked for. So one or more of such features as rail- or wagon-ways, canals, waste-disposal areas, specialist buildings for functions, equipment and workers, community housing and other social features could be expected in a meaningful pattern, ideally representing an industrial process. Falun, Sweden, is a good example of all that, yet it was not accepted as a World Heritage cultural landscape. Its inscription as a 'technological ensemble' seems rather to have missed the point – the point so pertinently taken at Blaenavon (Figure 26)

Several other topics of potential World Heritage interest might also well be expressed through cultural landscapes. Associations of a commercial nature, for example, almost invariably with cultural connotations, as in trade, are already touched on in the World Heritage List by including some individual towns in northern Europe's medieval Hanseatic League. This idea could be systematised and enlarged into cohesive, serial nominations of urban/hinterland/marine and island components to make up significant cultural landscapes. Indian/East African associations in this domain come to mind. Similarly, the idea of migration is surely one of undoubted 'outstanding universal interest'. One example

FIGURE 64. Representative of the potential outstanding cultural landscapes of South America, the canyon of the upper Pinturas River, Argentina, has been occupied since the ninth millennium BC and is the setting for the Cueva de las Manos where a suite of rock art expresses an intimate relationship with nature.

FIGURE 65.
Superimposed hand
stencils some five
thousand years old in
the Cueva de las
Manos, Alto Rio
Pinturas Area,
Argentina.

on a vast scale where it might be possible to assemble a 'landscape' of journeys, islands and landfalls interacting with nature in a long time-frame could be the peopling of Oceania from south east Asia. The peopling of the (pre-European) Americas is a similar broad-based, interdisciplinary idea on the grand landscape scale of the sort which World Heritage probably needs if it is to expand in the twenty-first century to become part of global consciousness rather than continuing primarily in nationalistic mode.

The military theme could also be expanded intellectually and spatially: one could envisage a 'campaign cultural landscape' following the route of a decisive military campaign or of a great war-leader like Alexander the Great in south west Asia in the fourth century BC, showing how natural factors influenced his campaign and how the great leader responded. Identified with similar discrimination, the landscapes of a few great writers and artists might also be considered, either the landscapes that inspired them or which they delineated, or the landscapes through which they passed on their 'quest' or travels, whatever they were. 'Classic' journeys like that of Robert Louis Stephenson and his donkey through the French Cévennes in the nineteenth century might be considered, as might associations between artist and particular landscapes as with Huang Gongwang and the Yuan landscape, China, in the late thirteenth–early fourteenth centuries.

In a way, however, such suggestions are but sub-sets of the grander concept of 'landscapes of ideas' (Figures 64, 65), a move onwards from 'sites with ideology' like the Hiroshima Peace Memorial, Japan, and Robben Island, South Africa. Ideas as such, however, already also underpin official cultural landscapes at religious landscapes e.g. Vat Phou, Laos (Hinduism), and Ambohimanga, Madagascar ('ancestor worship'). Several cultural landscapes on the World Heritage List are also based on, or strongly embody, abstract ideas, not just religious but ones such as 'royalty' (Kasubi, Uganda), 'solitude' (Skellig Michael, Ireland), 'aesthetics' (Mount Lushan, China) and 'human evolution' (Willandra Lakes Region, Australia; *cf.* Charles Darwin's house in London, Down House, itself of limited architectural interest, on the UK Tentative List in recognition of the fundamental ideas about evolution which were thought, researched and written inside it).

It may at first seem difficult to bring together the tangibility of landscape – earth and rock and water – with the intangibility of an abstract idea, but those examples indicate that it can be done. They suggest, moreover, that a more conscious approach to such juxtaposition, and embracing the concept of 'cultural landscape', could probably generate some innovative, stimulating additions to the World Heritage List. After all, the very words 'cultural land-scape' and 'World Heritage' are themselves mental constructs, differently construed by different cultures, through time and around the world. So, merely by identifying 'cultural landscapes', and in the case of World Heritage ones recognising in them qualifying 'values', we are in practice already bringing together the conceptual and the tangible.

'Associative landscapes' (category 3) was created precisely to give the freedom to think of 'landscapes of ideas', a concept which has been widely welcomed in regional expert meetings, in Africa for example. But it is a concept for all cultures, one within which to recognise that alongside the world of things there are worlds of ideas from oral traditions, folklore, art, dance and music, and thinkers, talkers, writers and poets. It is furthermore a concept which can in a very practical way, as the last decade has shown, stim-ulate international co-operation, local effort, better environmental understanding and wiser landscape management. We should be thankful that in cultural landscapes we have a wonderful idea, one whose memorable days as World Heritage lie in the future.

In practice World Heritage cultural landscapes have now begun to define themselves collectively (Chapter 11). They are characterised by, geographically, mountains, water, inhabited settlements and farming, and, intellectually, by historical and/or cultural significance, continuity and tradition, religiosity and aesthetics. Not all, of course, possess every one of those characteristics but all of them possess some of them, in different combinations. Only time will tell whether the first sample of 36 official cases has gone a long way towards defining the *genre* or whether early enthusiasm in bringing forward some ready-made nominations has biased the apparent nature of the phenomenon at this stage. A guess would suggest that the inscription of cultural landscapes is likely to have risen towards a hundred in the early years of the second decade of the twenty-first century, so the above list of characteristics can be both monitored and soon tested against a larger sample. Meanwhile, the proposal has been made that in fact there are about 100 cultural landscapes on the World Heritage List anyway (Chapter 11).

One increasingly reliable way of checking what is likely to be coming forward is the Tentative List (Chapter 10). It is a useful way of encouraging State Parties to be thinking seriously about the nominations they are likely to be making in future, and on what time-scale. From the World Heritage and cultural landscape point of view it is encouraging to know that several sites from sub-Saharan Africa are in mind, for example, Olduvai, Tanzania, and the former centre of the Monomotapa empire in northern Zimbabwe. The idea of the linear cultural landscape, already expressed in Europe in the pilgrimage route to Santiago de Compostella in north west Spain, is also being explored in Benin with a view to nominating the Slave Route of Abomey, a 117 km. road to the sea which 'totally integrates the historic memory of the slave trade in Benin. Its conservation is necessary for the safeguarding of the collective memory of humanity.' (Bocco 2000, 74). Among nominations to be considered in 2004 are 'The incense and spice road and the desert cities in the Negev', Israel, and, sounding very much like an example of the sort we have had in mind through this discussion, 'Sacred sites and pilgrimage routes in the Kii Mountain range, and the cultural landscapes that surround them.'

The preceding paragraphs have had to isolate topics and types of site and landscape in order to discuss aspects of World Heritage which could well come to official or academic attention. It is absolutely crucial, however, for those involved in such matters in an official or academic capacity to remember that such categorisations are merely tools to do a job. They do not represent the way in which most other people see the landscape or the historic environment. In general they see it as a totality, not divided up into such as buildings, archaeology, geology, woodland, urban sites and religious landscapes.

In truth, since we have to look after those identified as 'of universal value', we already have enough challenging landscapes and their issues to deal with without straying too far off-site. Two must suffice as examples, both already touched on earlier but mentioned again here. One is the ethical issue of whether we collectively through UNESCO, an international organisation working through the World Heritage *Convention*, for heritage reasons have in the last resort the right to inhibit, even prevent, 'normal' economic development – like acquiring basic facilities of water, electricity and hygiene – in archaic landscapes with communities living in undeveloped circumstances. The rice-growing montane communities of the Cordilleras in Luzon, the Philippines, is one apt and serious case in mind. The answer must be 'no' in principle, though in practice fortunately the issue may not be quite so clear-cut. We can, however, consider a range of economic and social strategies which may not necessarily impair the heritage interests.

This is also true in the second example where again, but even more so, the issue is now very much about people and not, in the first place, their material culture. We briefly discussed some aspects of the of the Central Sikhote-Alin region in the far east of the Russian Federation in Chapter 9. It contains a small population of hunter-gatherer people whose activities exploit the natural environment in a sustainable way and simultaneously have a significant effect upon flora and fauna. In this case the Udege characteristically live in a non-agricultural, or non-mechanized agricultural, economy within a significantly non-monumental lifestyle with minimal material culture. Other inscribed areas illustrate the same point: the inscriptions of the Three Parallel Rivers, China, and the Uvs Nuur Basin, Mongolia/Russian Federation, are recent examples. They all point to the need to consider in a global perspective, not whether to conserve 'Nature', a very proper and well-established activity, but whether or not 'preserving' our own species, characteristically as small, essentially non-Westernized indigenous populations in their 'natural' habitats, is the proper business of those implementing the World Heritage Convention. Whatever the debate, the continuance of the indigenous way of life is in the Central Sikhote-Alin case now under severe threat, both because of the small size of the population and because of external influences.

Given that the *Convention* was devised to protect natural and artefactual heritage, including landscape, it is, as the Venice Congress signalled, a significant move to place people at the centre of the heritage concern too. Not before time: one of the major lessons learnt from cultural landscapes as well as ordinary World Heritage Sites is that the best way in most cases to secure the future of that which we wish to maintain is to involve the residents. Conversely, it would follow in many case logically that if the people are sustained then, quite apart from humanitarian considerations, we have secured the best means of maintaining the heritage values which we wish to look after; but of course, important though that point is, our cultural heritage now equally embraces the 'software' of people and their intangibles as well as the 'hardware' of the monuments. That applies particularly to landscape, where both people and place exist and relate and develop symbiotically. Sikhote-Alin epitomises this.

Landscape designation stimulates thought, not least about the concept of World Heritage itself. Ideas about landscapes, on the World Heritage List or not, will continue to bubble up, reflecting personality, change and time. The way cultural landscapes are assessed for World Heritage purposes, in preparing the nomination, in evaluating the nomination and in managing the landscape thereafter, will have repercussions far beyond the hundred or so World Heritage cultural landscapes that can be envisaged as emerging in the early part of the twenty-first century. For one thing, 'A cultural landscape perspective explicitly recognizes the history of a place and its cultural traditions in additions to its ecological value' (Mitchell and Buggy 2000, 45) – a most valuable point to remember for anyone involved with landscape study, management and development. Even if God put it there in the first place, it has been modified to at least some extent, and of course often significantly, by human beings. It is far better in practice to start with an assumption that there is no such thing as 'pristine landscape', let alone 'pristine Nature'. 'There is nothing there' is in effect an inconceivable conclusion to expect from a serious examination of any area of land. Something will have happened there previously – in some sense there will be a history – and evidence of that 'something' may well be detectable, in the plant life quite as much as in archaeological evidence or documentation.

There may still be people there too, as is the case in every World Heritage cultural landscape so far. 'A landscape perspective also recognizes the continuity between the past and with people living and working on the land today' (*op. cit.*). In this perspective are seen not only the man-made structures on the landscape but the very structure of the landscape itself, with settlements, roads, tracks and pathways, and fields grafted on to geomorphological flexibility and geological fundamentals. From this come a distinctiveness and then, among people, a sense of place, cultural identity and traditions, ways of working that place in a particular fashion to enjoy a livelihood there. We, as external observers of this phenomenon, have to make it our business to understand these things, and not least to appreciate that together they overlay the landscape with intangible social and personal values.

A cultural landscape is also very close to ordinary people in that, conceptually and on the ground, its quality derives from its totality rather than from a string of particular elements. The cliché in this case is true: the whole is greater than the sum of its parts. Some cultural landscapes are conceived and designed by particular individuals; many of those designers, professionals like 'Capability' Brown, will be famous. But for the most part, far from being created by a famous person, cultural landscapes have been created by the great anonymous, and can be appreciated simply as the work of the common people. In other words, despite their name and any superior overtones suggested by the label 'World Heritage', most cultural landscapes are not elitist either as made or as now perceived.

Locally, as a consequence of World Heritage inscription, there are now expectations of us, all of us whether or not we live in a World Heritage cultural landscape. We are not just Kasubi or St Emilion villagers now; whether we like it or not, we are all global villagers, for World Heritage is meant for us all. Equally, those looking after its components are doing so, not just for the locality or their country, but for us all.

If we work in this World Heritage field, we have and will have our problems, of definition, management, interpretation and coping with wear and tear; it does not serve our cause well, nor that of the resource we would steward, when we expose our frailties to the watching world community – and watched we are being! I was asked in Canberra about the plans for Stonehenge and in Kingston, Jamaica, about the likely availability of the Hadrian's Wall

FIGURE 66.
Local children in 2003 beneath the cliff-face which, used and sanctified over centuries, has witnessed such violence at the end of the twentieth century and become the core of a World Heritage cultural landscape at the beginning of the twenty-first, Bamiyan valley, Afghanistan.

Management Plan as a model. We damage ourselves when we tie ourselves up in bureaucratic mishandling, indulge in episodes which are transparently driven by political expediency, or perpetrate inappropriate acts of uninformed development. Worse, sometimes we cannot even see that what we have done is unacceptable in a World Heritage context, and fail to raise our sights from the rigidity of institutional small-mindedness. We need to consider the rather grander concepts of the visionaries who thought of a world and its peoples discovering for themselves their diverse yet common past through landscape. World Heritage is both a mechanism to that end and an expression in practice of an ideal.

One of the consequences of World Heritage inscription is to underline the wisdom of the environmental mantra to 'think global, act local'. Perhaps, though it lacks the snappiness of the original, 'think noble, act global, stay local' might be adapted for cultural landscapes. Take Vat Phou as an example, a place 'floating' on water, with kilometres of channels, conduits and leats controlling the drainage through the landscape into the Mekong. It is impressive and iconographic in itself but, as should be the case with all cultural landscapes, it makes references to other parts of the human experience, even among contemporary communities. Canal-based irrigation, for example, was also developing elsewhere in the world in the first millennium AD. In the North American south-west, for example, the irrigation system of the desert-living Hohokam was ambitious from the outset and had allowed the creation of an agrarian economy by AD 500. In a global perspective, Vat Phou also shares many features in common with some principal sites of different but contemporary cultures developing in those centuries perceived in Western scholarship as 'Early Medieval'. In western Europe itself, for example, great religious complexes, also involving alignments, as at Cologne, Germany, Chartres, France, and Canterbury, England, were developing. A close parallel in terms, not of architectural form but of state formation, water management and road network within a core area containing built, religious complexes closely allied to natural phenomena, is at Chaco in New Mexico, USA, part of a civilization flourishing and fading at about the same time as that of the Khymer.

So my hope is that we can locally sort out our problems at Vat Phou and Hallstatt and Kasubi and Uluṟu, but do so with an eye to all the rest of us in the rest of the world, here now and yet to come. We, the people of the world, have to rely on locals to put matters right and, further, we expect them to do so on our behalf. We are watching – and we have every right so to do. As a local, however – and that means as a citizen of a signatory State Party – we must be aware not just of the formal requirements of the *Convention* but of the higher expectations of our behaviour. With cultural landscape we are dealing with something intellectually difficult, sensitive, and economically significant, in other words something which is fairly civilised. Let us be global villagers by all means; but let us be civilised ones who raise our game to meet others' expectations of us as we learn to look after, and enjoy, our very own landscapes for the world (Figure 66).

Notes to the Chapters

....

Note: this topic is a fast-developing one. Dates are therefore provided in the following Notes so that any student who so needs can judge what information was, or should have been, available to the author at the time of writing.

Chapter 1. Landscape and World Heritage

This chapter was drafted in May 2001, and revised in April, June, and again, July 2003. Essentially all its data are in the basic documents listed below or on the web (just key 'UNESCO World Heritage' or 'World Heritage cultural landscapes' into your search engine and start selecting from your hundreds of choices). www.unesco.org/whc/heritage.htmste is a good entry point, embracing the 'Global Strategy'; http://whc.unesco.org/archive/WHList03-ENG.pdf contains a list and basic details (in English) of all World Heritage Sites as at August 2003.

The World Heritage Centre is effectively the Secretariat and executive of the World Heritage Committee; UNESCO: United Nations Educational, Scientific and Cultural Organization. Both are at 7, Place de Fontenoy, 75352 Paris 07 SP, France. For the Centre, tel. +33 (0)1 45 68 15 71; e-mail wh-info@unesco.org; http://www.unesco.org/whc/heritage.htm

The three official Advisory Bodies to the World Heritage Committee are:

ICOMOS: International Council on Monuments and Sites, 49–51 Rue de la Fédération, F–75015 Paris, France. Tel. +33 (0)1 45 67 67 70; e-mail secretariat@icomos.org; www. icomos.org

IUCN: The World Conservation Union, Rue Mauverney 28, CH–1196 Gland, Switzerland. Tel. +41 (22) 999–0001; e-mail mail@iucn.org; www.iucn.org

ICCROM: International Centre for the Preservation and Restoration of Cultural Property, Via di San Michele 13, 1-00153, Rome, Italy. Tel. +39 06 585531; e-mail iccrom@iccrom.org; www. iccrom.org

List of general background documents (obtainable from the World Heritage Centre)

* *Convention concerning the Protection of the World Cultural and Natural Heritage* (UNESCO 1972)

* *Operational Guidelines for the Implementation of the World Heritage Convention (March 1999) (currently under review; new revised edition likely 2004)*

* *Glossary of World Heritage Terms*

* *Properties included in the World Heritage List*

The approved *Reports* of all World Heritage Committee meetings are available on the web (quotations throughout this text from the World Heritage Committee meeting of June–July, 2003, come from its draft *Report*, equivalent to minutes, available in early July 2003).

Key publications: World Heritage Cultural Landscapes

Barreda 2002; Cleere 2003; Fowler 2003b; Hajós 1999; Rössler 1998a and b, 1999, 2000; Rössler and Saouma-Forero 2000; von Droste, Plachter and Rössler 1995; von Droste, Rössler and Titchen 1998; WHC 2002, 2003b, 2003c. UNESCO 1962 is historically a starting point.

There are in addition reports on all the Regional Thematic Expert Meetings held on this topic from 1992 onwards: they are listed in Cleere 2003, section 3.3, with percipient commentary, and analysed in Fowler 2003b, Annex B. The foundation report is: WHC–92/CONF. 202/10/Add – *Revision of the Operational Guidelines for the Implementation of the World Heritage Convention: Report of the Expert Group on Cultural Landscapes, La Petite Pierre, France* (24–26 October 1992). Subsequent seminal meetings and reports include those on cultural landscapes in Africa in 1999 (WHC–99/CONF. 209/INF. 8; Rössler and Saouma-Forero 2000), on desert landscapes and oasis systems in 2001 (WHC–01/CONF. 208. INF. 10), on Asian rice culture and its terraced landscapes in Manila in 1995 (WHC–95/CONF. 203. INF. 8), on associative cultural landscapes in the Asia-Pacific region in 1995 (WHC–95/95/CONF. 203/INF. 9), on cultural landscapes in eastern Europe in 1999 (WHC–99. CONF. 209. INF14; see also Dömke and Succow 1998), and on cultural landscapes in the Andes in 1998 (Barreda 2002) and in Central America in 2000 (WHC–2000/CONF. 204/WEB. 4).

Cleere 2003, 3.4, also lists, with comment, ICOMOS studies, thematic and comparative, including such topics as fossil hominid sites, rock art, railways, coal-mining landscapes, industrial villages, canals and bridges, modern movement architecture, and a number of topics on a regional basis e.g. Islamic sites of Africa and Asia.

Both Cleere 2003 and Fowler 2003b also contain much other data supporting, but in general not repeated in, this book. At the time of going to press, the most up-to-date multi-author discussion of World Heritage cultural landscapes, and indeed of cultural landscapes in the world, is in the papers in the press from the cultural landscapes workshop at Ferrara in November 2002 (now published as WHC 2003c; Chapter 10 here; summarized in WHC 2003b, 138–41).

Chapter 2. The Idea of Cultural Landscape

This chapter was written in August, 2001 and fundamentally revised in June 2003. It draws on, and in places actually uses text from, several papers by the author during the 1990s–2001, notably an unpublished paper given to the National Trust Centenary Conference, Manchester, 1995 (Fowler 1995), and a keynote paper delivered at Oxford on 3 May 2000, to the ICOMOS UK 'Cultural Landscape' Conference, published as Fowler 2001. The Oxford Declaration on Landscape is published in Kelly *et al.* 2001. Reviews of the development of cultural and archaeological versions of landscape are provided by Aitchison 1995, most pertinently for present purposes and much used here, and in Haber 1995, Darvill 1997 and Williamson 1998. Pressouyre's (1996, 28–30) brief notice of cultural landscapes is procedural and legal rather than conceptual.

'Heritage' is itself an extremely emotive and powerful matter, and that will carry through to considerations of 'cultural landscape' quite as much as it has to individual archaeological sites and cultural property (see, for example, Stone and Molyneaux 1994 *passim*). Indeed, 'landscape' is a highly-charged subject in any case, involving matters across a range from life-style through property rights to aesthetics and cognitive perception (e.g. Appleton 1986; Shoard 1987; Renfrew 2003; *see* Chapter 12); so it was conceivable that in espousing the sub-set of 'cultural landscape', 'World Heritage' was about to enter a very interesting phase of its development (see Chapter 9). Embryonic tensions exist throughout von Droste *et al.* 1995, while Hajós 2000, among all its data about the Wachau, does not record considerable, articulated unease among the invitees at the symposium about the nature of the proposed nomination. The site became a World Heritage cultural landscape in 2000.

'Relict landscape', often archaeology by another name, is well illustrated, for example in Britain, in Fowler and Sharp 1990, Glasscock 1992 and Darvill 1996. The quotations about English landscape are from Keith 1974. The topic is discussed in Fowler 1997a. The quotation about Wicken Fen is from Adrian Colston, Reserve manager, as quoted in *The Guardian* newspaper, 2 May 2000, 9. As the proposal develops it will doubtless address questions of size by identifying very clearly its primary objectives, for example habitat, species or archaeological sustainability. Fyfield and Overton Downs, inside and outside the Avebury World Heritage site, are covered in Fowler 2000b; see also Chapter 7. The trends in the Causses area of Languedoc have already been discussed at some length in Fowler 2001. They are ranked in order of deleteriousness in the Notes to Chapter 10.

The six criteria for World Heritage cultural sites are given on pp. 4–5 of the text. The equivalent (slightly edited) four criteria for 'natural' sites are:

   (i) outstanding examples representing major stages of earth's history, including the record of life, significant ongoing geological processes in the development of land forms, or significant geomorphic or physiographic features;

   (ii) outstanding examples representing significant ongoing ecological and biological processes in the evolution and development of terrestial, freshwater, coastal and marine ecosystems and communities of plants and animals;

   (iii) contain superlative natural phenomena or areas of exceptional natural beauty and aesthetic importance;

   (iv) contain the most important and significant natural habitats for *in-situ* conservation of biological diversity, including those containing threatened species of outstanding universal values from the point of view of science or conservation.

A 'mixed site' has to meet one or more of both natural and cultural criteria; a cultural landscape must meet one or more cultural criteria but none of the natural criteria. Aspects of the latter, however, may well be in the minds of those assessing a potential cultural landscape in an IUCN perspective e.g. conservation of natural and semi-natural ecosystems, of biodiversity within farming systems, sustainable land-use and enhancement of scenic beauty.

Chapter 3. The First World Heritage Cultural Landscapes, 1993–95: Australasia and South East Asia

The account of Tongariro is heavily based on ICOMOS' evaluation report and Heuheu 1995, both of which are paraphrased as well as quoted.

The account of Uluru-Kata Tjuṯa is based on a personal visit and two published sources: Layton and Titchen 1995, and the Australian Government's (1994) *Renomination . . .* Both sources are paraphrased as well as quoted.

The account of the Cordilleras is based on a personal visit, my report to ICOMOS 1994, Villalon 1995 and Yuson 2000.

Chapter 4. Inscriptions, 1995–98: Europe and South West Asia

The account of Sintra is based on the original ICOMOS assessment of the nomination in 1995, the official documents about the site, and a visit and ICOMOS/IUCN report in 2000 by Gérard Collin and the author.

The accounts of Pyrénées-Mont Perdu, Spain/France, Hallstatt-Dachstein, Austria, and Portovenere, Italy, are based primarily on visits to the sites, official documents about the site in the ICOMOS Documentation Centre, Paris, and other material about the sites. The brief discussion of Lednice, Czech Republic, which the author has not visited, is derived from printed sources alone.

Chapter 5. The Idea Develops, 1999–2003

Much of this chapter was drafted in the autumn of 2001 when it took the story up to the decisions of the World Heritage Committee in December 2000. It was revised in early 2003 to update the story to December 2002 and completed in early July to take account of the decisions of the World Heritage Committee announced on 3 July 2003. The chapter is based on a mixture of personal knowledge, either from visits and/or involvement in the desk evaluation of the nominations, and on documentation as detailed above under Chapter 3 and 4. Much of the information comes from ICOMOS documentation, but see also Añon Feliu 1995 for Aranjuez; Liddell and Price 1992, Magãlhaes 1998 and Rosas 1998 for Alto Douro; WHC 2000b for vineyard landscapes; Rigol 2000 for Viñales; Dömpke and Succow 1998 for Dessau-Wörlitz and pastoral landscapes like Hortobágy; Hajós for Wachau and Rössler and Saouma-Forero 2000 for Africa. Trinder 1982 is relavent for industrial landscapes; see also Vanderhulst 1992. Note that despite all the relevant evidence for human/environmental interaction at Tsodilo, the site was not recognised as a World Heritage cultural landscape, nor were Kasubi Tombs (though, inconsistently, Colline Royale was).

Chapter 6. Britain and Cultural Landscapes

This chapter was significantly revised in June 2003. It incorporates material from four principal sources: recent and current experience/events; research for Fowler 2002 which familiarized the author with much current regional publication in Britain, referenced therein and not repeated in so much detail here; and two published papers. The first paper derived from a presentation by the author at the second 'expert meeting' on cultural landscapes organised by the World Heritage Centre at Templin/

Schorfeide, Germany, in October 1993. After discussion with David Jacques, it was published as a joint paper, Fowler and Jacques 1995, in von Droste *et al.* 1995, 350–63.

The second published paper originated as a presentation to an 'Expert Meeting on European Cultural Landscapes of Outstanding Universal Value' in Vienna on 21 April 1996. It was included in the cyclostyled 'Reader' of all the papers compiled for those attending but was otherwise unpublished until a revised and updated version of it appeared four years later as a free-standing paper (Fowler 2000a). Here we draw on it very selectively. Both papers have good bibliographies; see also Smith 1998. The Vienna 'Reader' itself, incidentally, contained and anticipated much of the development on cultural landscapes in Europe throughout the 1990s.

Scilly was one of my favourite stamping grounds in the 1980s; see Thomas 1985. My views on Orkney developed in particular from Fenton 1978, Renfrew 1985 and in fieldwork preparatory to Fowler and Sharp 1990. Renfrew (2003, 17–18) discusses the Ring of Brodgar and the surrounding, numinous area in personal and aesthetic terms, providing words which could well apply to other places where archaeology in context becomes cultural landscape: '... as a monument, its presence somehow transcends our knowledge or understanding. There is more to say, although we do not yet know how to say it.' It is this dimension which was eschewed in nominating Orkney for World Heritage status simply as a site, and it can only be hoped that during the course of the twenty-first century its deeper nature will come to be officially recognized.

My paragraph on the Severn estuary and mudflats subsumes years of research and publication by, in particular, Professor Martin Bell and Rippon (1996, 1997, 1999). A percipient view of the lowlands is in Fulford and Nichols 1992.

The archaeologically well known and significant highland/lowland dichotomy was first proposed in the present context by Fox 1933, following geographers' models. It was the basis of two major archaeological reviews in the 1970s (Evans *et al.* 1975 and Limbrey and Evans 1978, in one of which the model itself was re-interpreted in cultural terms (Fowler 1978). That the landscape is rather more complex has been cartographically demonstrated by the English Nature/Countryside Commission Character of England map (1996), with its 159 'Character Areas', and by Roberts and Wrathmell 2000.

A bibliography for Avebury is provided in the Notes to Chapter 7. Paintings of the area by Piper were exhibited at a retrospective at Dulwich Art Gallery, 2003, by Nash at the Walker Gallery, Liverpool, also in 2003, and by Inshaw are in the permanent exhibition at the Museum of the Wiltshire Archaeological and Natural History Society, Devizes, Wiltshire.

For Avebury, *see* the Notes to Chapter 7. Hadrian's Wall has, like Avebury, generated a huge bibliography. The simplest and most easily accessible entry point is Breeze and Dobson 1987 (or the latest available edition); Bidwell 1999 lists all substantial publications 1989–99. A new management plan was published in 2002.

For Cheviot, Mercer and Tipping 1994 report on recent research but no good comprehensive modern study of Cheviot exists so use has to be made of the relevant parts of Dixon 1903, Beckensall 2003 and Pevsner *et al.* 1992. For the Weald of Kent and Sussex, see respectively Everitt 1986 and Brandon 1978, Chapter VI.

State provision and the historic environment came up for governmental review in England in 2003. It is just possible that World Heritage may gain some formal status as a result.

Chapter 7. Landscapes of Stonehenge and Avebury

Stonehenge has generated a large library of its own (Chippendale 1994). As an archae-ological site, with excellent bibliography, it is best discussed in Cleal *et al.* 1995. The popular Atkinson 1979 is now unfortunately regarded as unsound. The issues the site and environs raise as a heritage property have been increasingly discussed over the last decade, beginning with Chippendale *et al.* 1990. A major contribution to the nature of the Stonehenge landscape was made recently by Ellison and Woodwards 1996. A management plan was published by English Heritage in 2000. Both its management and its research agenda are actively under consideration in 2003 and, as this book goes to press, the first phase of a new management regime has been put in place by the National Trust. Major decisions have to be made in the next few years about a proposed Visitor Centre (is it in the right place? Will it obtain planning permission?), about the main road passing just to the south of the monument (should it be put in a tunnel? If so, for what distance? And can it be satisfactorily approached by deep cuttings through the landscape at either end? Will it the road plans survive a public Inquiry?), and about the mode and degree of public access to be allowed to the land-scape and the monument.

Avebury, too, has generated its own considerable literature and also now enjoys the luxury of two excellent – each in its own different way – museological exhibitions on site. Otherwise, the best studies are two large scholarly tomes, Burl 1979 and Ucko *et al.* 1991, with Whittle 1997 providing modern insights into Silbury and the western part of the Avebury landscape. Evans *et al.* 1993 placed the site and the upper Kennet valley in their environmental context. Fowler 2000b provided detailed discussion of its eastern landscape; Figure 15.3 therein, based on a map prepared by the former Royal Commission on the Historical Monuments of England, provides a good and accurate cartographic statement about the downland east of Avebury village. Fowler and Blackwell 2000, in synthesizing the last in a 'popular' book, attempted an interpretive narrative of the area; a 'biography' (not 'bibliography') of the henge monument and the area is now published in Pollard and Reynolds 2002. Its own research agenda, covering the monuments and its landscape through all periods, was published in 2001 (AAHRG 2001) and is being kept under review; its excellent original management plan (English Heritage 1998) is currently being reviewed. All these publications themselves carry extensive bibliographies.

The management of cultural landscapes is covered extensively in ICCROM forth-coming. See also Notes to Chapter 10 below.

Chapter 8. Cultural Landscape Values: Europe and the British Isles

This chapter is based on an invited, heavily illustrated and largely extemporised pres-entation in Amsterdam to a symposium on the future of World Heritage called by the World Heritage Centre, March 1998. A written version of the presentation (Fowler 1998b), here only slightly edited, was published in the Proceedings (von Droste *et al.* 1998). Different angles on Europe's landscapes are now available in Rössler 2001a, Clark *et al.* 2003 and at pcl.eu.de.

'... with humanity's relationships with Nature as with the interactions of both in the landscape': see Barker 1985, Birks *et al.* 1988, Braudel 1986, Brongers 1973, Chardin 1966, Cronon 1983, Goudie 1990, Mitchell 1976, Rackham 1986, 1990, Thomas 1955.

For DNA see Jones 2001.

Willis (1976, 43) provided the gem about the Alpine penny-cress; the Jutland fen is quoted from Glob 1971, 105. For Fyfield and Overton, see Fowler 2000b and Fowler and Blackwell 1998, 2000, *passim,* for sarsens and sheep, Figure 16 for daisies. For Dartmoor, Italian centuriation and Stowe respectively see Fleming 1988, Bradford 1974 and Jacques 1983. The Burgundy vignerons come from Megret and Collin 1995, 310, crofting landscapes from Dodgson 1988, and the Banawe rice terraces from Villalon 1995. Good entry points into the considerable Caussenard literature are Marres 1935, Martel 1936, Bonniol and Saussol 1995, Fowler 1998a. Megret and Collin 1995, 309–10, provide a preliminary essay on the area's nomination. For the Biferno valley, see Barker 1995.

Fowler and Jacques 1995 discuss the Lake District's 'associative value', now embraced within a comprehensive re-assessment (2003) of the District's values for the various interests involved in bringing forward a re-nomination for inscription as a World Heritage site. The bold course would be to nominate it as a category 3 cultural landscape under criterion (vi) alone; but a more cautious approach would involve its nature as a category 2b cultural landscape in World Heritage terms with claims under criteria (iii) and (iv). 'Honesty' at Bede's World, Jarrow, England, is explained in Fowler and Mills 2003.

Chapter 9. Contentious Landscapes

Much of the factual content here comes from ICOMOS evaluations.

Good 'dispute' material is available almost daily in the media, characteristically related to 'natural' events' like flood and fire, to tourism, and to the ignorance/philistinism/avariciousness of public authorities; and in book form in, for example, Layton 1989; Gathercole and Lowenthal 1990; Boniface and Fowler 1993, especially Chapters 7, 9, 11; Tunbridge and Ashworth 1996; Renfrew 2000; Brodie *et al.* 2001 and Cotter *et al.* 2001.

World Heritage publications involving contention include von Droste *et al.* 1995, 1998, and Fielden and Jokilehto 1998.

The Bend of the Boyne, a World Heritage site, was re-examined in 2004 in the light of developments there since inscription. For Hadrian's Wall, *see* the Notes on Chapter 6. The Kakadu contention led to a 140-page publication by the Australian Government in 1999.

The Loire has also generated its own extensive literature, but it is as well introduced in Michelin 1996 as in any other accessible publication. There is, however, far more to it than the chateaux, e.g. the cities of Orléans and Tours within the World Heritage site: see Préfecture 2000. Much of the material here comes from personal experience in carrying out an evaluation mission to the Loire on behalf of ICOMOS and from my subsequent report and, encouraged by the WHC and the local authorities, my continuing involvement in the area.

For Vall de Boí, see Fontova and Carme Polo nd. For the 'Golden Age of Northumbria', see Hawkes 1996 and Hawkes and Mills 1999.

The Cordilleras, Philippines, cultural landscape was put on the List of World Heritage in Danger in 2000, not as a criticism of the local authorities but in general to alert the world to the serious situation now existing in that landscape and specifically to help trigger a course of remedial action there. The World Heritage

Committee receives a 'state of conservation' report each year on subsequent developments and – as with all sites it has placed on its 'In Danger' List – decides annually whether or not improvement is such that the site can be removed from the List. The Cordilleras were retained on this List in 2003, as were, for example, Angkor, Cambodia, the Old City of Jerusalem and its Walls, Timbuktu, Mali, and the Everglades, USA. Yellowstone was, however, one of the three sites removed from the 'In Danger' List, much to the relief of the USA, but among the five simultaneously added were Kathmandu Valley, Nepal, and the just-inscribed Bamiyan Valley, Afghanistan (Plate 12; Figure 66).

The need for a thematic study of agricultural landscapes for World Heritage purposes is further discussed in Fowler 2001 and Cleere 2003, and is one of the recommendations in Fowler 2003b.

Chapter 10. Conserving Cultural Landscapes

The management of World Heritage sites is authoritatively covered in Fielden and Jokilehto 1998 and of World Heritage cultural landscapes specifically and extensively in ICCROM (forthcoming). Management plans for UK sites such as Stonehenge and Hadrian's Wall are available on the web. For the management of rural landscape more generally, though from an historic/archaeological angle, *see* Brown and Berry 1995 and Grenville 1999. Both contain many useful, up-to-date bibliographical references, and the latter contains a paper, Fairclough 1999a, specifically on 'Protecting the cultural landscape' (though it does not mention World Heritage). While both volumes derive from British experience, most of the general principles touched on are valid elsewhere. Equivalent management volumes and papers stem from other regions of the world, especially from Australia and the USA, and from other points of view, notably that of nature conservation: for cultural landscapes especially, useful studies and entry points into other bibliographies are, for example, Jeschke 1999, Mitchell and Buggey 2000, Munjeri 2000, Parks Canada 2000 and Phillips 1995. Urban conservation has its own enormous literature, as does the study and conservation of standing buildings, both often facets of cultural landscape even if most of the World Heritage examples are primarily rural (Chapter 1 and 2). Clark 2001 is a recent and extremely useful entry into these fields and again, although primarily about English material, with much detail which need not concern people elsewhere, its principles, methodology and bibliography are widely relevant.

Many, and to an extent, repetitive, management issues occur throughout the basic World Heritage cultural landscape volumes, von Droste and Rössler 1995, WHC 2003c and Fowler 2003b. WHC 2003b, published in July 2003, provides a general conspectus of current thinking about World Heritage and the management of its Listed sites going into the twenty-first century. Separate sections within it now make available in hard-copy the full text of the reports from the Workshops preceding it (my quotations come from the duplicated 'Conclusions' of each meeting presented to the Congress in November 2002). The proceedings of the Ferrara Workshop have now been published (WHC 2003c). 'Cultural Landscapes: the challenges of conservation' is at WHC 2003b, 138–141; 'Monitoring World Heritage' (not summarized in the text here) is at WHC 2003b, 150–151b. Its conclusions and proposals are in general in line with the thrust in this chapter e.g. 'Monitoring is an essential part of World Heritage site management and should be understood not as externally imposed control, but as providing information to aid management processes and conservation planning.' One of its six 'operational concerns' touches on an aspect not mentioned at all here, IT: 'to establish a thematic, on-line network for World Heritage monitoring in order to exchange experiences and to create an accessible knowledge management system …' 'Risk preparedness' is dealt with in Stovel 1998. A good example of periodic reporting developing in practice is provided by WHC/Korea 2001.

A good example of identifying potential World Heritage sites well in advance, through expert meetings as well as through formal Tentative Lists, is provided by a Workshop held in New Delhi in 1987. A *Preparatory Study* for it reviewed 18 countries in South and South-East Asia and listed 34 strong candidates from 10 countries. Twenty have since been inscribed on the World Heritage List (Cleere 2003, 3.4.2.6), the most recent the Bamiyan Valley in 2003. Similarly, in terms of influence if not yet quantitatively, an Expert Meeting on 'Routes as part of our Cultural Heritage' in Madrid in 1994, was the seminal meeting on the subject (WHC–94/CONF. 003/INF. 13). It identified categories of route e.g. trade and faith, and themes e.g. military campaigns, as well as specific routes e.g. trades routes from Asia to Europe, slave routes across and from Africa. It also promulgated ideas which resonate through current thinking e.g. Fowler 2003b and Cleere 2003 (from which, in section 3.4.3.2, the detail of this example is quoted).

Cleere (2003, 2.1.1.9) defines 'religious properties' as 'any form of property with religious or spiritual associations: churches, monasteries, shrines, sanctuaries, mosques, temples, sacred monuments (ruined or intact), landscapes, sacred groves and other landscape features, etc., from all periods.

The Dutch National Commission for UNESCO, in collaboration with the Dutch Ministry of Education, Culture and Science, organised a specialist conference in Amsterdam, 21–24 May 2003, in order to reflect upon the specific challenges to the management of World Heritage Sites in the wake of the Venice Congress, and to discuss possible lines of action. Its title was 'Managing a Sustainable Future for World Heritage: … Linking Universal and Local Values'. Its key words were cultural diversity; local communities; traditional knowledge; development; capacity building – all clear indications of the intended thrust. The written 'background' to this occasion is itself interesting in that it articulates much of the current thinking about management in relation to World Heritage sites, six months after the very public expressions of idealism and pragmatism at Venice (WHC 2003b). We quote with only minor editing:

[Begins by quoting *Guidelines* 1999, para. 24(b)(ii)]. [In 1992] 'For the first time in the history of the World Heritage Convention traditional management mechanisms and systems of customary land tenure were deemed acceptable for a World Heritage Site. Only in 1998 [were] the *Operational Guidelines* changed accordingly to allow a traditionally managed natural site, East Rennell (Solomon Islands), to be inscribed on the World Heritage List.

Article 8 of the *Convention on Biological Diversity (Rio de Janeiro, 1992)* states that each State Party will "subject to its national legislation, respect, preserve and maintain knowledge, innovations and practices of indigenous local communities embodying traditional lifestyles relevant for the conservation and sustainable use of biological diversity and promote their wider application with the approval and involvement of the holders of such knowledge, innovations and practices and encourage the equitable sharing of the benefits arising from the utilization of such knowledge, innovations and practices".

Furthermore, the *Nara Document on Authenticity* (1994) acknowledges that "judgements about values attributed to cultural heritage, as well as the credibility of related information sources, may differ from culture to culture, and even within the same culture. (...) the respect due to all cultures requires that heritage properties must be considered and judged primarily within the cultural contexts to which they belong".

The *Seville Strategy for Biosphere Reserves* (1995) identified two directions, amongst its key issues:

* "Reflect more fully the human dimensions of biosphere reserves. Connections should be made between cultural and biological diversity. Traditional knowledge and genetic resources should be conserved and their role in sustainable development should be recognized and developed".

* "Promote the management of each biosphere reserve essentially as a 'pact' between the local community and society as a whole. Management should be open, evolving and adaptive. Such an approach will help ensure that biosphere reserves – and their local communities are better placed to respond to external political, economic and social pressures".

Point 14 of the Action Plan of the *Universal Declaration on Cultural Diversity* (2001) encourages cooperation between Member States for "respecting and protecting traditional knowledge, in particular that of indigenous peoples; recognizing the contribution of traditional knowledge, particularly with regard to environmental protection and the management of natural resources, and fostering synergies between modern science and local knowledge".

At the 24th Session of the World Heritage Committee (Helsinki 2001) ... "numerous participants affirmed that local communities have an essential role in the conservation of certain World Heritage properties and that a network would favour the exchange of information and experience concerning their protection. The Committee encouraged professional research and an exchange of views on this subject".

The *Budapest Declaration 2002* recognizes heritage in all its diversity and states that the World Heritage Committee will "seek to ensure an appropriate and equitable balance between conservation, sustainability and development, so that World Heritage properties can be protected through appropriate activities contributing to the social and economic development and the quality of life of ... communities" and will "seek to ensure the active involvement of ... local communities at all levels in the identification, protection and management of ... World Heritage properties".

The participants at the International Workshop ... on World Heritage Site Management [Padua, *see* text, and WHC 2003, 158–160] recommended that local communities, including those of indigenous cultures, participate in the conservation of World Heritage, and that their needs be integrated in management planning.

In the light of this background, the presentations will aim to investigate the ways by which local communities can contribute to their sustainable economic and social development, as well as to sustainable management of World Heritage properties. In this context, the effect of changing social and economic conditions, such as globalisation and modernisation (including migration streams, mass tourism, new media, liberalisation of markets for cultural goods and service), will also be considered.'

The Conference itself was a successful occasion, not least because of the strong representation from Africa and South America; and a report has been forwarded to the World Heritage Committee. Proceedings should be published. Meanwhile, we note the emphasis on local involvement, especially where local communities are 'indigenous' (though, as I always like to point out in these contexts, 'indigenousness' is a quality not limited to the developing world and that I too am 'indigenous' in England, closely involved in the management of World Heritage sites). The note also clearly brings out that the nature of 'management' is itself a developing concept; it is definitely not a set of rigid mechanisms set in stone for general application. Its identification of a close relationship between the sustainable conservation of World Heritage sites and 'changing social and economic conditions' is also welcome – and realistic. But sadly, it also has to be recognised that in many World Heritage situations where, for diverse reasons, theory and practice have hardly yet reached first base, this is really advanced thinking.

The trends in the Causses area of Languedoc (Fowler 2001), ranked in order of deleteriousness, are:

   i. enclosure, that is the fencing in, characteristically with electric wire, of the unenclosed sheep pastures, fundamentally changing the outstanding characteristics of this landscape, its visual openness, its sense of space and its physical accessibility on foot

  ii. the erection of large, prefabricated, modern sheds, usually for sheep shelter, sheep-milking and manure management, characteristically insensitively sited and cumulatively now a major visual, late 20th century element of the landscape

 iii. the piecemeal ploughing up of old pasture, driven by EU grant payments to produce temporary cereal Europe does not need, here botanically and archaeologically disastrous, visually detrimental and pedologically dangerous in an area of tremendous rain-storms, shallow soil and fast run-off

  iv. road-improvements, ostensibly to make it easier for milk-tankers to visit farms each day and also making it possible for large tourist buses to drive through landscape and villages they could not previously reach and to which they contribute nothing except visual intrusion

   v. new houses (in an area with hundreds of empty and semi-ruinous vernacular buildings), built with non-local materials and characteristically sited insensitively (usually for those inside to gain a good view) outside existing villages

  vi. the continual erection of new signage, not so much the formal, directional road signs but the proliferation of additional signs marking recently-invented tourist routes and territorial imperialism of recently-invented official organizations

This happens to be the particular combination of factors in this particular case. Practitioners will recognize a familiar clumping-effect, even if their particular factors are different. I wrote Fowler 2001 and pp.174–76 here before France nominated the area as a World Heritage cultural landscape.

Funding aspects of World Heritage are now helpfully brought together in WHC 2002a.

Chapter 11. Reviewing the Achievement: World Heritage Cultural Landscapes, 1992–2003

The text of this chapter is the product of several origins and revisions. Basically, a paper on the first ten years of cultural landscapes was drafted in anticipation in May, 2001, and privately circulated. It was then revised for a so far unpublished volume based upon papers given at a session on World Heritage at the World Archaeological Congress in South Africa in 2001. It was then updated in 2002 and a revised version, including data from the WHCommittee's meeting of June 2002, was prepared for inclusion in Fowler 2003b. Some matter, especially Table 7, appears in the summary of that, Fowler 2003a. The version here, somewhat amended yet again, includes data up to 3 July, 2003. The figure of 36 official World Heritage cultural landscapes was supplied on request by e-mail by the WHC on 3 July 2003, and has since been confirmed on the web. This version omits columns 1–4 and 1–6, since the relevant analysis of the use of natural and cultural criteria in the inscription of World Heritage cultural landscapes is now in Table 8 here. This version (Table 9) omits columns 1–4 and 1–6, since the relevant analysis of the use of natural and cultural criteria in the inscription of World Heritage cultural landscapes is now in Table 8 here.

The concept that much of the world's terrestial surface is 'cultural landscape' in the sense that it has been affected by human beings to at least some degree – not quite the same as the World Heritage sense, *see* Chapter 2 – is explored and implied by such as Birks *et al* 1988, Simmons 1989, and McKibben 1990. For World Heritage cultural landscapes as samples, *see* Rössler 1999 and WHC 2003; for the hundred or so cultural landscapes on the World Heritage List as at June 2002, *see*, Fowler 2003b, Annex C.

Key references for some of the landscapes mentioned can be identified from full titles of publications listed in the Bibliography e.g. Añon Feliu 1995 for Aranjuez, Spain; Holzknecht 1998 for Dessau-Wörlitz, Germany.

For mountains generally, and their values, *see World Conservation 2002*, and Bernbaum 2001; and in South East Asia, UNESCO World Heritage Centre 2001.

Chapter 12. 'A Global, Noble Concept?'

This chapter was originally drafted in the autumn of 2001 and revised in June 2003. It draws on, and is complementary to, Fowler 2003b, but is essentially original to this book.

Examples of relevant academic studies are Donkin 1979, Conklin 1980, Barreda 2002 and Fowler 2002. Rigol 2000 discusses Cuban cultural landscapes. The debate about 'natural' habitat and indigenous people is illumined by van der Hammen 2003.

For mountains and water, see Rössler 2001b and Bernbaum 2001; for 'landscape of ideas' in Africa, see Rössler and Saoma-Forero 2000 generally and Munjeri 2000 specifically. For war and heritage, see English Heritage 2003. For everything, read Simmons 1997; though his eco-cultural approach, and the functional-evolutionary process underpinning much of this book, up to and including contemporary landscape, are not apparently embraced by the quite narrow perception of 'Modern Heritage' as conceptualized, presumably out of unawareness, largely by architects for WHC 2003d.

A UNESCO Convention for the Safeguarding of the Intangible Heritage was signed in October, 2003. Nominations to the World Heritage List to be considered in 2004 are at://terra.hq.int.unesco.org/doccen/SITES/2003/index-2004.htm.

Bibliography

This Bibliography includes items not referenced in the text or Notes but provided here as part of the background to the topic.

AAHRG (2001) *Archaeological Research Agenda for the Avebury World Heritage Site*, Salisbury: Wessex Archaeology

Aitchison J. (1995) 'Cultural landscapes in Europe: a geographical perspective' in von Droste *et al.,* 272–88

Allison G., Ball S., Cheshire P. C., Evans A. W. and Stabler M. J. (1996) *The Value of Conservation?* London: English Heritage

Añon Feliu C. (1995) 'Aranjuez: Nature, agriculture and the art of the Landscape', in von Droste *et al.,* 295–306

Appleton J. (1986) *The Experience of Landscape*, Hull: University of Hull Press

Appleton J. (1994) *How I Made the World: Shaping a view of Landscape*, Hull: University of Hull Press

Ashmore W. and Knapp A. B. eds (1999) *Archaeologies of Landscape. Contemporary Perspectives*, Oxford: Blackwell

Atkinson R. J. C. (1979) *Stonehenge*, Harmondsworth: Penguin (3rd edn)

Australian Government (1999) *Australia's Kakadu. Response by the Government of Australia to the UNESCO World Heritage Committee regarding Kakadu National Park*, Canberra: Environment Australia

Barker G. (1981) *Landscape and Society. Prehistoric Central Italy*, London: Academic Press

Barker G. (1985) *Prehistoric Farming in Europe*, Cambridge: Cambridge University Press

Barker G. (1995) *A Mediterranean Valley. Landscape Archaeology and Annales History in the Biferno Valley*, London: Leicester University Press

Barreda E. M. ed. (2002) *Paisajes Culturales en los Andes*, Paris: World Heritage Centre, UNESCO

Beckensall S. (2003) *Prehistoric Northumberland*, Brimscombe Port, Stroud: Tempus Publishing

Bender, B. ed. (1993) *Landscape Politics and Perspectives*, Oxford: Berg

Bergeron L. (2001) *Les Villages Ouvriers comme Eléments du Patrimoine de L'Industrie*, Paris: ICOMOS-TICCIH (Occasional Papers for the World Heritage Convention)

Bernbaum E. (2001) 'Sacred mountains of the World Heritage', *World Heritage* 23, 4–23

Berry A. Q. and Brown I. W. (1995) *Managing Ancient Monuments: an Integrated Approach*, Mold: Clwyd County Council

Bidwell P. ed. (1999) 'Hadrian's Wall 1989–1999: a summary of … research …', Handbook … Twelfth Pilgrimage of Hadrian's Wall, 1999, Newcastle upon Tyne

Birks H. H. *et al.* eds (1988) *The Cultural Landscape – Past, Present and Future*, Cambridge: Cambridge University Press

Bocco J. (2000) 'Slave route' in Rössler and Saouma-Forero, 74–78

Boniface P. and Fowler P. J. (1993) *Heritage and Tourism in 'the Global Village'*, London: Routledge

Bonniol J.-L. and Saussol A. eds (1995) *Grands Causses. Nouveaux Enjeux, Nouveaux Regards. Hommage à Paul Mares*, Fédération pour la Vie et la Sauvegarde du Pays des Grands Causses, Millau

Bibliography

Bradford J. (1975) *Ancient Landscapes. Studies in Field Archaeology* Bath: Chivers

Brandon P. ed. (1978) *The South Saxons*, London and Chichester: Phillimore

Braudel F. (1986) *L'Identité de la France* Les Editions Arthaud, Paris (English edition *The Identity of France. Volume I. History and Environment*, 1989, London: Fontana)

Breeze D. and Dobson B. (1987) *Hadrian's Wall*, Harmondsworth: Penguin

Bridgewater P. and Hooy T. (1995) 'Outstanding cultural landscapes in Australia, New Zealand and the Pacific: the footprint of man in the wilderness' in van Droste *et al.*, 162–169

Brodie N., Doole J. and Renfrew C. (2001) *Trade in Illicit Antiquities: the destruction of the World's Archaeological Heritage*, Cambridge: McDonald Inst Monog

Brongers J. A. (1973) *1833: Reuvens in Drenthe*, Nederlanse Oudheden IV, Rijksdienst voor het Oudheidkundig Bodemonderzoek, Amersfoort

Burl A. (1979) *Prehistoric Avebury*, Newhaven and London: Yale University Press

Chardin T. de (1966) *Man's Place in Nature*, London: Collins

Chippendale C., Devereux P., Fowler P. J., Jones R. and Sebastian T. (1990) *Who Owns Stonehenge?*, London: Batsford

Chippindale C. (1994) *Stonehenge Complete*, London: Thames & Hudson

Clark J., Darlington J. and Fairclough G. eds (2003) *Pathways to Europe's Landscape*, Lohr a. Main, Germany: EPCL

Clark K. (2001) *Informed Conservation. Understanding Historic Buildings and their Landscapes for Conservation*, London: English Heritage

Cleal R. M. J., Walker K. E. and Montague R. (1995) *Stonehenge in its Landscape. Twentieth-century Excavations*, London: English Heritage (Archaeological Report 10)

Cleere H. (1995) 'Cultural landscapes as World Heritage', *Conservation and Management of Archaeological Sites* 1, 63–68

Cleere H. (1999) 'Cultural landscapes and the World Heritage List: development, definitions, and problems', in Hajós, 17–24

Cleere H. (2003) *Analysis of the World Heritage List and Tentative Lists: Cultural and Mixed Properties. A Study carried out by ICOMOS at the Request of the World Heritage Committee 2002*, Paris: ICOMOS

Cobham Resources (1993) *Landscape Assessment Guidance*, Cheltenham: Countryside Commission

Comptroller and Auditor General (1992) *Protecting and Managing England's Heritage Property* London: HMSO

Conklin H. C. (1980) *Ethnographic Atlas of Ifugao. A Study of Environment, Culture and Society*, Yale University Press

Cosgrove D. and Daniels S. eds (1988) *The Iconography of Landscape. Essays on the Symbolic Representation, Design and use of Past Environments*, Cambridge: Cambridge University Press

Cotter M., Boyd B. and Gardiner J. eds (2001) *Heritage Landscapes: Understanding Place and Communities*, Lismore NSW: Southern Cross University Press

Council of Europe (2000) *European Landscape Convention and Explanatory Report*, Strasbourg

Countryside Commission (1987) *The Lake District Declaration*, Cheltenham: Countryside Commission

Countryside Commission (1988) *Protected Landscapes: Symposium Proceedings*, Cheltenham: Countryside Commission

Cronon W. (1983) *Changes in the Land. Indians, Colonists, and the Ecology of New England*, New York: Hill & Wang

da Silva J. C. and Luckhurst G. (1997) (4th edn) *Sintra, A Landscape with Villas*, The Genius of the Place Collection, Ediçäes Inapa

Darvill T. ed. (1987) *Ancient Monuments in the Countryside. An Archaeological Management Review*, London: English Heritage

Darvill T. (1996) *Prehistoric Britain from the Air*, Cambridge: Cambridge University Press

DCMS (1998) *UNESCO World Heritage Sites. A Consultation Paper on a New United Kingdom Tentative List of Future Nominations* issued by the Secretary of State, Department for Culture, Media and Sport, August 1998, London

DCMS (1999) *World Heritage Sites. The Tentative List of The United Kingdom of Great Britain and Northern Ireland*, London: Buildings, Monuments and Sites Division, Department for Culture, Media and Sport

Denevan W. (1992) 'The pristine myth: the landscape of the Americas in 1492', *Ann. Assoc. Am. Geog.* 82, 369–85

Dixon D. D. (1903) *Upper Coquetdale, Northumberland*, Newcastle upon Tyne: Redpath (Alnwick: Sandhill Press, reprint 1987)

Dixon P. (1994) 'Field systems, rig and other cultivation remains in Scotland: the field evidence', in Foster and Smout, 26–52

Dodgson R. A. (1988) 'The ecological basis of Highland peasant farming, 1500–1800 AD' in Birks *et al.*, 139–151

Dömke S and Succow M. eds (1998) *Cultural Landscapes and Nature Conservation in Northern Eurasia. Proceedings of the Würlitz Symposium, March 20–23*, Bonn: Narturschutzbund Deutschland (NABU), AIDEnvironment, and the Nature Conservation Bureau

Donkin R. A. (1979) *Agricultural Terracing in the Aboriginal New World*, Tucson, Arizona: University of Arizona Press for Wenner-Grenn Foundation for Anthropological Research, Inc, Viking Fund Publications in Anthropology 56

Edroma E. (2001) 'The notion of integrity for natural properties and cultural landscapes', in Saouma-Forero, 50–58

English Heritage (1996) *Hadrian's Wall World Heritage Site Management Plan*, London: English Heritage (revised 2002)

English Heritage (1998) *Avebury World Heritage Site Management Plan*, London: English Heritage (currently being revised)

English Heritage (2003) *The Archaeology of Conflict*, Conservation Bulletin 44

Evans J. G. (1999) *Land and Archaeology: Histories of Human Environment* in the British Isles, Stroud: Tempus Publishing

Evans J. G., Limbrey S. and Cleere H. eds (1975) *The Effect of Man on the Landscape: the Highland Zone*, London: Council for British Archaeology

Evans J. G., Limbrey S., Maté A. and Mount R. (1993) 'An environmental history of the Upper Kennet Valley, Wiltshire, for the last 10,000 years', *Proc Prehist Soc* 59, 139–95

Everitt A. (1986) *Continuity and Colonization. The Evolution of Kentish Settlement*, Leicester: Leicester University Press

Everson P. and Williamson T. eds (1998) *Archaeology and the Landscape*, Manchester: Manchester University Press

Faegri K. (1988) 'Preface' to Birks *et al.*, 1–4

Fairclough G. (1999a) 'Protecting the cultural landscape: national designation and local character', in Grenville, 27–39

Fairclough G. ed. (1999b) *Historic Landscape Characterisation. "The State of the Art", Papers from a seminar held at the Society of Antiquaries, Burlington House, London, 11 December 1998*, London: English Heritage

Fairclough G., Lambrick G. and McNab A. (1999) *Yesterday's World, Tomorrow's Landscape. The English Heritage Historic Landscape Project 1992–94*, London: English Heritage

Fenton A. (1978) *The Northern Isles: Orkney and Shetland*, Edinburgh: Donald

Fielden B. and Jokilehto J. (1993) *Management Guidelines for World Cultural Heritage Sites*, Rome: ICCROM

Fleming A. (1988) *The Dartmoor Reaves: Investigating Prehistoric Land Divisions*, London: Batsford

Fleming A. (1998) *Swaledale: Valley of the Wild River*, Edinburgh: Edinburgh University Press

Fontova R. and Carme Polo M., nd *Romanesque of Vall de Boí*, Barcelona: Dissenys Culturals

Foster S. and Smout T. C. eds (1994) *The History of Soils and Field Systems*, Aberdeen: The Cultural Press

Fowler P. J. (1978) 'Lowland landscapes', in Limbrey and Evans, 1–12

Fowler P. J. (1983) *The Farming of Prehistoric Britain*, Cambridge: Cambridge University Press

Bibliography   Fowler P. J. (1995) 'Cultural landscapes' (unpublished paper read at National Trust Countryside Centenary Conference, Manchester)

Fowler P. J. (1997a) 'Writing on the countryside' in Hodder I. *et multi al.* eds, *Interpreting Archaeology. Finding Meaning in the Past*, London: Routledge (pb edn of 1995 hb), 100–109

Fowler P. J. (1998a) 'Moving through the landscape', in Everson and Williamson, 25–41

Fowler P. J. (1998b) 'Cultural and natural values of archaeological landscapes of Europe and the British Isles', in von Droste *et al.* eds, 100–114

Fowler P. J. (2000a) 'Cultural landscapes of Britain', *Internat J Heritage Studies* 6, 201–12

Fowler P. J. (2000b) *Landscape Plotted and Pieced. Field Archaeology and Local History in Fyfield and Overton, Wiltshire*, London: Society of Antiquaries, Research Report 64

Fowler P. J. (2001) 'Cultural landscape: great concept, pity about the phrase' in Kelly *et al.*, 64–82

Fowler P. J. (2002) *Farming in the First Millennium* AD. *British Agriculture between Julius Caesar and William the Conqueror*, Cambridge: Cambridge University Press

Fowler P. J. (2003a) 'World Heritage Cultural Landscapes 1992–2002: a review and prospect', in WHC (2003c) 16–32

Fowler P. J. (2003b) *World Heritage Cultural Landscapes 1992–2002*, Paris: UNESCO World Heritage Centre

Fowler P. J. and Blackwell I. (1998) *The Land of Lettice Sweetapple. An English Countryside Explored*, Stroud: Tempus (hb only)

Fowler P. J. and Blackwell I. (2000) *An English Countryside Explored. The Land of Lettice Sweetapple*, Brimscombe Port, Stroud: Tempus (pb)

Fowler P. J. and Jacques D. (1995) 'Cultural landscapes in Britain' in von Droste *et al.*, 350–63

Fowler P. J. and Mills S. (2003) 'Bede's world: an early medieval landscape. A late 20th-century creation with 7th-century fields and buildings', in Jameson J. H. ed., *The Reconstructed Past: The Value of Reconstructions in the Public Interpretation of Archaeology and History*, Walnut Grove, California: Altamira Press

Fowler P. J. and Sharp M. (1990) *Images of Prehistory*, Cambridge: Cambridge University Press,

Fox C. F. (1933) *The Personality of Britain*, Cardiff: National Museum of Wales

Fukuyama F. (1992) *The End of History and the Last Man*, New York

Fulford M. and Nichols E. eds. (1992) *Developing Landscapes of Lowland Britain. The Archaeology of the British Gravels: A Review*, London, Soc. Antiquaries, Occasional Paper 14

Gathercole P. and Lowenthal D. eds. (1990) *The Politics of the Past*, London: Unwin Hyman

Glasscock R. ed. (1992) *Historic Landscapes of Britain from the Air*, Cambridge: Cambridge University Press

Glob P. V. (1971) *Danish Prehistoric Monuments. Denmark from Stone Age to the Vikings*, London: Faber & Faber

Goudie A. (1990) *The Human Impact on the Natural Environment*, Oxford: Blackwell (3rd edn)

Grenville J. ed. (1999) *Managing the Historic Rural Landscape*, London: Routledge

Haber W. (1995) 'Concept, origin and meaning of "Landscape"', in von Droste *et al.*, 38–41

Hajós G. ed. (1999) *Monument – Site – Cultural Landscape exemplified by The Wachau* (Proceedings of an International Conference, 12–15 October, 1998, Dürnstein, Austria), Verlag Berger, Vienna

Harrison F. (1991) *The Living Landscape*, London: Mandarin

Haverkort B. and Millar D. (1994) 'Constructing diversity: the active role of rural people in maintaining and enhancing biodiversity', *Etnoecologica*, Vol. II, No. 3, 1994, 51–64

Havinden M. (1981) *The Making of the English Landscape: The Somerset Landscape*, London: Hodder and Stoughton

Hawkes J. (1996) *The Golden Age of Northumbria*, Warkworth: Sandhill Press

Hawkes J. and Mills S. eds (1999) *Northumberland's Golden Age*, Thrupp, Stroud: Sutton Publishing

Hayes D. and Patton M. (2001) 'Proactive crisis-management strategies and the archaeological heritage', *Internat J Heritage Stud* 7, 2001, 37–58

Holzknecht A. (1998) 'The Desai-Wörlitz Garden Realm and the challenge of sustainability', in Dömke and Succow, 51–53

Hoskins W. G. (1955) *The Making of the English Landscape*, London: Hodder and Stoughton

ICCROM (forthcoming) *Guidelines for the Management of World Heritage Cultural Landscapes*, Rome

ICOMOS (1993) *Cultural Tourism*, Colombo, Sri Lanka: International Scientific Symposium, 10th General Assembly, Central Cultural Fund Publication no. 133

IUCN (1978) *Categories, Objectives and Criteria for Protected Areas*, Gland, Switzerland, and Cambridge, UK: IUCN

IUCN (1994a) *Guidelines for Protected Area Management Categories*, Gland, Switzerland, and Cambridge, UK: IUCN

IUCN (1994b) *1993 United Nations List of National Parks and Protected Areas*, Gland, Switzerland, and Cambridge, UK: IUCN

IUCN (2000) IUCN Commission on Environmental Law 2000, *Landscape Conservation Law: Present Trends and Perspectives in International and Comparative law*, Gland, Switzerland and Cambridge, UK: IUCN Environmental Policy and Law Paper no. 39

IUCN, UNEP and WWF (1991) *Caring for the Earth*, Gland, Switzerland, and Cambridge, UK: IUCN

Jackson J. B. (1952) 'Human, all too human geography', *Landscape* 2, 5–7

Jacques D. (1983) *Georgian Gardens. The reign of Nature*, London: Batsford

Jacques D. (1995) 'The rise of cultural landscapes', *Internat J Heritage Studies* 1, 91–101

Jacques D. and Fowler P. (1995) 'Conservation of landscapes in post-industrial countries' in von Droste *et al.*, 412–19

Jellicoe G. and S. (1975) *The Landscape of Man. Shaping the environment from prehistory to the present day*, London: Thames and Hudson

Jeschke H.P. (1999) 'How to maintain UNESCO cultural heritage landscapes … in federal European nations' in *Shaping the Land I*, Trontheim: Department of Geography, University of Trontheim, 278–97

Johnson N. and Rose P. (1994) *Bodmin Moor. An Archaeological Survey. Vol 1: The human landscape to c. 1800*, English Heritage/RCHM, London

Jones M. (2001) *The Molecule Hunt. Archaeology and the search for ancient DNA*, London: Penguin

Keith W. J. (1974) *The Rural Tradition. A Study of the Non-fiction Prose Writers of the English Countryside*, Toronto: University of Toronto Press

Kelly R., Macinnes L., Thackray D. and Whitbourne P. eds (2001) *The Cultural Landscape. Planning for a Sustainable Partnership between People and Place*, London: ICOMOS-UK

Layton R. ed. (1989) *Conflict in the Archaeology of Living Traditions*, London: Unwin Hyman

Layton R. and Titchen S. (1995) 'Uluru: an outstanding Australian Aboriginal cultural landscape', in von Droste *et al.*, 174–181

Le Berre M. (2000) 'Cultural landscapes in Africa – genesis', in Rössler and Saouma-Forero, 44–58

Liddell A. and Price J. (1992) *Port Wine Quintas of the Douro*. Lisboa: Quetzal

Limbrey S. and Evans J. G. eds (1978) *The Effect of Man on the Landscape: the Lowland Zone*, London: Council for British Archaeology

Lucas P. H. C. (1992) *Protected Landscapes; a Guide for Policy-makers and Planners*, London: Chapman and Hall

Macinnes I. ed. (1999) *Assessing Cultural Landscapes: Progress and Potential*, Edinburgh and London: ICOMOS UK, Proceedings of a Seminar held in Longmore House, Edinburgh, in February 1998, Gardens and Landscapes Committee

Magalhães V. (1998) *Port and Douro wines*. Lisboa: Chaves Ferreira

Marres P. (1935) *Les Grands Causses*, Thèse de Lettres, 2 vols., Editions Arrault et Cie, Tours

Martel E.-A. (1936) *Les Causses Majeures* Editions Artières et Maury, Millau

Mathieson A. and Wall G. (1982) *Tourism: Economic, Physical and Social Inputs* London; Longman

Bibliography

Mayson R. (1999) *Port and Douro*. London: Faber & Faber

McKibben B. (1990) *The End of Nature*, Harmondsworth: Penguin Books

Megret A. and Collin G. (1995) 'Cultural landscapes in France' in von Droste *et al.*, 307–315

Melnick R. Z. (1984) *Cultural Landscapes: Rural Historic Districts in the National Park System*, Washington D.C.: National Park Service, U.S. Department of the Interior

Mercer R. and Tipping R. (1994) 'The prehistory of soil erosion in the Northern and Eastern Cheviot Hills, Anglo-Scottish Borders' in Foster and Smout, 1–25

Michelin (1996) *Châteaux of the Loire*, Watford: Michelin Tyre plc

Mitchell F. (1976) *The Irish Landscape* London: Collins

Mitchell N. and Buggey S. (2000) 'Protected landscapes and cultural landscapes: taking advantage of diverse approaches', *J George Wright Forum* 17, 1, 35–46

Munjeri D. (2000) 'Cultural landscapes in Africa', in Rössler and Saouma-Forero, 35–43

P&A (1993) 'Landscapes in a new Europe: unity in diversity?' (Blois Conference proceedings), *Paysage & Amenagement* 23 (March 1993)

Parks Canada (2000) 'An approach to Aboriginal cultural landscapes', http://parks canada.pch. gc.ca/aborig/sitemap_e.htm

Pereira P. and Carneiro J. M. (1999) *Pena Palace*, London: Scala Publishers

Pevsner N. *et al.* (1992) *Northumberland* (*Buildings of England*), London: Penguin

Phillips A. (1995) 'Cultural landscapes: an IUCN perspective', in von Droste *et al.*, 380–92

Phillips A. (2000) 'Practical considerations for the implementation of a European Landscape Convention', in IUCN, 17–25

Phillips A. (2001) 'The nature of cultural landscapes: a nature conservation perspective', in Kelly *et al.*, 46–63

Plachter H. (1999) 'The contributions of cultural landscapes to nature conservation', in Hajós, 93–115

Pollard J. and Reynolds A. (2002) *Avebury: The Biography of a Landscape*, Brimscombe Port, Stroud: Tempus

Préfecture (2000) Préfecture de la region Centre, *Proposition d'inscription au Patrimoine Mondial de l'UNESCO du Val de Loire – Paysages Culturels, Dossier complémentaire*, Orléans: Préfecture de la region Centre

Pressouyre L. (1996) *The World Heritage Convention, Twenty Years Later*, Paris: UNESCO Publishing

Priore R. (2001) 'The background to the European Landscape Convention', in Kelly *et al.*, 31–37

Rackham O. (1986) (1st edn) *The History of the Countryside*, London: Dent

Rackham O. (1990) *Trees and Woodland in the British Landscape*, London: Dent

RCAHMScot (1990) Royal Commission on the Ancient and Historical Monuments of Scotland, *North-East Perth. An Archaeological Landscape*, London: HMSO

RCHM (1959) Royal Commission on the Historical Monuments of England, *A Matter of Time*, London: HMSO

Renfrew C. ed. (1985) *The Prehistory of Orkney*, Edinburgh: Edinburgh University Press

Renfrew C. (2000) *Loot Legitimacy and Ownership*, London: Duckworth

Renfrew C. (2003) *Figuring It Out. What Are We? Where Do We Come From? The Parallel Visions of Artists and Archaeologists*, London: Thames & Hudson

Ribeiro J. C. ed. (1998) *Sintra World Heritage*, Sintra: Sintra Municipality

Rigol I. (2000) 'Cultural landscapes in the Caribbean,' in Hoof H. de ed., *La patrimoine culturel des Caraïbes et la Convention du patrimoine mondial*, Paris: Édition du Comité des travaux historiques et scientifiques, UNESCO, 259–76

Rippon S. (1996) *Gwent Levels: The Evolution of a Wetland Landscape*, York: Council for Britisih Archaeology, Res Rep 105

Rippon S. (1997) *The Severn Estuary: Landscape Evolution and Wetland Reclamation*, Leicester: Leicester University Press

Rippon S. (1999) 'Romano-British reclamation of coastal wetland', in Cook H. and Williamson

T. eds, *Water Management in the English Landscape. Field, Marsh and Meadow*, Edinburgh: Edinburgh University Press, 101–21

Roberts B. and Wrathmell S. (2000) *An Atlas of Rural Settlement in England*, London: English Heritage

Rosas J. A. R.-P. (1998) *O vinho do Porto: notas sobre a sua história, produção e tecnologia*. 5th ed Porto: Instituto do Vinho do Porto

Rössler M. (1998a) 'The World Heritage Convention', in *Landscapes: The Setting for our Future Lives, Naturopa* 96, 19 (Strasbourg: Council of Europe)

Rössler M. (1998b) 'Landscapes in the framework of the World Heritage Convention and other UNESCO Instruments and Programmes', in Dömpke and Succow, 24–32

Rössler M. (1999) 'Cultural landscapes in the framework of the *Convention Concerning the Protection of the World Cultural and Natural Heritage* (World Heritage Convention, 1972)' in Hajos, 25–32

Rössler M. (2000) 'World Heritage cultural landscapes', *J George Wright Soc* 17, 1, 27–34

Rössler M. (2001a) 'World Heritage cultural landscapes in the European Region', in Kelly *et al.*, 38–45

Rössler M. (2001b) 'Sacred landscapes: new perspectives in the implementation of the cultural landscape concept in the framework of the UNESCO World Heritage Convention', in UNESCO World Heritage Centre, 27–41

Rössler M. and Saouma-Forero G. (2000) *The World Heritage Convention and Cultural Landscapes in Africa. Expert Meeting – Tiwi, Kenya, 9/11 March 1999*, Paris: UNESCO

Saouma-Forero G. ed. (2001) *Authenticity and Integrity in an African Context. Expert meeting – Great Zimbabwe – 26/29 May 2000*, Paris: UNESCO

Sauer C. O. (1925) 'The morphology of landscape', *University of California Publications in Geography* 2.2, 19–53

Shoard M. (1987) *This Land is Our Land*, London: Paladin

Simmons I. (1989) *Changing the Face of the Earth: Culture, Environment, History*, Oxford: Blackwell

Simmons I. G. (1997) *Humanity and Environment: A Cultural Ecology*, Harlow: Longman

Smith C. (1998) *UNESCO World Heritage Sites. A Consultation Paper on a New United Kingdom Tentative List of Future Nominations*, London: Department for Culture, Media and Sport

Stone P. G. and Molyneaux B. L. eds (1994), *The Presented Past. Heritage, Museums and Education*, London: Routledge

Stovel H. (1998) *Risk Preparedness: A Management Manual for World Cultural Heritage*, Rome: ICCROM

Svobodova H. ed. (1990) *Cultural Aspects of Landscape*, Wageningen: Pudoc

Thomas C. (1985) *Exploration of a Drowned Landscape. Archaeology and History of the Isles of Scilly*, London: Batsford

Thomas W. L. ed. (1955) *Man's Role in Changing the Face of the Earth*, Chicago: Wenner Gren Foundation

Titchen S. M. and Rössler M. (1995) 'Tentative lists as a tool for landscape classification and protection', in von Droste *et al.*, 420–427

Trinder B. (1982) *The Making of the Industrial Landscape*, London: Dent

Tunbridge J. E. and Ashworth G. J. (1996) *Dissonant Heritage: The Management of the Past as a Resource in Conflict*, Chichester: Wiley

Ucko P. J. *et al.* (1991) *Avebury Reconsidered. From the 1660s to the 1990s*, London: Unwin Hyman

UNESCO (1962) *Recommendations Concerning the Safeguarding of the Beauty and Character of Landscapes and Sites*, Paris: UNESCO

UNESCO (2002) (Map of) *World Heritage 2002*, Paris: UNESCO

Van der Hammen M. C. (2003) *The Indigenous Resguardos of Colombia: Their Contribution to Conservation and Sustainable Forest Use*, Amsterdam: IUCN Netherlands

Vanderhulst G. ed. (1992) *Industry, Man and Landscape*, Brussels: TICCIH-Belgium

Bibliography   Villalón A. (2001) 'Spiritual values versus the reality of the physical survival at the rice terraces of the Philippine Cordilleras', in WHC, 189–203

Villalon A. F. (1995) 'The cultural landscape of the rice terraces of the Philippine Cordilleras', in von Droste *et al.*, 108–113

von Droste B., Plachter H. and Rössler M. eds (1995) *Cultural Landscapes of Universal Value – Components of a Global Strategy*, Jena: Gustav Fischer Verlag

von Droste B., Rössler M. and Titchen S. eds (1998) *Linking Nature and Culture ..., Report of the Global Strategy Natural and Cultural Heritage Expert Meeting, 25 to 29 March 1998, Amsterdam*, Amsterdam: Directory for Cultural Heritage, Ministry for Education, Culture and Science, The Netherlands

Wagner P. L. and Mikesell M. W. eds (1962) *Readings in Cultural Geography*, Chicago: University of Chicago Press

WHC (1999) Intergovernmental Committee for the Protection of the World Cultural and Natural Heritage, *Operational Guidelines for the Implementation of the World Heritage Convention*, Paris: UNESCO, World Heritage Centre (WHC–99/2, revised March 1999)

WHC (2000) *Properties Inscribed on the World Heritage List*, World Heritage Centre, Paris (WHC. 2000/3, Jan. 2000)

WHC (2001) *Thematic Expert Meeting on Asia-Pacific Sacred Mountains, 5–10 September 2001*, Paris and Tokyo: UNESCO World Heritage Centre

WHC (2002a) *Investing in World Heritage: Past Achievements, Future Ambitions. A Guide to International Assistance*, Paris: UNESCO World Heritage Centre: World Heritage Papers 2

WHC (2002b) UNESCO World Heritage Centre and the Secretariat of the Hungarian World Heritage Committee eds, *World Heritage Expert Meeting on Vineyard Cultural Landscapes, 11–14 July 2001, Tokaj, Hungary*, Budapest

WHC (2003a) *Cultural Landscapes* (web page in October 2003 listing the official 36 current World Heritage cultural landscapes under 'Global Strategy' @ www.unesco.org/whc/heritage.htm)

WHC (2003b) UNESCO World Heritage Centre 2003, *World Heritage 2002. Shared legacy, common responsibility* ([proceedings of] an International Congress organized by UNESCO's World Heritage Centre and Regional Bureau for Science in Europe ... with the support of the Italian Government on the occasion of the 30th anniversary of the World Heritage Convention ... Venice, Italy, 14–16 November, 2002), Paris: UNESCO, World Heritage Centre

WHC (2003c) *Cultural Landscapes: The Challenges of Conservation*, Paris: UNESCO World Heritage Centre: World Heritage Papers 7

WHC (2003d) *Identification and Documentation of Modern Heritage*, Paris: UNESCO World Heritage Centre: World Heritage Papers 5

WHCC (2003) *Cultural Landscapes: The Challenges of Conservation*, Paris: UNESCO World Heritage Centre: World Heritage Papers 7

WHC/Korea (2001) UNESCO World Heritage Centre, the Korean National Commission for UNESCO and the Cultural Properties Administration of the Republic of Korea 2001, *UNESCO Regional Workshop for the Preparation of Periodic Reports on the State of Conservation of World Heritage Cultural Sites in Asia, July 11–13 2001, Gyeongju, Republic of Korea*, Seoul: Korean National Commission for UNESCO and the Cultural Properties Administration

Whittle A. (1997) *Sacred Mound, Holy Rings. Silbury Hill and the West Kennet Palisade Enclosures: a Later Neolithic Complex in North Wiltshire*, Oxford: Oxbow Books, Monograph 74

Williamson T. (1998) 'Questions of preservation and destruction', in Everson and Williamson, 1–24

Willis A. J. (1976) 'Natural history and ecology', in Atthill R. ed. *Mendip. A New Study*, Newton Abbot: David & Charles, 38–49

Woodward A.B. and P. J. (1996) 'The topography of some barrow cemeteries in Bronze Age Wessex', *Proc Prehistoric Society* **62**, 275 on

Yuson A. A. (2000) 'Dancing anew on the stairways to heaven', *The UNESCO Courier*, December 2000, 31–33

Index

....

References to illustrations in **bold**; to plates preceded by '**pl.**'